ELLA FITZGERALD
A LIFE THROUGH JAZZ

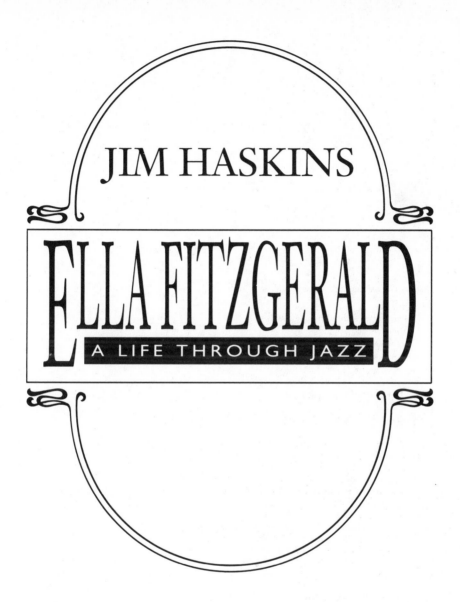

JIM HASKINS

ELLA FITZGERALD

A LIFE THROUGH JAZZ

NEW ENGLISH LIBRARY

British Library Cataloguing-in-Publication Data

Haskins, Jim
  Ella Fitzgerald: A life through jazz.
  I. Title
  781.65092

  ISBN 0-450-48796-2

Published by New English Library,
a hardcover imprint of Hodder and Stoughton,
a division of Hodder and Stoughton Ltd,
Mill Road, Dunton Green, Sevenoaks, Kent TN13 2YA
Editorial Office: 47 Bedford Square, London WC1B 3DP

Photoset by Rowland Phototypesetting Ltd
Bury St Edmunds, Suffolk

Printed in Great Britain by St Edmundsbury Press Ltd
Bury St Edmunds, Suffolk

To Leo and Geri

Contents

	Acknowledgements	8
1	The Orphan's Gift	10
2	Stomping at the Savoy	27
3	'A-Tisket, A-Tasket'	41
4	Bandleader	58
5	On Her Own	74
6	Settled	92
7	On the Granzwagon	112
8	The Songbooks	129
9	Time Out	142
10	Fine and Mellow	156
11	The *Grande Dame* of Vocal Jazz	172
	Selected Bibliography	189
	Ella Fitzgerald's Grammy Awards	190
	Discography	191
	Notes	261
	Index	269

Acknowledgements

I am grateful to the following people for their help with this book: Patricia Allen-Browne, the late Eddie Barefield, Keter Betts, Geri Branton, Dave Burchfield, Charline Burgess, Pam Day, Bill Doggett, Tommy Flanagan, E. E. Gariepy, Leslie Gourse, Gene Grissom, Milt Jackson, *Jazznews International*, *Jazz Notes*, Hank Jones, Arthur Josephson, Ann L. Kalkhoff, Connie Kuhns, the late Mel Lewis, Marian Logan, Norman Matulef, Marvin Millis, James Moody, Beverly Peer, Maurice Prince, Roger Ramirez, Mr and Mrs Irving Randolph, Mr and Mrs Abe Rothstein, Phil Schapp, Victoria Secunda, Raymond Trent, George Wein. A special thank you to Kathy Benson.

1 The Orphan's Gift

For more than half a century, Ella Fitzgerald has enjoyed a place in the hearts of music-lovers all over the world, and her staying power is no mystery. Her voice, which she calls a gift from God, is remarkable. For many years, it was thin and girlish. Only in the last two decades or so has it deepened to a dark contralto. But it has remained immediately identifiable as her voice alone.

She has managed to adapt to the changes in her voice, not to mention changes in musical styles and tastes, because of her incredible musicianship, the ability to 'play' the voice like an instrument. As critic John Rockwell wrote in *The New York Times* in 1986, 'She can not only hit whatever note she wishes, bending and coloring it at will, but she knows just the *right* note to select from the dizzying possibilities flying past her in the heat of a jazz improvisation. The way she can shade a pitch, or slither up and down a chromatic scale, or pick out the most piquantly expressive note in a chord, reveals a consummate musician, however informal her training.'[1]

And finally, there is her style. Over the years, critics have complained of a lack of real emotion in her singing, a dearth of passion. She could never have been a blues singer and, mercifully, rarely tried. What she did try – and successfully – was to balance and blend jazz and pop singing. What she lacked in depth she made up for in technique. Her uncanny sense of rhythm, the precision of her articulation, and her focused, defined artistic personality helped her to weather the vagaries of musical taste in a professional career now approaching its sixth decade.

Until very recently, Ella and her voice aged gracefully. Her girlish ebullience may have been a survival mechanism initially, but it served its purpose. Ella was the girl next door when many white fans wouldn't sit next to someone of her race on a public bus. Later, she was a favourite aunt, and still later, an icon. Through it all, she has never felt secure in her identity either offstage or on, and that may well be the major tragedy of an otherwise star-studded career. The hundred-plus albums, thirteen Grammy awards, national and international honours aside, Ella Fitzgerald is still a frightened, insecure little girl who has always been less inclined to lead her life than to be led by it and who has been so wary of revealing her private self that after more than a half century as a public figure she is one of the world's least-known personalities.

Ella Fitzgerald was born on April 25, 1918, in Newport News, Virginia. She never knew her father who, according to Ella legend, died not long after she was born. Her few memories of him are anecdotes her mother told her which, in her child's mind, became confused with actual experiences. Her mother, Tempie, did tell her that when her father was alive the Fitzgerald household was filled with music; her mother sang, her father played guitar, and in the days before radio they made music for family and friends, and for each other. After her father died, the music stopped for a while and Ella never had the opportunity to relate to a male at her youngest and most impressionable age. Ella's mother didn't have the luxury of worrying about that. Her concern was how she was going to support herself and her daughter. At length, she joined the postwar black migration north, to Yonkers, New York, where she had a sister.

Yonkers, just up the Hudson from the Bronx (the northernmost borough of New York City), was a thriving industrial town after the war. Little Ella and her mother moved in with Ella's aunt, Virginia Williams. Tempie Fitzgerald found work in a laundry and eventually started a catering business on the side. Soon, she began dating a man who worked as a ditchdigger and chauffeur, and after a time she and little Ella moved in with him. Ella's new 'stepfather' apparently treated her well, and after a while she had a little half-sister. She speaks of a warm family life where there was love and hope.

The neighbourhood in which they lived was typical of a northern mill town whose need for relatively unskilled labour attracted immigrants and blacks from the South. There was a 'sporting house' down the street as well as a Numbers parlour or two. It was racially mixed, and blacks lived without incident alongside newly-arrived immigrants who had also sought out the job opportunities in Yonkers. Young Ella's neighbours and classmates were mostly Italian, but she does not recall feeling different as a child. Her friends' parents were still too new to the country and too concerned with making a living and learning the language to have recognised its class stratification and realised how they could manipulate it. Ella was eleven when she was called 'Nigger' for the first time. The boy was a newcomer at school, and in response Ella pushed him, knocking him down. But her schoolmates thought she had hit him and were suitably impressed. Ella was a small girl, and her classmates respected her for besting the new kid.

At home, there was music again, and Ella learned the popular songs her mother sang and discovered that she herself liked to sing and dance. It was soon apparent that Ella had an 'ear' for music, perfect pitch, a good voice, and an excellent sense of rhythm. Encouraging her, Tempie Fitzgerald decided to pay for piano lessons, somehow eking out the necessary five dollars per lesson from the household budget. But Ella spent more time watching in fascination as her teacher played than she did playing herself. When her mother realised that she was playing the same tunes over and over she decided that the five dollars she'd been paying for Ella's piano lessons could be better spent, so she stopped the lessons.

The family often lacked money: 'We didn't have much,' says Ella. 'We came up at a time when you had to stand in line for a bag of horse meat. But we shared everything we had.'[2] When she was not in school, she helped out in whatever ways she could, running errands for neighbours at first. When she was old enough, about seven or eight, she acted as lookout for the local 'house', keeping a keen eye out for the cops and knocking on the door when she saw one, warning the girls inside. 'I was just a kid, of course,' she has said, 'and didn't realise that kind of thing was wrong. I just thought I was helping those women buy shoes.'[3] Later, she 'ran Numbers', picking up the daily bets from households in the neighbourhood and taking them to the local Number Hole.

With what she brought in, and the rest of the family's income, the household could afford a gramophone and, occasionally, new records to play on it. Now, Ella's mother sang along with the popular white singers of the day, among them the Boswell Sisters – Connee, Martha and Helvetia out of New Orleans – whose close harmony would be copied by the Andrews Sisters and other female groups, not to mention black male groups like the Mills Brothers, who would become integral parts of swing-band performances. Connee Boswell, lead singer and arranger for the group, classically trained and a cello, piano and saxophone player, was Ella's favourite, and while many jazz purists pooh-poohed the Boswell Sisters' style, it should be pointed out that they pioneered the use of the voice as an instrument and were the first to infuse popular singing with elements of jazz. White records were far more plentiful and easy to obtain than records by blacks. Ella's favourite black singers included Mamie Smith, Ethel Waters and the Mills Brothers on the early black labels like Okeh and Black Swan, and songs like 'Down Home Blues' and 'Oh Daddy'. One didn't go down to the record stores to buy these ten-inch wax discs but purchased them from the trunks of cars driven by black entrepreneurial types or from the back rooms of black-run neighbourhood enterprises like greengrocers'. The local sporting house was a good source for black records as well.

A great variety of musical fare was available on the radio, which every self-respecting home had. There were two networks, CBS and NBC. Duke Ellington and his orchestra broadcast instrumental jazz nightly from the Cotton Club, the posh, whites-only nightclub in Harlem to the south. Ella's tastes, however, leaned more toward popular white music. Her favourite show was Arthur Tracy's on CBS. Tracy billed himself as 'The Street Singer', which obviously had a different connotation at that time than it does today, since he favoured songs like 'Marta (Ramblin' Rose of the Wildwood)' and 'The Wheel of the Waggon is Broken'. Popular songs and novelty songs, in which the lyrics were more important than the instrumentation, were Ella's taste as a teenager, and this taste proved to be formative. Her ability to sing the popular songs of the day stood her in good stead as a member of the glee club in junior high school and a frequent performer in school shows. During lunch hours, she and her girlfriends would sometimes sneak away to a local theatre to listen to white singers like Dolly Dawn with George Hall's orchestra, and she would incorporate what she heard into her repertoire.

Ella's interest in music did not at that time distract her from her school work. She says that she was a good student in junior high school: 'Actually, I thought I was going to be a doctor or something like that, 'cause I was pretty good in Latin in school, and everything was all right 'till all my friends were taking the easier course. And I got bored with trying to learn Latin, and I let that go.'[4]

In those days, some kind of creative instruction was part of the curriculum. Ella was required to take either art or music. As she was 'no good with a paint brush', she chose music, and learned the rudiments of sight reading, but only enough to get by – a cursory musical education that she would later regret.

The church, cradle of so many great black singing talents, seems not to have been an influence on her. Rather, the influence was the music she heard on records and the radio. She was especially intrigued with unique vocal styles, and her skill in vocalising made her a natural mimic. When she was in junior high, she heard the 'growl' style made popular by Louis Armstrong, Fats Waller and others, and soon had mastered it. 'I got in a couple of school plays,' she says, 'and there was a song called "Sing You Sinners", and I used to try to growl that. The kids liked me when I did that, and then I got a little big-headed.'[5]

One day she was walking home with her mother after appearing in a school play. A fellow student approached to congratulate her on her performance, and Ella ignored her schoolmate. Her mother slapped her, saying, 'Don't you ever go around where you don't speak to somebody. If a man is lying in the gutter and he speaks to you, you say hello. You never know who will get up and help you. Don't you ever do that again.'[6] That public humiliation at a particularly impression-able time stayed with her, she says, and forever after she remembered that incident, and her mother's stern warning.

In terms of her self-image, a little big-headedness about her singing talent was probably good for young Ella, for she had little physically to be proud of. Ella was no beauty, and recognising that reality can be difficult for a teenager. Her face was plain, with small eyes above high cheek bones and a generous nose and mouth. Short in stature and thick in build, she had incongruously skinny legs. It was her mother who assured her that her singing talent was a gift from God equal to if not greater than physical beauty, which was another reason why her mother became so angry with Ella when she assumed the attitude that her singing talent was a right, rather than a privilege.

Not only did Ella love to sing, she also enjoyed jazz dancing. While she and her girlfriends practised steps to the latest dance crazes, like the Black Bottom and the Suzy-Q, tap was her favourite form. She and her cousins or girlfriends often went to the local theatre to watch professional dancers like Bill 'Bojangles' Robinson and Eddie Rector. As these top dancers were usually billed as 'Direct from Connie's Inn', or with some other reference to the big Harlem clubs, it was logical that Ella would soon cross the Harlem River to see what was going on there.

The roar of the 1920s might have been muted in Yonkers, but there is no way that the excitement of Harlem in the 1920s and 1930s era would not have reached above the Hudson. With the passage of the Volstead Act in 1919 and the start of Prohibition, it hadn't taken larcenous types long to realise that big money could be made in bootleg liquor. Harlem, formerly a sylvan suburb of Manhattan, had recently become the new base for black Manhattanites, who'd been forced out of Hell's Kitchen and other midtown neighbourhoods by newly-arrived ethnic minorities. The race riot after the 1910 Jack Johnson-Jim Jeffries heavyweight bout had nudged blacks uptown, while the economic reality of overbuilding in Harlem in the wake of the promised new elevated subway line had provided the apartments for blacks to live in. Once the venerable Abyssinian Baptist Church moved uptown to Harlem, the midtown black populace was quick to follow.

Southern blacks migrating to New York City either headed voluntarily or were steered to Harlem, and by the early 1920s a major cultural explosion, the Harlem Renaissance, was in progress. The relatively new music called jazz was both one of the major producers and products of this cultural awakening. An outgrowth of the syncopated rhythms of ragtime, jazz carried syncopation over to harmony and orchestration. It had begun to develop long before World War I and was cradled in the towns along the Mississippi like New Orleans, where the coming together of black and Creole musicians in the saloons and gambling houses of the legally sanctioned prostitution district of Storyville led to the development of a musical ensemble in which the trumpet or cornet carried the melody and brasses, piano and drums, bass and banjo in various combinations provided the rhythm.

Music historians differ on how jazz got its name. Early on, it was called 'razz' music or 'spasm' music. Chicagoans claim that the term 'jazz' originated there around 1912 with the popularity of a trombone player named Jasbo Brown, called 'Jas', whose nickname was soon applied to his music. Whatever its origin, the term was in general use by World War I.

By this time, jazz was developing from a vaudeville novelty into a fashionable musical style, primarily because it was becoming danceable and thus more accessible to the larger public. The danceability of jazz was nowhere more evident than in *Shuffle Along*, an all-black show that opened at the 63rd Street Theater in midtown Manhattan in 1921, and if the beginning of the Harlem Renaissance can be traced to a single event, it is this show.

The exuberant dancing in *Shuffle Along* inspired whites to look northward to Harlem with new interest. Soon, an adventurous few were travelling uptown to see what else was going on up there. Before long, clever bootleggers had started opening high-class speakeasies in Harlem, inaugurating its era as a playground for whites as well as, incidentally, creating a white audience for Harlem writers and pictorial artists.

At clubs like the Cotton Club and Connie's Inn, the clientèle were all white but the waiters and entertainers were all black. While aware, sometimes painfully, of the hypocrisy of such arrangements, the black entertainers were delighted to have jobs, and ordinary blacks were just as delighted to see that at least some of their race had made it. Duke Ellington and his orchestra became the house band at the Cotton Club, and in 1927 WHW, a small local radio station, began to broadcast a nightly session of Ellington's music. Columbia Broadcasting System (CBS) soon followed with national broadcasts, and every black household with a radio tuned in nightly as a matter of racial solidarity, not to mention enjoyment of good entertainment. Ella reserved the hours of the Cotton Club broadcasts for radio listening and dreamed of the glamorous world that the Cotton Club represented.

The Stock Market crash of 1929 did not dim the lights of Harlem for several years, and by the time she was in her early teens Ella and her girlfriends were taking the train to Harlem to go to the small black clubs that had no cover charge and weren't sticklers for the age restrictions that prevailed at the more high-class clubs. Their favourite spot was the Savoy Ballroom, Harlem's biggest and most popular dance hall. It was also a place where their parents felt they were safe, for a strict standard of order was maintained by the Savoy's burly, tuxedo-clad bouncers, who dealt swiftly with any troublemakers.

Housed on the second floor of a block-long building on Lenox Avenue between 140th and 141st Streets, where formerly had been old streetcar barns, the Savoy had opened its doors on March 6, 1926. Owner Moe Gale and manager Charles Buchanan, both well versed in hyperbole, billed it 'The World's Most Famous Ballroom'. They proved to be prescient, as it became just that.

Its dance area was the largest in Harlem, measuring fifty feet by two hundred feet. It was nicknamed 'the Track' early on, possibly because to some it resembled a race track and probably because dancers left tracks on its frequently paste-waxed floor. Its entertainment repertoire was vast. Visiting singers and dancers held forth on a stage that could be elevated above dance floor level when in use and then lowered so as to augment the dance floor area. Dancer Eddie Rector made a special opening-night appearance. But the Savoy's major claim to fame was that it consistently featured and was built originally to accommodate two bands, with bandstands on either side of the dance floor.

Fess Williams and His Royal Flush Orchestra was one of the original bands. 'Professor' Stanley Williams of Kentucky, whose 'title' was soon shortened to 'Fess', was a showman *par excellence* and wore a diamond-studded suit and top hat to accord with the name of his orchestra. He was so popular with the Savoy crowds that the Ballroom put on a 'Fess Williams Night' during which 2,500 copies of his latest record for the Harmony label were given away free.

The Charleston Bearcats (later called Duncan Mayor's Savoy Bearcats) were the other 'house band' on opening night, in addition to which Fletcher Henderson's Roseland Orchestra appeared as guest band. A crowd of over five thousand attended.

In the early days, the two bands politely shared entertainment duties; when one finished its set, the other took over. Their primary purpose was to play for the dancers, and if the dancers did not dance exuberantly when a band played, that group was not invited back. But by 1927, battles of the bands had become standard fare, and during those battles, dancers were often too entranced to go out on the floor.

One of the most famous early battles, on May 15, 1927, pitted New York against Chicago. Fletcher Henderson's and Chick Webb's bands represented New York, Fess Williams' (by this time his was the house band at the Regal Theater in Chicago) and King Oliver's bands did the same for Chicago. Lenox Avenue was jammed for blocks, and the riot squad was called out to keep order.

An even greater attraction was the North versus South event which pitted three bands from each region against one another. Representing the South were Cab Calloway and The Missourians, Johnson's Happy Pals from Richmond, Virginia, and Ike Dixon from Baltimore. From the North were Duke Ellington and His Orchestra, Charlie Johnson's Paradise Band from Small's Paradise (a favourite Harlem club), and Fess Williams and His Royal Flush Orchestra.

Almost from the beginning, the dancers at the Savoy Ballroom were themselves a major part of the entertainment, and in the 1930s the ballroom's slogan was changed to 'The Home of Happy Feet'. In the course of its thirty-year-plus history, the club cradled some of the most popular new dances, including the Suzy-Q, Peckin', Truckin', and the Congeroo. The most famous came shortly after the club opened. Following Charles A. Lindbergh's solo flight across the Atlantic in 1927, the Savoy became an incubator of the Lindy Hop, a dance done by couples whose movements mimicked the take-off and landing of a plane (the female being the plane). But the regular dancers at the Savoy never lacked creative stimulation, for the club was a showcase for the legions of 'eccentric' dancers who were popular in the 1920s and 1930s.

Ella's favourite was Earl 'Snakehips' Tucker, whose speciality was the Snake Hip, a southern-based dance in which the head and shoulders were kept stationary while a flow of undulating rhythm rippled from the chest to the heels. Tucker could twist his haunches and thighs into unbelievable contortions. Ella found that she could successfully mimic Tucker, and her dream was one day to be an eccentric dancer. That she did not look graceful in repose, that her skinny legs seemed overburdened by a comparatively hefty torso, broad shoulders, and a fleshy neck and jaw, did not over-concern her. She knew that a transformation occurred when she started to dance.

She began her dancing career in school shows, and when these did not provide a sufficient outlet for her talents, continued on the streets of Yonkers, where she would tap dance for passersby and receive contributions. 'My cousins would say, "Let's go to the movies,"' she has said, 'and I'd end up dancing in the streets and people would give

Ella was a plain, awkward teenager when she began her career as a contestant at various Harlem theatre amateur nights.
Ken Whitten Collection

us money. At that time, they used to have block parties and I'd go and dance.'[7] After a time, she became something of a local celebrity.

Later, when they were older, the girls plied their dancing trade on the streets of Harlem, especially around Seventh Avenue in the 130s, known as 'Black Broadway', where sidewalk entertainers were permanent fixtures.

The Depression had, if anything, increased the numbers of these itinerant performers. Well received, and able to earn train fare for their efforts, Ella and her friends talked often and excitedly of becoming professional performers like Whyte's Lindy Hoppers, a popular group of the time. They would have made the obligatory pilgrimage to the Tree of Hope, an old elm that stood at the corner of Seventh Avenue and 131st Street. Over the years, it had become known among Harlem show people as a sort of living Aladdin's lamp, for it was believed that if people rubbed its bark and made a wish, the wish would come true. Plans to widen Seventh Avenue in 1934 included cutting down the tree, but the tap dancer Bill 'Bojangles' Robinson, then the unofficial 'Locality Mayor' of Harlem, succeeded in preserving the stump, later to have it installed as a monument complete with plaque on the enlarged Seventh Avenue.

Aware that none of them was likely to be the object of a miraculous 'discovery', Ella and her friends talked about entering an amateur night contest at one of the clubs in Harlem. An offshoot of the Depression, like flagpole-sitting and marathon dancing, amateur nights gave talented people a chance to be discovered and audiences an opportunity both to vent their frustrations by participating in public humiliation and to experience vicariously the triumphs of ordinary people like themselves. First introduced on Wednesday nights at the Harlem Opera House in 1930, amateur nights had become so popular by 1933 that many other Harlem theatres had adopted them.

Amateur nights were so integral to Harlem nightlife that it was theoretically possible for a determined would-be star to appear in an amateur contest somewhere nearly every night from Monday through Thursday. Friday and Saturday nights were reserved for shows featuring more established talents.

With the proliferation of amateur contests, Ella and two of her girlfriends decided to stop talking about entering one of them and do it. Evidently they never considered forming a dance team. There were no teams of three black dancers in show business, and although dancing duos, a holdover from the old 'two-Colored' rule of white vaudeville, were legion, Ella and her friends did not form a duo from their threesome. Instead, each considered herself an individual dancer, and when they decided at last to try an amateur night, none wanted to compete against the others. So they drew straws to see who would enter the next amateur contest at the Harlem Opera House, and Ella drew the short one.

The Harlem Opera House, 209 West 125th Street, the first theatre north of Central Park, had been built by Oscar Hammerstein at the end of the nineteenth century. It was eventually taken over by the B. F. Keith vaudeville chain and used for variety acts until 125th Street, which for a time had remained a white outpost amidst an increasingly black Harlem, had become the centre for black entertainment. By 1930 the HOH was featuring all-coloured performers. Its Wednesday-night amateur contests were among its major attractions, and since its amateur nights were the best known, Ella and her friends thought first of the Harlem Opera House.[8]

Ella submitted her name as a dancer, the talent at which she considered herself best, and then tried to control the rabid stage fright that she would suffer the rest of her life as she waited backstage for her turn. She couldn't back out now – her girlfriends would call her chicken if she didn't perform. Peeking out from behind the side curtains, she nearly fainted, for the act before her was also a dancing act – a pair of agile, acrobatic sisters who were real crowd-pleasers. How could she follow them? She could barely move when her name was called and her act introduced as a dance act.

'My legs turned to water and a million butterflies played tag in my stomach,' she recalled later. 'They almost had to shove me onstage, and when I looked where I thought the audience should be, all I saw was a big blur.' The orchestra began to play. Ella's mind willed her body to move, but it refused to cooperate. The audience murmured impatiently. From offstage, the emcee whispered, 'Do *something*.'[9] In panic, Ella realised she was not even capable of running off the stage.

Then reason took over. If she could not move, she could at least sing. The strains of a Connee Boswell song came into her consciousness, and haltingly she uttered the first line of 'Judy'. The orchestra, familiar with the popular tune, picked it up, helping her along. The audience stopped shifting impatiently in their seats as a remarkably clear tone came out from the stage, each note true. As her confidence grew, Ella relaxed and let her body sway to the song's easy, swinging rhythm, and by the time it ended the audience was cheering and Ella had reached a turning point in her life. 'Once up there,' she recalled, 'I felt the acceptance and love from the audience – I knew I wanted to sing before people the rest of my life.'[10]

So comfortable was she on that stage that she immediately launched into another Boswell Sisters song, 'The Object of My Affection.' The audience response was equally effusive. She would have sung more, but at that point the emcee reappeared and gently led her from the stage.

Amateur contests were judged by acclamation, and at the end of the evening it was Ella who received the loudest response from the audience. She won a cash prize of $25, later remarking ruefully, 'It was the hardest money I ever earned.'[11]

Coincidentally, that same year another young woman whose dream was to be a dancer wound up beginning her career as a singer in Harlem. Billie Holiday, born Eleanora Fagan in Baltimore in 1915, arrived in Harlem in the early 1930s and auditioned as a dancer at Jerry Preston's Log Cabin at 168 West 133rd Street in 1933. Informed she was no dancer, she tried again, this time as a singer, and was hired at a salary of $12 a week. It was there that John Hammond, Yale graduate and former businessman-turned music columnist and producer, discovered her and arranged for her to record for the first time, although those 1933 records did not sell well.

Ella, emboldened by her first success, and eager to feel again the surge of love and acceptance from an appreciative audience, entered other amateur contests. In one, Ella tried to introduce a new song, 'Lost in the Fog' by Jimmy McHugh and Dorothy Fields, who had become famous for their writing for the Cotton Club shows in the late 1920s. Unfortunately, the pianist mixed up the chording and Ella herself stumbled over a phrase. 'I mean, I *really* got lost,' she later said, making a play on the song's title. Neither the pianist nor Ella was able to regain enough composure to finish the song. The Harlem audience, already famous for giving absolutely no quarter to performers who couldn't make the grade, happily booed Ella off the stage, a potentially shattering experience for an insecure teenager.[12]

But Ella persevered. Telling herself not to make the same mistake again, she returned to the small repertory she knew best, and that she assumed most pianists could follow.

She next entered an amateur contest at the new Apollo Theater, located at 253 West 125th Street. The former Hurtig and Seamon's Burlesque, whose stage had been graced in earlier days by Sophie Tucker and Fannie Brice, was owned by Sidney Cohen, who also owned a small theatre called the Apollo Burlesque a few doors down and directly above the Harlem Opera House. In 1933, ironically the same year that Prohibition was repealed and the era of the speakeasy ended, newly-elected Mayor Fiorello LaGuardia began a campaign against burlesque in the city as ribald and indecent. Hurtig and Seamon's was driven out of business, as was the Apollo. Attempting to cut his losses, Sidney Cohen closed the small theatre that had housed the Apollo Burlesque and reopened the former Hurtig and Seamon's as the 125th Street Apollo Theatre, which would feature lavish revues.

Sidney Cohen, with his manager Morris Sussman, now set out to compete with the Harlem Opera House, a few doors east on 125th Street. Beginning with its inaugural show on January 26, 1934, the Apollo featured name jazz bands as well as its own amateur night.

Ella's performance at the Apollo amateur night went off without a hitch. She would sing, she said, and once again she did tunes popularised by the Boswell Sisters. She won that amateur-night contest as well.

She entered yet more contests. Occasionally she added the popular song, 'Believe It, Beloved', copyrighted in 1934 by J. C. Johnson and introduced by Fats Waller, to her standard Boswell Sisters fare. She realised that the number of contests she could enter was finite, and that at some point she would have made the rounds, but it was all she could do. She had no connections in show business, and thus far no one had 'discovered' her. She had to keep on taking advantage of whatever opportunities for exposure were open to her and hope they would lead to something more.

One amateur night, Benny Carter was in the audience. The New York-born, multi-instrumentalist, composer and arranger was then leading his own orchestra, and he recognised the specialness of Ella's voice. 'Here was this young lady, maybe fifteen or sixteen, with an astonishing talent,' he says. 'What she had, which you could see immediately, was good taste. She also had honesty and a style of her own. Perhaps there were some slight suggestions of Connee Boswell, but she wasn't copying anybody. I knew she was exceptional, and the years have proven me right.'[13]

Carter was not using singers at the time, but felt she would be an asset to a big band that did. So he introduced her to John Hammond, who was himself sufficiently impressed by Ella's voice to agree to arrange, with Carter, an audition with Fletcher Henderson.

Henderson enjoyed the distinction of having been the first band-leader to divide his orchestra into sections by instrument, thereby creating greater opportunities to control and vary the sounds in ways not possible before. Harlem had had large orchestras since around 1910, but they had not been true jazz bands, for neither the instru-mentation nor the arrangements allowed the players the opportunity to improvise. Around 1923, Henderson, with the help of violinist Allie Ross and arranger Don Redman, who could now take a song and divide its parts among the various instruments, began to section off the instruments and encourage improvisation. By 1927 Henderson's band was in residence at the big Roseland Ballroom downtown on Broadway and considered the best big band from Harlem. After playing for dancing at Roseland, they would go uptown to appear in Harlem's late-night clubs, where they discarded their arrangements and jammed.

Other big bands had soon adopted Henderson's format, which led to the development of swing, the musical style that defined the 1930s in the same way that jazz had defined the 1920s.

A development of the big-band style of the late 1920s, swing was characterised by a steady, pulsing rhythm that took precedence over melody. Even more danceable than melodic jazz, it emphasised instrumental sections and depended on complex arrangements. But musically, swing was never as exciting as 1920s jazz, because the swing bands became too popular. Expensive to support, they required financial backers who wanted a quick return on their money. The bands were heavily promoted, and personalities began to overshadow the music. Bandleaders became stars in their own right, and the music they played was more and more influenced by public taste than the other way around.

The cult of personality soon extended to band singers, who often eclipsed even the leaders in popularity. With swing, 'girl singers' became more important to big bands. All the most popular bands had them, and Carter and Hammond believed that Ella was just the sort of girl singer who would appeal to Henderson.

Together, they accompanied her to Henderson's home on Striver's Row, the most fashionable part of Harlem (Seventh Avenue to Eighth

Avenue, 138th to 139th Street), where Duke Ellington and other successful blacks lived and which featured a row of apartment houses designed earlier in the century by noted architect Stanford White. Ella, awed by her surroundings and more than a little nervous, sang her standard songs with her interpretation of swing, which Henderson felt was too much like the white interpretations of swing that the Boswells peddled. There was no heart to it. Henderson told her he'd get in touch with her later, but she never heard from him.

While Benny Carter and John Hammond continued to be interested in young Ella, they had their own agendas and could not spend much time helping her. Resignedly, she decided to return to the amateur contest circuit.

Not long afterwards, Ella got another opportunity when she auditioned for Arthur Tracy's radio show on CBS, 'The Street Singer', and was offered a contract. Being a minor, she had to have her mother sign the contract for her. Ella legends conflict as to whether her mother ever actually signed the contract, but shortly after it was proffered, Ella's mother died suddenly. Even if she had signed the contract, her death made it null and void because of Ella's minority.

The loss of her mother was an indescribable blow to Ella. The two had been close, and her mother had supported her in her efforts to build a career in entertainment, advising her on her presentation, insisting on clear enunciation, lending her own few 'good' dresses for Ella's amateur night performances. Ella had been able to turn to her mother with her problems, her insecurity about her looks, her frustration at not being 'discovered'. Her mother had comforted her with calming words – 'That's okay, honey, you'll do just fine' – and with mother wisdom – 'It isn't where you come from, it's where you're going that counts.'

Her erstwhile 'stepfather' was either gone by then or unable or unwilling to take the responsibility of raising two girls in the midst of the Great Depression. Whatever her relationship with the man was or had been, it did not give her the positive attitude toward men that she would need in order to form intimate and long-lasting partnerships later on. Ella and her sister moved in with her aunt, Virginia Williams.

An enduring aspect of Ella legend has it that for a time Ella lived at the Riverdale Orphanage, but that story appears to have been concocted by some overzealous public relations type. There were no blacks in public relations at the time, a significant failing when it came to creating fictions about the lives of black entertainers – any black would have known that black people did not send their children to orphanages; that someone, whether relative or friend, always took in orphaned children.

As early as 1949, an article in the black newspaper *Our World* stated, 'Press agents have since capitalized on . . . her mother's death for all its tear-jerker appeal [and] have spread the legend that Ella spent some dismal years in an orphanage. They have even concocted the story that Ella made a rope out of bed sheets and stole away from the orphan home. Actually Ella was brought up by relatives living in New York.'[14]

Much of Ella's private life is shrouded in mystery, and she resolutely refuses to discuss her childhood in any depth, but it is known that she dropped out of high school. At the time, finishing school wasn't important to a young girl bent on pursuing a singing career. In later years, however, Ella deeply regretted her lack of formal education and would stiffen when anyone around her referred to high school dropouts. 'You never know,' she would say, 'one of these kids may have something but not the money or means to finish.'[15]

For Ella, the only thing that made sense at the time she dropped out of school was singing, soaking up from audiences the love she could find nowhere else. Remembering her mother's wise words, she refused to become discouraged.

Every chance she got, she hung around the Harlem theatres. 'I used to go to a theater on 148th Street all the time,' she says. 'I'll never forget. My legs were so skinny, I used to wear boots so nobody could see the bottom of my legs. They would see me coming, and they'd say, "Oh, here's that little chick with them boots on!" If it was summer, winter, spring, "Here come those boots. There she is again."'[16]

Ella laughed right along with them. While she may not have been able to afford a pair of shoes, the fact that the boots made people laugh proved to her that a plain girl doesn't get much attention unless she is a funny girl. 'I used to be very self-conscious,' she said more than half a century later. 'I used to wish I was pretty. My cousin Georgia always taught me that if you *smile*, people will like you.'[17] Clowning and girlish ebullience seemed to work well for her, and she would use it most of her life to mask a profound insecurity. She knew that the one big thing she had going for her was her voice, her gift from God. Her problem was how to make that work for her.

2 Stomping at the Savoy

Ella went back to the Harlem Opera House, which was engaged in fierce competition with the Apollo and trying to distinguish its amateur contests from others by offering to the winners a week's engagement. There, at the scene of her first triumph, Ella won her first professional engagement at a salary of $50 for the week. Rather than try to get an adult to sign her contract for her, sixteen-year-old Ella simply added two years to her age and discarded the status of minority – at least in terms of age.

Her debut at the Harlem Opera House as a paid performer occurred during the week of February 15, 1935. Ella appeared on a bill head-lined by Tiny Bradshaw and his orchestra. Other performers on the bill were Mae Alix, Eddie Hunter, Billy Higgins, the 3 Sams, and George Booker. According to Ella, 'They put me on right at the end when everybody had their coats on and were getting ready to leave. Tiny said, "Ladies and gentlemen, here is the young girl that's been winning all the contests," and they all came back and took their coats off and sat back down again.'[1]

Ella did not have suitable clothing for her debut, so Tiny Bradshaw and the chorus girls at the Harlem Opera House pooled their re-sources and bought a gown for her, probably getting it from one of the 'merchandising men' who plied hot gowns to the girls backstage at the numerous Harlem clubs. Ella didn't care where it had come from. What mattered most to her was that people had cared enough about her to want her to look right. She cherished that gown, and would have occasion to be grateful for it again when she got her next professional engagement.

Not long after she completed her week's work at the Harlem Opera House, Ella got a chance to meet Chick Webb, whose band had taken over as the 'house band' at the Savoy from Fess Williams and His Royal Flush Orchestra after that band had enjoyed the distinction for several years. According to Ella legend, it was Bardu Ali who actually saw her perform at the HOH and who made it his business to introduce her to Webb. Ali, a singer, was also the front man for the Webb band, for Webb had neither the inclination nor the physical attributes necessary for such a job.

Webb, born William Henry Webb in Baltimore in 1909, was such a tiny child that early on he was given the nickname 'Chick'. While still a child, he had contracted tuberculosis of the spine, which, combined with a childhood fall down a flight of stairs, rendered him permanently deformed. Hunchbacked and stiff-legged, he was born too early to be helped by modern rehabilitative techniques; but one of his doctors, noting that he had a strong sense of rhythm, suggested that he take up drums as a way to exercise and strengthen his shoulders, arms and hands. Given the excuse that drumming on anything within reach was therapy, Chick banged on household items while dreaming of a real set of drums. He earned the money for his first drum set by selling newspapers, later boasting that he had sometimes sold three thousand in a day.

By the time he was fifteen Webb was a virtuoso on the drums, and so that year, 1924, he went north to New York City, a hunchbacked, four-foot-tall dwarf who, according to Garvin Bushell (who later played with the Webb band), probably could not read or write his name.[2] But he had a fantastic memory, could remember a complete arrangement after hearing it just once, and was determined to get a job with a big orchestra. Accompanying him was his Baltimore boyhood friend, John Trueheart, who played guitar and who would live up to his name by remaining with Webb for the rest of Webb's life. Neither could read music; they simply memorised the arrangements they heard.

Although he was crippled by tuberculosis of the spine, Chick Webb became known as a great dance drummer.
Ken Whitten Collection

Sincerely
Chick Webb

Duke Ellington got them their first job, at the Black Bottom Club. Ellington, born Edward Kennedy Ellington in 1899 and raised in Washington, DC, had arrived in New York with his band the previous year and opened at the Lafayette Theater on March 25, 1923. Ellington took credit not only for getting Webb his first job but also for elevating Webb to the position of bandleader. By 1926, Ellington knew so many musicians that other musicians would come to him for pick-up bands. He was leading a small band at the Kentucky club at Broadway and 49th Street when he received one such request. He and Sonny Greer, his drummer, went up to Harlem and assembled a group of five or six musicians, including Chick Webb as drummer. Ellington recalled:

> 'Now, you're the bandleader,' I said to Chick.
> 'Man, I don't want to be no bandleader,' he answered.
> 'All you do is collect the money and bring me mine.'
> 'Is that all I have to do?'
> 'Yeah.'
> 'Okay, I'm a bandleader.'[3]

The seventeen-year-old Webb called his first band the Harlem Stompers, and they were good enough to get some steady engagements and even to record in 1927, although the sides were never issued. When the band went into the Roseland Ballroom later that year, Webb changed the name of his group to the Roseland Band.

Unfortunately, Benny Carter came along in 1928 and took half of Webb's personnel away from him, promising them better gigs and more money. In those early years, Webb frequently lost personnel to other bandleaders. Musicians moved around a lot, and the makeup of most big bands was fluid, but Webb seems to have been harder, and more often, hit than most.

Webb was a great guy to work for because he was so easy-going and kind that his musicians were not afraid to leave him. Webb would lend his musicians money, pay their hospital bills, and hire them back after they had left him. Moreover, as a bandleader, he was among the best. According to music historian Barry Ulanov, 'He'd always stand at the side during rehearsals of new numbers and have section bits, figures, solos played over and over again until he was familiar with every bar in every arrangement. On the stand, if a musician or a section muffed something, he'd turn around and hum the right passage correctly, note for note, to the singer or group offenders.'4

In the late 1920s Webb formed a group he called the Jungle Band, which in 1929 recorded two titles for Brunswick, 'Dog Bottom' and 'Jungle Mama', that are now regarded as nascent jazz classics. The group's members changed over the next few years, but Webb's musicianship, as well as his leadership, continued to develop, and by the early 1930s he had a superb orchestra and a reputation as a dance-drummer.

According to Duke Ellington, 'Some musicians are dancers, and Chick was. You can dance with a lot of things besides your feet . . . Chick Webb was a dance-drummer who painted pictures of dances with his drums.'5 It did not matter that Webb's own feet and legs were practically useless and that his bass drum had special pedals for his feet, because he would not have been able to reach them otherwise. His sound made listeners want to dance. It even made his musicians feel good. According to Teddy McRae, who played tenor sax in the Webb band for a time, 'He could make you play whether you felt like it or not. You could come to work tired, he'd make you feel good.'6

In 1933, the Webb organisation became even stronger. Edgar Sampson, a composer, became Webb's chief arranger and second alto sax player that year; trombonist Sandy Williams and trumpet player Taft Jordan came on; and John Kirby arrived from Fletcher Henderson's orchestra as tuba and bass player. These men, together with Webb and others, formed a rhythm section that was pure swing, and not coincidentally it was in that year that Moe Gale engaged the Chick Webb Orchestra as the resident orchestra at the Savoy Ballroom, at the same time becoming manager of the Chick Webb band.

By the time Chick Webb went into the Savoy on a permanent basis, many swing bands had added male singers. For Webb, this development was especially welcome, because it meant that a singer could act as front man, engaging in the requisite patter, introducing the numbers, etc. For Webb, climbing up to and down off the 'throne' of his specially-built drumset according to the prevailing schedule at the Savoy, was in itself agony: the band usually played from 7.30 to 9.30, rested while the second band took over from 9.30 to 10.30, and then alternated hourly until 2 a.m. Approaching front-and-centre stage to announce numbers was beyond him. So his male singer took on those chores.

Especially good at it was Bardu Ali, who stepped into the role of putative leader while Webb drummed. Ali's father was Egyptian and he had been part of a tumbling act with his brother called the Ali Brothers. According to Garvin Bushell, Ali really couldn't sing, but he was handsome and knew how to conduct.

At the time Bardu Ali saw Ella at the Harlem Opera House, he was doing the announcing for Webb and Charlie Linton was the featured singer with the Chick Webb Orchestra. Formerly of the Linton Brothers, a gospel quartet out of Cheraw, South Carolina, Dizzy Gillespie's hometown, Charlie had eventually struck out on his own. His voice, according to Dizzy Gillespie, was high. He found a home with the Chick Webb band, and remained with Webb until Webb's death. Although Ali talked excitedly about the girl with the voice like a horn, in Webb's opinion, Charlie Linton was enough. He didn't see the need for singers at all, but the public seemed to want them, and the key to success was pleasing the public. He was not alone among bandleaders in his lack of enthusiasm for girl singers. According to the jazz magazine *Swing*, 'Ask any ten bandleaders as to their pet headache . . . nine will answer "girl vocalists" . . . Yes, girl vocalists are a nuisance.'[7]

Distinguished as such because in earlier times big-band vocalists were exclusively male, 'girl vocalists' required separate dressing rooms, cleaner language, and presented all sorts of problems for a band travelling on the road, including separate quarters. They could also be a source of dissension among the guys in a band by favouring some more than others. Moreover, in the opinion of many band-leaders and sidemen, they did not understand jazz, were not serious musicians, and were superfluous. But they were becoming in-creasingly more important to big-band entertainment, and Bardu Ali did not forget Ella, or his feeling that Chick Webb needed a girl singer.

Not long afterward, Webb took his orchestra into the Apollo Theatre for a week's engagement. Toward the end of the week, Ella was there, too, scheduled to appear in yet another amateur hour and hoping to get a professional booking. Bardu Ali saw her standing in the wings, wearing what looked like men's shoes and munching on a hot dog. He approached her, told her he had heard her sing, and invited her to Chick Webb's dressing room so the bandleader could hear her. Ella, who had often danced at the Savoy to Chick Webb's swinging music, needed no coaxing.

Dozing in his dressing room between shows, Webb was not pleased at the interruption, but he was too kind not to listen to Ella sing 'The Object of My Affection'. 'I always thought my music was pretty much hollering,' joked Ella, 'but he didn't.'[8] Webb realised that she had a superb voice and perfect pitch, and something told him to pay close attention to this girl. According to George Wein, founder of the Newport (now JVC) Jazz Festival, 'He tried to get some alternate opinions. Most of the musicians didn't understand why Chick was so high on her. But he heard something, and he was right.'[9]

At first, Webb wasn't sure what to do with her. It occurred to him, however, that he and his orchestra were scheduled to play a fraternity party at Yale the following evening and that Ella, with her white pop singer style, might go over very well. He called Moe Gale with that suggestion. Moe Gale came over to the Apollo to have a look at Ella. He looked, and said to Chick Webb, 'You're kidding.'

The girl was definitely plain, even awkward. She dressed in clothes that looked like charity handouts and affected a little-girl demeanour that may have softened the hearts of some men but not Moe Gale's. Gale announced that he would not pay her for any kind of booking. So, Bardu Ali and Chick Webb pooled their resources to pay Ella for the Yale gig.

Ella knew nothing of these behind-the-scenes doings. All she knew was that Mr Ali and Mr Webb liked her, and that she was going to go with the band to New Haven the next day.

Shy Ella kept to herself as the band bus made its way to New Haven. Most of the musicians ignored her, as musicians were wont to do unless a girl was very pretty. Their attitude changed somewhat after Ella began to sing. Her white-sounding style went over well with those Yale college guys and their dates, who crowded around the bandstand after her set and called for more. Webb was convinced that Ella could be an asset on such occasions, but he wasn't sure how she would go over at the Savoy.

He decided to try her out for a week. Moe Gale refused to pay her. He didn't know how Webb could even think of putting a girl who looked like that up on the bandstand. 'She looked incredible,' he recalled years later, 'her hair was dishevelled, her clothes just terrible!' Webb responded to Gale's scepticism by saying, 'Mr Gale, you'd be surprised what a beauty parlor and some make-up and nice clothes can do.'

At least Charles Buchanan, manager of the Savoy, was in Webb's, and Ella's, corner. Recalling the night Chick Webb first brought Ella to the Ballroom, he described her as 'young, simple, an orphan': 'I said to Chick, "I'll put ten dollars, and you put ten dollars." We pooled the twenty dollars and hired Ella. The second week we paid her fifty dollars. The third week we dressed her up.'[10]

By that third week, Webb had decided to make Ella his girl singer, sharing vocal duties with Charlie Linton. He also became her protector, the first of several men who would serve that crucial function in the life of a timid and insecure woman. Webb talked the problem of Ella's being underage over with his wife, Sallye, and they decided to become Ella's legal guardians.

Sallye Webb was white. According to Mrs Irving Randolph, wife of a Webb band member in the late 1930s, she did not fraternise with the band members, nor take much interest in the business of the band. 'She was no Gladys Hampton,' says Mrs Randolph. Gladys Hampton essentially managed her husband Lionel's band for years. 'Gladys Hampton was an educated woman,' continues Mrs Randolph, 'and of course Sallye was no comparison to Gladys Hampton. Sallye was just a white woman, that's all, and Chick liked her, and that was that.'[11]

Sallye Webb took an interest in the young, shy Ella, however, and under her tutelage Ella began to pay attention to her looks. She did have one thing going for her – brown skin. Even the most talented and beautiful girl singers didn't make it on a stage in those days if they were dark-skinned. She acquired a neat, short haircut, learned how to use makeup, and dressed in soft, becoming styles. Within a few months, she had adopted tweezered eyebrows and taken to wearing flowers in her hair à la Billie Holiday.

Holiday, three years older than Ella, was enjoying considerable success by this time. In 1933, she'd made her first recordings with Benny Goodman, and in 1935 she'd recorded several sides with Goodman's pianist Teddy Wilson. (While billed as Teddy Wilson and His Orchestra, the musicians were simply a group culled from Goodman's band. Wilson did not form his own band until 1940.) She'd played a week at the Apollo Theater in April 1935 and made a return engagement for two weeks in August. She'd even made a brief appearance in a short East Coast film titled *Rhapsody in Black* with Duke Ellington's Orchestra. While weighing in at over two hundred pounds, much heftier than the one hundred and thirty-pound Ella, she had a definite style and carried herself with ladylike dignity. In fact, she had already acquired the nickname 'Lady'.

Billie Holiday became close friends with many members of the bands she worked with. Ella and the 'boys in the band' coexisted. While some sources say that the musicians became protective of her and called her 'Sis', members of the band in the early years do not recall such closeness. Says saxophonist Garvin Bushell, who was with Webb when Ella joined the band, 'It was pretty lonesome for her, because none of us paid her any mind. She was big and gawky. She never made an impression on anybody.'[12] Says bass player Beverly Peer, 'We went our way, she went hers.'[13]

Ella was pleasant but remained shy and kept her distance. It wasn't her style to try to be 'one of the boys', as Sarah Vaughan and Dinah Washington would, using even saltier language and telling even raunchier jokes than the men did. Nor did she feel comfortable enough with men in general to flirt with them. Ella remained aloof and, perhaps taking another cue from Billie Holiday, acted the lady.

Such a lady was Ella, in fact, that she was rather nonplussed when people called her by her first name: 'It used to bother me when people I didn't know came up and called me Ella,' she says. 'It seemed to me they should say, "Miss Fitzgerald," but somehow they never do.'[14]

Chick Webb had no real need for a girl singer, except as window dressing. His style was instrumental music, and he continued to perform and record as if his singers were essentially superfluous. In fact, for Webb, just about anything but music was superfluous. George Wein featured a resuscitated Webb band at the Newport Jazz Festival in 1978. 'I interviewed all the surviving members of the band in 1978,' says Wein. 'What I learned was that Chick Webb was probably the most intensely involved with music of any jazz musician who ever lived. His musicians could never remember him saying, "Who won the game today?" never heard him talk about the weather or a restaurant or anything except what he thought the band should play that night.'[15]

Webb recognised that Ella was a young, naïve girl with an un-polished talent, and he had no interest in catapulting her to a featured role that she might not be able to handle. According to Ella, 'He used to tell me, you never want to be someone who goes up fast, because you come down the same way. And you meet the same people coming down as you do going up.'[16]

He brought her along slowly, letting her sing a couple of choruses during each set, always uptempo tunes, because he didn't feel she was ready yet for ballads. She had trouble sustaining notes, and Webb decided she wasn't breathing correctly. At one point, he considered hiring a voice teacher for her, but the prospective teacher assured Webb that Ella already had a style, and formal instruction might ruin it. Because Ella never received formal instruction in voice, her breathing and thus her phrasing were poor technically. But her voice had a clarity and a native instrumentality that no amount of coaching could engender. In fact, as the teacher understood, lessons might adversely affect those qualities.

At first, Ella didn't mind having so little time on the bandstand. When she wasn't singing, she was on the floor dancing, and to her mind it was the best of all possible worlds to dance and get paid while doing it.

Even singing so little, Ella was noticed. Mary Lou Williams, the great jazz pianist, recalled, 'One night, scuffling around Harlem, I fell in the Savoy. After dancing a couple of rounds, I heard a voice that sent chills up and down my spine (which I never thought could happen). I almost ran to the stand to find out who belonged to that voice, and saw a pleasant-looking, brown-skinned girl standing modestly and singing the greatest. I was told her name was Ella Fitzgerald and that Chick Webb had unearthed her from one of the Apollo's amateur hours.'[17] A musician like Williams recognised right away the hornlike quality of Ella's voice, as well as its tremendous, two-and-a-half-octave range.

Webb allowed Ella to record two songs early on, and for Ella it was a memorable experience going into the New York recording studios of the new Decca label (with which Webb had signed a contract the previous year) on June 12, 1935, and seeing how records were made. Because the sounds were recorded directly on wax discs, there were no 'takes'. If you messed up, the disc was ruined and had to be melted down. If every member of a group didn't start at exactly the same time, the disc also had to be scrapped. Every bit of background noise was picked up on the disc, so recording studios were airless and hot. Recalls Lionel Hampton of recording sessions in 1929, 'There was a huge microphone in the middle, and the musicians moved up close or far away from it, depending on what kind of sound they wanted. That was the 1929 version of "mixing". The engineer sat over in a corner trying to get the sound on wax, and you usually didn't get a good cut the first time, so you had to do it over and over until you got it.'[18]

One song Ella did that first recording session was 'Love and Kisses' by composer J. C. Johnson and lyricists George Whiting and Nat Schwartz. It has since disappeared, as did many songs recorded by black artists in those days, for music publishers did not give their best songs to black singers. However, it had a short life on jukeboxes in black clubs. Ella was fascinated by the idea that she had actually made a record that people could hear, although being underage she had a hard time hearing it on jukeboxes in bars. Soon after the record was released, the band was in Philadelphia. Ella wanted to hear her record at the local beer garden, but she knew she couldn't get in. She recalled, 'So I had some fellow who was over twenty-one go in and put a nickel in while I stood outside and listened to my own voice coming out.'[19]

Ella had more opportunities to hear her own voice in October of 1935, when she was featured on two of the five sides of the Webb group recorded: 'Rhythm and Romance' and 'I'll Chase the Blues Away'.

While the Webb band played some outside engagements, their primary home was the Savoy Ballroom where by 1935 Webb was the undisputed 'King of the Savoy'. There was nothing like steady work to keep a group of musicians together, and Webb no longer regularly lost musicians to other bandleaders. A group of musicians who work together consistently can create a more polished sound than a group who are unused to one another. But the popularity of the band derived primarily from Webb himself, who by 1936 was beginning to assert himself more and more as a soloist.

By the same year, however, the importance of singers to bands was beginning to overshadow their instrumentation. Demanded by audiences, singers added a dimension to a band's performance that ordinary people who had no hope of understanding pure jazz needed. Along with singers came lyrics, to which the average person could relate better than to instrumentation, no matter how clever or lyrical.

Moreover, a singer, male or female, was out front, not hidden behind an instrument, and thus more accessible to audiences. All the commercially successful bands had singers – Ellington had Ivie Anderson, Basie Jimmy Rushing, Goodman Helen Ward. Charlie Linton was still with Webb, and Ella was getting more time on stage. When she wasn't singing, she would usually stand at the side of the band, and as the various sections blew their ensemble phrases, she'd sing along with each one, often gesturing with her hands as though she were leading the band. In so doing, she was furthering her musical education, training her voice's instrumentality.

Another aspect of Ella's musical education came with the famous 'battles' of bands at the Savoy that most often pitted the Webb band against another led by a major bandleader. A born scrapper, which

was no doubt why he had come so far despite his physical handicaps, Webb had been battling other bands since the 1920s when his band had only eight pieces – including Elmer Williams on tenor sax, Johnny Hodges on alto sax, Bobby Stark on trumpet, Slats Long on trombone, and Leon England on bass. According to Duke Ellington, 'Webb was always battle-mad, and those eight guys used to take on every band that came up to play [at the Savoy]. And most times they did the cutting, regardless of the fact that half the time the other bands were twice the size. But the unforgettable and lovable Webb ate up any kind of fight, and everybody in the band played like mad at all times. They figured out a bunch of original numbers, and it was generally too bad for the guy on the opposite stand.'[20]

Ironically, one of Webb's few losses was to the Ellington Orchestra in a battle that was one of the most famous in the history of the Savoy. Ellington had been loath to do battle, saying to Webb, 'Look, man, we got the place full, we ain't gettin' no more money, why knock our brains out?'[21] But Webb, perhaps eager to show his early mentor what he had been able to accomplish in the years since, and clearly determined to outdo what was considered by many to be the best band in the country (although not the most commercially success-ful), persisted. Ellington gave in, and knocked Webb's socks off.

With each set, the two bands played louder and faster, and it was only when the playing of the Ellington orchestra actually shattered several windows in the club that Webb conceded defeat. It was a lesson for Webb that he wasn't quite ready to take on the top band in the country, and it was a lesson for Ella that no matter how good a musician you were, there was always a higher plane.

But she was impatient to get the experience she knew she needed. She was so eager to sing that at times she couldn't keep herself off the bandstand. She pleaded with Webb to let her do more singing. Webb was still struggling to fit his new 'girl singer' into what remained a basically instrumental format, especially at the Savoy. He still thought first of Charlie Linton when it came to ballad singing, and once assigned Linton to sing a ballad that had been especially arranged for Ella. Ella reportedly burst into tears. It was a frustrating time for her. She had no allies among the musicians. She had no offers

Taken under Chick Webb's wing, Ella, shown here with Webb Orchestra vocalist Charlie Linton in 1935, blossomed into an attractive young woman.
Frank Driggs Collection

39

from other bandleaders. Even if such an offer had come her way, however, she would have entertained no serious thoughts of leaving Webb. She was grateful to Webb for giving her a chance.

Early in 1936, Webb got his own radio show, a thirty-minute weekly broadcast from the Savoy on NBC called 'Gems of Color'. In this format, a girl singer made sense, and with the popular audience in mind he featured Ella frequently, especially on novelty numbers. The audience response was good enough to cause Webb to start thinking more seriously about the commercial possibilities of her voice.

Her exposure on radio may also have led to Ella's being asked to fill in for Billie Holiday on a session with Teddy Wilson and His Orchestra in March 1936, when Holiday was playing some out-of-town theatre dates with the Jimmie Lunceford band. Ella's renditions of 'My Melancholy Baby' and 'All of My Life' sold as well as Wilson's recordings with Holiday usually did, although British fans of the Holiday-Wilson recordings were reportedly disappointed.

The month following Ella's recording session with Wilson, Webb decided to give her another opportunity to record with his band. At a session at the Decca studios on April 7, 1936, four of the sides recorded featured Ella, and the songs were primarily ballads. Ella was overjoyed, and believed she had reached a milestone in her nascent career.

3 'A-Tisket, A-Tasket'

On April 25, 1936, eighteen days after the first Webb recording session to feature her on vocals, Ella celebrated her eighteenth birthday. She no longer needed a legal guardian and could sign her own contracts, although her professional relationship with Webb was not that formal. She was making $50 a week with Webb by now, a substantial income by Harlem standards, enabling her to dress well and to live comfortably. She moved out of the Webb home and into a room of her own.

While she helped out her sister and her aunt, her time and her money were hers to do with as she pleased, and when she was not singing with Webb she could be found in the audiences of various clubs and theatres, listening to both instrumentalists and vocalists whom she admired. It was her misfortune, however, to have reached her majority and achieved financial independence at a time when the bloom was off the Harlem rose.

The Depression had cast a long shadow over Harlem by this time. In fact, by 1934, according to the interracial organisation, the National Urban League, eighty per cent of Harlemites were on relief. 'Last hired and first fired', as the saying went, residents could not afford to pay the prices charged by the white-owned Harlem stores. Nor could they get jobs in those stores, or on the city-operated buses that plied the local boulevards. The pride and energy of the 1920s and early 1930s had given way to despair and increasing anti-white resentment, which had exploded in March 1935.

One of Harlem's worst riots to date was sparked by an incident at the Kress department store on 125th Street. A sixteen-year-old black Puerto Rican youth named Lino Rivera was caught shoplifting a ten-cent knife by a white employee. The two scuffled outside the store, attracting a crowd of onlookers; and within minutes the rumour spread that a white man was beating a black boy. Someone threw a brick through a white-owned store window, and like spontaneous combustion whole blocks of Harlem were engulfed in looting and burning.

This was hardly the way to keep white downtowners and out-of-towners coming to Harlem. The long soup lines were too depressing anyway. Since the repeal of Prohibition in 1933, Harlem nightlife had steadily lost its attraction; the exotic newness of the Harlem Renaissance had palled. When the fabled Cotton Club closed its doors on February 16, 1936, and moved downtown, it was the end of an era.

Not being the correct skin colour, nor having the money to patronise the Cotton Club, Ella was not affected by this event. But she could see the nightlife of Harlem fading and was aware that the downtown clubs were picking up the slack. West 52nd Street was becoming the new centre for innovative music. Billie Holiday opened at the Onyx Club there in September 1936. Ella felt that she, too, was ready for greater exposure.

On October 29, 1936, when the Webb band recorded four more sides for Decca, Ella showed she was ready. On 'If You Can't Sing It, You'll Have to Swing It', more popularly known as 'Mr Paganini', Ella mispronounced the Italian composer and violinist's name, calling him 'Mr Pagganinny'. But she also took a musical risk and scatted one line in the song. It may have been the first time – at least on record – that she did so, a harbinger of the vocal mastery that would elevate many relatively banal songs to near classics.

Scatting, originated by Louis Armstrong back in 1926, involved substituting nonsense syllables for a song's lyrics. Only singers with control of the instrumentation of their voices could scat successfully. Ella would become a master at the form.

For this and other reasons, Benny Goodman continued to be impressed with Ella's voice. He invited her to appear on his segment of the NBC radio show, 'Let's Dance' (the show featured three bands – 'hot', 'sweet' and 'rhythm'; Goodman's was the hot band). He also asked her to record with him for RCA Victor. Webb had no objection, and on November 5, 1936, less than a week after her October 29 session with Webb, Ella happily sang on three cuts for Goodman – 'Goodnight My Love', 'Take Another Guess', and 'Did You Mean It?'.

Unfortunately, neither Webb nor Goodman – and certainly not Ella – had any idea of the legal ramifications of that innocent session. The songs became hits, and Decca stepped in to protest, charging that Ella had breached the contract between Webb and Decca by recording with Goodman. At Decca's insistence, Ella's name was taken off the record labels. This may be why some discographies list Helen Ward as the vocalist on those cuts.

Who had a contract with whom meant little to musicians in New York in the 1930s. They wanted to record together, so they did. A musician in a band could bill himself as an orchestra leader for recording purposes, and the real orchestra leader didn't mind at all. Ella couldn't understand why she couldn't record with whomever she wanted, for after all, she had signed no recording contract with Decca. Decca, however, maintained that its contract with Webb covered all of Webb's personnel, and now that Ella was becoming more and more popular, Decca intended to exercise its right of exclusivity over her.

Ella was indeed becoming popular. On November 18, 1936, she recorded for the first time as a headliner, something she had been pushing for. Billed as 'Ella Fitzgerald and Her Savoy Eight', she fronted Taft Jordan on trumpet, Sandy Williams on trombone, Pete Clark on clarinet, Teddy McRae on tenor and baritone sax, Tommy Fulford on piano, John Trueheart on guitar, Beverly Peer on bass, and Webb on drums, and recorded two cuts for Decca, 'My Last Affair' and 'Organ Grinder's Swing'.

The next day they did two more cuts, 'Shine' and 'Darktown Strutters' Ball', which they had performed on Webb's radio broadcasts from the Savoy and were never among their proudest accomplishments. Both were racist novelty tunes of the sort that Decca believed would appeal to whites, like the darkey souvenirs one could buy at carnivals. Black entertainers went along with this racist exploitation – playing 'jungle rhythms', singing blue material – because whites controlled most aspects of the music business. Black bands had to work with white managers because there were no opportunities for black managers. White record companies controlled the major markets and therefore the type of material recorded. The music business was so segregated that record companies frequently had black singers record for black audiences the same songs that white singers had recorded for white audiences. Called 'covers', these records were then sold in the 'race music' sections of record stores and played on the 'race music' stations. Covers were also a feature of the white record business – if a white singer had a hit song, one or more other white singers would record 'covers' of it. But the reasons were not the same. Fortunately for Ella, she arrived on the entertainment scene when the more flagrantly racist songs were beginning to lose favour.

Ella Fitzgerald and Her Savoy Eight recorded about twice a year for the next two years. As her confidence as a singer grew, she even tried her hand at songwriting. 'You Showed Me the Way', with music by Webb, McRae and trombonist Benny Green, and lyrics by Ella, was first recorded on January 25, 1937, by Teddy Wilson and His Orchestra, with Billie Holiday on vocals. It was a particular source of pride to Ella to have her singing idol record her song.

Holiday had just finished a second engagement at the Onyx Club on West 52nd Street and was ensconced for three months at Uptown House, a basement club on Seventh Avenue and 134th Street in Harlem. Ella went there to hear her as often as she could, but she still had not got up the courage to speak to Holiday.

The waning of Harlem as a playground for whites was bad news for the operators of the Savoy Ballroom, who were concerned about losing business. By 1937 the Ballroom had instituted a policy of inviting white bands to play opposite Webb's on Sundays. On May 11, 1937, the guest band was Benny Goodman's, the first appearance at the Savoy for the 'King of Swing'. According to legend, twenty thousand people were turned away that night. The riot squad and the fire department were called out to keep order. Shortly before the show began, Chick Webb spoke to Ella and his musicians, saying, 'This is the turning point of the band. You know how much this means to me.'

That night, the Webb organisation played as they never had before. Ella did her part, and it's said that while she sang the audience of four thousand locked arms and swayed to her swinging sounds. But the real kicker was Webb's extended drum solo, which brought a thunderous ovation.

The barriers against integrated bands performing together were still intact – only Benny Goodman travelled with two black musicians, Teddy Wilson and Lionel Hampton, and they were part of the Benny Goodman Quartet which played separately, never at the same time as the big band. But now there was greater fluidity in recording. Black and white musicians frequently recorded together, and Benny

Goodman, among others, had recorded with black singers like Billie Holiday and Ella. June Richmond worked regularly with Jimmy Dorsey's band, and Billie Holiday would soon begin travelling with Artie Shaw and his orchestra. Ella wondered if she would have more chances to record with white bands.

Still, Ella had begun to reach a white audience. The music magazine *Down Beat*, founded in 1935, the majority of whose readers were white, conducted an annual readers' poll to identify the most popular musicians and singers. Published in its first issue of the new year, the poll for 1937 awarded top male vocalist honours to Bing Crosby and female vocalist honours to the teenager Ella Fitzgerald (Mildred Bailey was second, Billie Holiday third). At the end of the year, the readers of the British music publication *Melody Maker* accorded her the same honour. Ella's was a miraculous success story – from an orphan in man's shoes to one of the top female singers in just over two years – and she owed it all to Chick Webb.

Webb was well known for helping other musicians. A young Dizzy Gillespie was with Teddy Hill's band when it went into the Savoy in 1937. Mario Bauza was then playing first trumpet for Webb, and he took an interest in Gillespie. Gillespie later recalled, 'Chick Webb liked me, too. He used to let me sit in Taft Jordan's place and take solos, and I think I was the only one he used to let sit in like that. Of course, I could read very well by that time.'[1]

But in the case of Ella Fitzgerald, Chick Webb really hit the jackpot. She was the one who made the Chick Webb orchestra famous. 'This is it,' Webb reportedly said, 'I have a real singer now. That's what the public wants.'[2]

Some jazz historians, notably Gunther Schuller, feel that Webb essentially sold out to commercialism by featuring Ella on more and more records. In a footnote in his book, *The Swing Era*, Schuller writes that '. . . once Ella's popularity had been established, the Webb band recorded only sixteen instrumentals, as opposed to fifty-seven vocals (*not* even counting the two dozen titles recorded under her name and the Savoy Eight). The vast majority of these vocals were by Ella, and of dubious merit. Younger readers, who know Fitzgerald only as a single in the fifties and sixties and a magnificent ballad and scat singer performing real jazz materials, will have no idea of the idiotic, often trashy songs she sang in her early career.'[3]

But while such criticism might have hurt Ella if she'd heard it, she would not have been dissuaded from continuing to sing exactly the same material. What mattered to her was singing, and feeling the love that only her audiences could bestow.

Ella's increasing popularity as a singer did wonders for her social life, for it made her more attractive to the male hangers on, the 'groupies' of the 1930s who enjoyed basking in the reflected light of even the dimmest stars. Ella had plenty of young, attractive men, according to band members of the time. They ran errands for her, escorted her to clubs, consistently praised her singing, and offered her advice on her career. But Ella was justifiably wary of their intentions. She saw the invisible strings and the potential for exploitation. The appreciation of audiences was genuine.

Nearly as genuine was the appreciation of other bandleaders who envied Webb and wished they had a singer like Ella. After Ella won the *Down Beat* and *Melody Maker* polls, Jimmie Lunceford offered her a job at $75 per week, more than what Webb was paying her.

Lunceford was the most academically trained and one of the classiest black bandleaders. He'd earned a BA in music at Fisk University in Nashville, Tennessee, and done graduate work at Fisk and at New York's City College. He had then taken a job teaching music at Manassa High School in Memphis and organised his first band with students in his class. When they graduated and went on to Fisk, Lunceford went with them, taking a position as an assistant professor of music. During the next four years, the band played frequently in the South, and upon the students' graduation Lunceford took them to New York. They played at the Cotton Club in Harlem in the spring of 1934 and launched a career as a big band.

Ella admired Lunceford and appreciated his offer of more money, as well as his promise that she could sing the ballads that Webb denied her the opportunity to sing. But she felt an intense loyalty to Webb (whom she still called Mr Webb), without whom she believed she might still be stuck on the amateur-night circuit. Moreover, Ella was not good at adjusting to change; she preferred the known to the unknown. In the end, Lunceford withdrew his offer, out of respect for Webb; and Webb, reminded of how sought-after Ella was becoming, raised her salary from $50 to $125 per week.

Around that time, he also gave Ella a ring. 'I thought it was something he wanted me to try on for size for his wife,' she has said, 'but he said it was for me.'[4] It was as if to seal their bond, and Ella never again considered breaking it.

She established no such bond with the Webb band musicians,

however. Webb encouraged her to hang out with the guys to develop the instrumentation of her voice; when they jammed, she should jam with them. But while she seemed to enjoy jamming with the musicians onstage, she was not part of their after-hours sessions. At one point she decided that she, too, should play an instrument and took up the accordion; but the fellows were reluctant to carry it around for her, so she dropped the idea.

According to bassist Beverly Peer, not much had changed since Ella had first joined the Webb organisation. 'Ella always kept to herself and really didn't have much to do with the musicians. Whenever we stopped playing, nobody knew where she disappeared to. Most of the musicians didn't really care much for her personality. I don't think she was really nasty, but she was insecure and so she came off as being nasty. Nobody messed with her. We just went right on about our business, and she went on about hers.'[5] Ella was far more comfortable with her family and old friends than in trying to make new friends. She kept her private life separate from her professional life.

Personalities aside, Webb's sidemen continued to resent the increased prominence that their leader was giving to a girl singer, which naturally detracted from the earlier emphasis on musicianship. Although the band's billing was now Chick Webb and his Band with Ella Fitzgerald, or sometimes even Ella Fitzgerald with the Chick Webb Band, Ella wasn't the only reason why the Webb group was at the height of its popularity. The brass section was enjoying considerable fame in itself. Dubbed the Five Horsemen by their fellow band members, these musicians – Taft Jordan, Mario Bauza, and Bobby Stark on trumpet, and Nat Story and Sandy Williams on trombone – attracted crowds around the bandstand at the Savoy when they did 'St Louis Blues' and 'Stardust' and 'Tiger Rag'.

Alto sax and clarinet player Garvin Bushell had played with Webb in the early 1930s, then left to join Cab Calloway, who paid him better. When he rejoined Webb in 1937, he accepted a lower salary in order to be part of the music the Webb band was playing: 'Musically, it was much more pleasurable with Webb than with Cab. The arrangements were better, and featured the band more. The sections had a better quality of sound. And in order to feature Webb, we had to play some uptempo ballads.'[6]

Chick's solos were better than ever, and so it was the musicians as well as Ella who earned a sustaining programme on NBC ('sustained' by the network rather than by sponsors) with the Ink Spots titled 'The

The Chick Webb Orchestra in 1937. Back row, from left: Wayman Carver, John Trueheart, Tommy Fulford, Taft Jordan, Nat Story, Sandy Williams, Charlie Linton, Teddy McRae, Chauncey Haughton. Front row: Mario Bauza, Beverly Peer, Chick Webb, Louis Jordan, Bardu Ali.
Ken Whitten Collection

Good Time Society', which remained on the air for several months. It was also the Webb organisation as a whole that was sought after by venues other than the Savoy. The band frequently played guest engagements elsewhere in New York and in other East Coast cities.

But Webb still considered Ella the key to success, especially in attracting white audiences, which was essential to the band's commercial well-being. Black audiences could not support a large organisation like Webb's. Garvin Bushell believes that the reason why Webb fired Louis Jordan, who sang like Louis Armstrong, was that Jordan was overshadowing Ella. 'Ella's one problem was that she didn't have a tremendous amount of personality on stage. She couldn't put on a number like Louis Jordan, who was in the band when I joined. Louis would go out and just gas, break up the show. Nobody could follow him. Louis was overshadowing Ella, so Chick decided to fire him.'

The band was at the RKO Theater in Boston in early 1938. Says Bushell, 'Chick decided to get rid of Louis without giving notice. Louis was always hollering, "If you don't like what I do, fire me!" I heard this down the hall, after the show. I remember Chick said, "Well, that's exactly what I'm going to do" . . . And that was the best thing that ever happened to Louis, because he got a job at the Speedway in New York – that's where he started his Tympany Five – and that was it.'[7]

By the time he fired Louis Jordan, Webb was letting Ella do more singing. The swing era was in full blossom, and even the prodigious Tin Pan Alley songwriters couldn't keep up with the demand for songs to be recorded in swing tempo. Webb started letting Ella do more ballads, although he still didn't think she was ready. Aware that her ballad style needed work, as often as she could Ella went to hear Billie Holiday, who was then singing with Artie Shaw's band. Ella visited the Roseland Ballroom in 1938 to hear Billie and the two singers had their first real talk.

Often compared by musical pollsters, Fitzgerald and Holiday were worlds apart in style and life experience. While both had had difficult childhoods, Holiday's had been far more tragic than Ella's and Holiday nursed her wounds with booze and dope. Already she had a reputation for unreliability, but when she felt like singing she could tear your heart out. Ella, on the other hand, could be counted on to turn in a good performance every time. But her singing lacked emotional depth. She kept her feelings to herself, her need for self-protection stronger than her need to communicate. Far from reaching out to her listeners, she bade her listeners reach out to her. Her singing came from her vocal chords; she did not allow it to emanate from her soul.

If Ella's singing lacked emotional depth, it was marked by marvellous clarity, as is evident on the recordings she did in early 1938. In January, she recorded two sides: 'It's Wonderful' and 'I Was Doing All Right'. In the early spring, she did six sides: 'This Time It's Real', 'What Do You Know About Love?', 'You Can't Be Mine (And Someone Else's Too)', 'We Can't Go on This Way', 'Saving Myself for You' and 'If You Only Knew'. They were good ballads, and Ella sang them nicely. But it was a novelty song that really catapulted Ella to fame.

During an engagement at the RKO Theatre in Boston – possibly the same engagement during which Webb fired Louis Jordan – Webb was hospitalised with a flareup of his tuberculosis. Ella and the band carried on without him. One day at rehearsal she was sitting at the piano trying to come up with a song she could sing to Webb to cheer him up. Noodling around with two fingers, she began to sing the words to a nursery song she remembered from primary school, where the children sang it as they played a little game called 'Drop the Handkerchief'.

> A-tisket, A-tasket
> A brown and yellow basket
> I wrote a letter to my mummy,
> On the way I dropped it.
> I dropped it, I dropped it.
> Yes, on the way I dropped it.
> A little girlie picked it up
> And put it in her pocket

Al Feldman, a pianist who had been arranging for Webb for a couple of years and who would later change his name to Van Alexander and successfully lead his own band, happened by. Intrigued by the ditty Ella was singing and picking out on the piano, he sat down with her, and shortly they had created a novelty song. When Ella sang it for Webb, he liked it so much that he gave her the go-ahead to try it out on stage. She did so while the Webb group was still in Boston, and the audience loved it.

Novelty tunes were still very popular. Most of the top singers and groups had recorded at least one, including Maxine Sullivan's rendition of 'Loch Lomond', Larry Clinton's 'Dipsy Doodle', Rudy Vallee's 'The Whiffenpoof Song', and the Andrews Sisters' 'Bei Mir Bist Du Schön', of which Ella had recently recorded a cover for the black audience. 'A-Tisket, A-Tasket' fitted right in with such fare.

Back in New York, Ella celebrated her twentieth birthday on April 25. About a week later, with the Webb band, she went into the Decca recording studio for her twelfth time in three years. Webb wanted to record 'A-Tisket, A-Tasket' but Jack Kemp, Decca's A&R (Artists and Repertory) man, was not impressed with it, complaining that it was just a children's song. He couldn't imagine who would buy it. Webb assured Kemp that the song had gone over well with audiences. Kemp relented, and the song was one of four sides recorded during that May 1938 session.

The band recorded the song much as they had rendered it in live performances, with an engaging repartee that went:

> Was it green?
> No, no, no no!
> Was it red?
> No, no, no, no!
> Was it blue?
> No, no, no, no!
> Just a little yellow basket.

Backed by a song called 'Liza', the record – Ella's twenty-seventh for Decca – was released soon afterward and almost immediately made the record charts. The Lucky Strike Hit Parade was then in its third year. Georgia Gibbs sang the song on the show, and it soon became number one. It was the biggest hit of the summer, on the charts for seventeen weeks and number one on the Hit Parade. By September it had sold over a million copies, a landmark even then, although at the time the industry was not dispensing gold records.

Why the song was so popular is anybody's guess. One would have to explain why 'The Whiffenpoof Song' was such a hit, or the novelty singer Slim Gaillard's 'The Flat Foot Floogie With the Floy Floy' (Gaillard was famous for his hep-cat expressions, like 'O-voutie, orooney'). The gathering clouds of war in Europe produced a sense of unease, and novelty songs offered an escape from the pressures of the real world. Ella had displayed no clever market analysis in coming up with the song; she'd just been noodling around, trying to cheer up Webb. She was as surprised as anyone else that the song was such a hit.

As a songwriter, Ella was eligible to join ASCAP (the American Society of Composers, Authors, and Publishers), which she did, becoming the youngest member in its history. She would prove that she was no flash-in-the-pan as a novelty songwriter, following 'A-Tisket, A-Tasket' with 'I Found My Yellow Basket', 'Chew, Chew, Chew', 'Oh, But I Do' and other songs.

The Webb band went on tour that summer, capitalising on the popularity of 'A-Tisket, A-Tasket'. They performed several times in Boston, where the song had first been well received.

One couple who are long-time Ella fans remember her and the Chick Webb Orchestra at the small club in the Gardner Hotel in Boston. 'She would sit at the edge of the stage swinging her rather hefty right arm in time to the music,' they recall. 'The number everyone waited for was "A-Tisket, A-Tasket".'[8]

Another fan remembers seeing Ella in performance right after she had recorded the song: 'They were appearing at the RKO Boston Theater, coupled with some forgettable movie. For me, the band and its young vocal star eclipsed all else. During the movie interval, an equally devoted young girl, with whom I'd been dancing in the aisles, suggested that we try for autographs at the stage door. We were allowed to wait in a small corridor while a postcard-sized photo of the band was being signed by the musicians. At that point Ella appeared to receive a sales pitch from a suave gentleman who had a Boston bull terrier puppy available at a modest price. He held up the dog, which was certainly appealing, but Ella was the principal focus of our interest. She, too, was taken by the pup, but declined, citing the band's rootless wanderings as a drawback. As I watched her, trans-fixed by her nearness, I noted that she seemed almost diminutive, and of a proportion that a large pair of hands could span her waist. A really appealing young woman, soft-voiced, and gracious in her rejection of his offer. The girl and I stumbled out with our autographed pictures and felt clad in reflected glory.'[9]

It's interesting how different people who saw Ella at about the same time remember her size. In the eyes of one, she had a rather hefty arm, and in the eyes of another she was almost diminutive. Photographs from that time reveal an Ella of generous proportions, but not fat, and with a comparatively trim waist. Ella was one of those women whose size depends on the eye of the beholder.

The Webb band made its first trip to the West Coast that summer. For Ella, it was a rehearsal for later trips into the South, for Los Angeles was as racist as a southern town in those days and rigidly segregated. The band played mostly white clubs, which did not admit blacks. One of the few engagements at which blacks could hear them was at a small bowling alley at 48th and Central Avenue in the heart of the black section of town, the only bowling alley in the city open to blacks. At the time, Ella could not imagine herself ever living there.

Back on the more liberal East Coast, the Webb band began playing at white clubs more often, thanks to the popularity of Ella. It was the first black band to perform at New York's exclusive Park Central Hotel. Ella, who was always nervous on stage, felt especially shaky about this engagement. Wearing a sequin-studded gown with chiffon streamers, matching sequined armlets, and gripping the standing microphone tightly, she made it through her set and received great applause from the mink and pinky-ring set.

The Webb Orchestra also headlined at the Paramount Theater on Broadway, another bastion of white entertainment. The audience at the Paramount went wild over Ella, jumping from their seats to touch her and, on one occasion, even ripping her gown in their eagerness.

But Ella was most comfortable at the Savoy, which she and the band considered 'home' and where she was at last beginning to develop an easier stage presence. One fan of many years recalls taking the 'A' train up to Harlem and the Savoy on several occasions. But one evening stands out: 'Ella and Chick Webb were in residence, and I think the Savoy Sultans completed the double bill. Ella was wearing a white satin evening gown, white slippers, and her long fingernails were painted white. I was standing in front of the bandstand, and as she finished one of her numbers she looked down at me, waved, and said, "Nice to see you again." Whether she was just being friendly or did remember my face (I had seen her a month or so previously on one of the band's "one-nighters") I'll never know.'[10]

Meanwhile, Chick Webb's health was growing steadily worse. There were times when he could barely finish a set. Irving Randolph, who had left Webb to join Cab Calloway's band by then, but who caught Webb as often as he could, recalls, 'He had to have a little break in between, and he had a fella who used to sit in for him. That guy would come in and play for a little while when Chick didn't feel too good. Then Chick would take over. Then he would rest a little while again.'[11] On several nights, Webb fainted after the end of a show. But he pooh-poohed all expressions of concern about his health with, 'I'm gonna be so well in another couple of months. Besides, I gotta keep my guys working.'[12]

Moe Gale kept pressuring Webb to take the band and Ella on another tour to capitalise on the continuing popularity of 'A-Tisket, A-Tasket' as well as of the popularity of its sequel. Webb, whose condition was growing progressively worse, was reluctant. However, he eventually agreed to a five-week tour, to begin in June 1939.

It was Ella's first tour ever in the South. The group rode by bus from New York down to Washington, DC, for an engagement on a river-boat out on the Potomac River. Webb was so ill he could barely play. The following day he was rushed to Johns Hopkins Medical Center in Baltimore. Tim Gale, brother of Moe and the tour arranger, suggested that the band continue south without Chick, who would rejoin the tour as soon as he was able. The band knew the arrangements. Bardu Ali would continue in his role as conductor. Gale found Bill Beason to take over on drums. The band went on to Alabama.

'Touring the South with Chick [Webb's band] was better than with Cab,' recalls Garvin Bushell. 'The black people accepted Ella and Chick more than they did Cab Calloway; the whites went for Cab. Therefore . . . we had more social activity – we were invited to parties and social affairs. With Cab, sometimes blacks didn't even know we were in town.'[13]

For a black band, touring in the South was difficult, no matter how well known or liked the leader. A group of blacks on a southern highway was a group of blacks, period, and white hostility was palpable, not to mention downright dangerous. A white service station would sell you gas, but you couldn't use the restroom. A white truck-stop diner might sell you some food out the back door, but you had better stay away from the front door. Finding suitable lodgings was a constant worry. There were no black hotels, except in a few of the large cities, and white hotels were off-limits. The black boarding houses that catered to railroad men were usually squalid and dangerous; but some boarding houses of a better class would refuse musicians, since show people had a poor reputation among some segments of the black community. Often, a band ended up spending the night on the bus. Any black entertainer who toured frequently in the South learned to build up a network of friends and

By 1939, Ella had joined the roster of famous female jazz singers. She is shown here at the Savoy Ballroom with Mildred Bailey and Helen Humes, laughing with big band leader Count Basie.
Franks Driggs Collection

contacts who could be relied upon to provide lodging for a night and an occasional home-cooked meal.

Ella enjoyed that time in the South, in spite of the attendant problems. It was her first opportunity to know firsthand how popular her records were in that region, among both whites and blacks. While they played for more white audiences than black, there was no mistaking the warmth and acceptance from black audiences. But it was to be a short tour. Ella and the band were playing at a Masonic Temple in Montgomery, Alabama, when Tim Gale called the band members together at the intermission and announced that Chick Webb was dead.

Doctors at Johns Hopkins Medical Center had discovered that Webb had pneumonia. Unfortunately, he had been too frail to treat, and the doctors had decided to let him die at home. He had clung to life for nearly a week. Then, on June 16, he had asked his mother to lift up his head so he could see the friends and relatives who surrounded his bed. 'I'm sorry,' he said, 'I gotta go,' and then he died.[14]

His body was laid out in a casket in the little house where he had often stayed with his uncle, and it was on view for several days. Other friends and relatives and fans gathered in Baltimore. The drummer Gene Krupa, then with Benny Goodman, had come as soon as he had heard the news. He sat by the casket for hours, sobbing. The funeral, at the Waters African Methodist Church, was huge, for thousands came to mourn Webb's passing. Traffic was stopped all across the city for the funeral procession, which numbered eighty cars. Ella stood at the casket and sang 'My Buddy', ordinarily a rather silly, maudlin tune that suddenly took on great power as sung by Ella with the intense love and sense of loss that she felt. There wasn't a dry eye in the church by the time she finished.

'He was always in pain, but no one ever knew it,' she said of Webb. 'If he'd have taken the same time he applied to helping people, and rested, he'd have lived longer than his twenty-nine years. And there was so much music in that man.'[15]

Ella had lost her protector, and she would miss him deeply. But he had launched her career. In three short years, she had gone from a nobody singing in amateur contests to a singer of number one selling records.

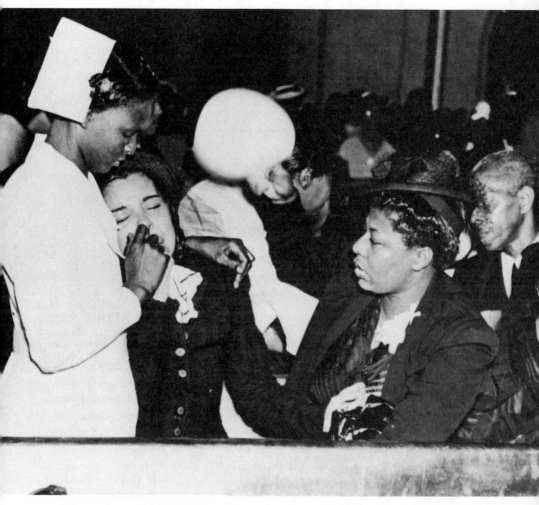

*Ella comforts Chick Webb's widow at his funeral in Baltimore, Maryland,
June 20, 1939.*
UPI/Bettmann

4 Bandleader

Ella had little time to mourn the death of Chick Webb. Says Beverly Peer, 'She never skipped a beat, was back the next day. She was thinking about her future. All the musicians were thinking about their future.'[1]

Moe Gale advised them to remain together. They had the southern tour to finish. Charlie Buchanan wanted them back at the Savoy, and Milt Gabler of Decca was still interested in recording them. From Gale's, Buchanan's, and Gabler's business points of view, there was much to be exploited about Webb's band now that he was gone. People would show up just to hear what it sounded like without him and would be more than a little interested in its progress.

There was no argument about how to restructure the group. Ella was the obvious titular leader, the one with the most name recognition. The band took the name Ella Fitzgerald and Her Famous Orchestra. Moe Gale issued a statement to the press that read, 'In accordance with Mr Webb's wishes, Miss Fitzgerald has succeeded to the leadership of the band.'

Webb's drum set, which had always occupied centre stage, was moved back. The Chick Webb logo – a crown with the initials CW – that had decorated the bass drum and the musicians' boxes – gave way to a basket with the initials EF. At twenty-one, Ella was now one of the youngest big bandleaders in the world, not to mention one of the few women.

There is a wonderful photograph of Ella as a bandleader that shows clearly Ella's position with the band after Webb's death. Smiling coyly, head hunched down into her shoulders, conductor's baton resting against her neck, her attitude is, 'Isn't this cute? I'm playing bandleader.' She made no effort to assert any real influence over the band or its material – and would have been foolish to do so – and with that understood, the musicians went along with the arrangement. Putting Ella out front was a marketing decision, it made good business sense. The goal for everyone involved was to keep the band working. 'I really didn't direct the band that much,' Ella said later. 'I wasn't of age to be a leader. They had Bardu direct. They let me feature one or two numbers.'[2]

Saxophonist Teddy McRae became musical director and hired Edgar Sampson as arranger. The rest of the fourteen-piece group included: Dick Vance and Taft Jordan on trumpet, George Matthews, Nat Story, and Sandy Williams on trombone, Garvin Bushell on clarinet, Hilton Jefferson on alto sax, Wayman Carver on alto sax, tenor sax, and flute, Tommy Fulford on piano, John Trueheart on guitar, Beverly Peer on bass, and Bill Beason on drums.

By the end of June, the band was back at the Savoy and back at the Decca recording studios cutting a Chick Webb memorial album of ten sides, nine of the ten featuring Ella. One of those sides became her next big hit. It was Edgar Sampson who found 'Stairway to the Stars' for Ella. With lyrics by Mitchell Parish, who had also written 'Stardust', and music by Frank Signorelli and Matt Malneck, it was a lush, romantic ballad, and Ella showed how much she had improved her ballad style by singing to perfection.

Ella Fitzgerald and Her Famous Orchestra remained in residence at the Savoy Ballroom through 1939, recording eleven sides from the Savoy in December 1939, beginning with the opening theme, 'A-Tisket, A-Tasket', and ending with the closing theme, 'Swing Out'. On one of the songs, ' 'Tain't What You Do (It's the Way That You Do It)', she did some scatting, ending one of her phrases with the word 'rebop', which some musicologists regard as the first appearance of the name that was first applied to the innovative music being played by Dizzy Gillespie and Charlie Parker.

The nascent bebop, which the style eventually came to be called, evolved from swing at a time when swing was beginning to lose its popularity. Played by small groups rather than big bands, and improvised rather than orchestrated, it was music by musicians for musicians – whether lay audiences liked it or not was beside the point. Unpopular with such audiences at first, it would gain greater favour later when singers like Ella took it up.

Not long after the band recorded those sides in December 1939, it lost its favoured position at the Savoy. Erskine Hawkins, fresh on the heels of his big hit, 'Tuxedo Junction', proved to be more popular with the Savoy crowd, and Ella had to look for another gig.

By 1940 there were few other places to go in Harlem. Connie's Inn had followed the Cotton Club downtown. Other clubs had closed. Even the Savoy was having trouble maintaining a loyal clientèle. Worse than the Depression was the aftermath of Prohibition. Once liquor was again legal, there was no profit in it for the mob operators of the big, whites-only clubs. Gangsters started fighting turf wars over control of prostitution and loan-sharking, and when gun battles between rival mobs began to claim innocent lives, average citizens no longer considered the streets of Harlem safe. Those who didn't have to be on them stayed away.

Simultaneously, there were changes occurring in the big band business. The market was glutted with big bands, very few of them with a sound that was in any way distinctive. According to Paul Eduard Miller, writing in *Down Beat*, 'The public is now saturated; most swing bands prior to '39 have made good financially . . . as for the rest, even those organised years ago, their financial success, to put it optimistically, is only mediocre.' Black bands, always on less firm ground than white bands, suffered especially. Wrote Miller, 'The truth is that the public will absorb a very limited number of negro bands . . . Ella Fitzgerald, et cetera, are practically out of the picture as far as the public are concerned.'[3]

But the news of Ella's demise as a bandleader was premature. Moe Gale was convinced that her name was still big enough to carry the band. In the January 1940 issue of *Down Beat* she was voted most popular female vocalist for the fourth straight year, and Gale reasoned that she would continue to draw audiences.

In February 1940, Ella and Her Famous Orchestra went into the Famous Door on West 52nd Street, New York's new jazz centre. The narrow brownstones that had once housed speakeasies now hosted in

Ella playing band leader. While she became the titular head of the Webb band after Chick's death, she had neither the maturity nor the skill to lead a band.
Ken Whitten Collection

the space of a few blocks most of the biggest names in jazz. Unfortunately, the Famous Door closed without paying Ella and her band the money owed them.

New York jazz was in considerable flux. Added to the glut of big bands was the plethora of black musicians in New York at the time. With Hitler's invasion of Poland in September 1939 and France's declaration of war against Germany three days later, black American musicians who'd found a haven in Paris after World War I realised they had to leave. There was no question in their minds that if Paris fell, they would be shipped off to concentration camps. In fact, only the bravest were still in Paris by 1940.

Pianist Roger Ramirez arrived from Europe and briefly joined Ella's band. Prior to going to Europe, he'd played with Willie Bryant's band at the Savoy and the Apollo. 'I'd been playing with Monty Martin, Kaiser Marshall, John Russell – we opened up at the Polish Pavilion in the Paris Exposition,' he says.

> The clouds of war were gathering then, and everybody was trying to get out. I had a time getting out of the country. Charlie Buchanan sent money over there to get me home. I don't know how it happened, but there I was with the band.
>
> Tommy Fulford was playing piano with the band then. Tommy and I had gone to junior high school together . . . I filled in for him and played a couple of dates. I remember one – we went there on our own private bus. We were supposed to play some ball, and the band all had on tuxedos and everything, and when we went to the ball we saw this big watermelon backdrop![4]

As Ramirez's recollection indicates, black bands operated under special hardships when they played in white venues. Not only did they have to use the kitchen entrance and the freight elevator, but they were expected to bow to prevailing racial stereotypes. Such indignities rankled with Ella and the musicians, but they came with the territory. Objecting meant not working.

'When I joined the band,' Ramirez continues, 'Chick had died, and Ella took over. Louis Jordan was the [real] leader of the band; he was the straw boss. The band went to Baltimore to play a memorial for Chick.'[5]

The Baltimore engagement was a special show to benefit the Chick Webb Memorial Recreation Center Fund. More than eight thousand people turned out for it, including the governor of Maryland and former heavyweight boxing champion Joe Louis. A number of other entertainers contributed their talents to the cause. Peg-Leg Bates, who danced on a real peg leg, did his 'one-legged dancing fool' routine, and the Nicholas Brothers, Fayard and Harold, did their acrobatic splits down a grand staircase. Teddy Hill's band played, and the Ink Spots sang their hits. But the act that got the greatest applause was Chick Webb's old orchestra and former protégé.

Later, seated next to Webb's widow, Sallye, Ella said, 'What Chick did for me and the boys can never be repaid. The fellows in the band and I can only hope our small contribution will help make Chick Webb's dream come true.'[6] Eight thousand paying guests, at $1.50 per person, contributed a gross take of $9,200.

Back in New York, the band reorganised. Says Garvin Bushell, 'They got rid of Bardu and were going to bring in Eddie Barefield and put him in front of the band. They wanted to emulate a Benny Goodman setup [Goodman, with his clarinet solos, was the most popular bandleader of the time]. When I heard Barefield was coming – so they wouldn't need me as a clarinet player – I put in my notice, and beat them to the punchline.'[7]

Eddie Barefield, born in Iowa, had started his musical training on bass. 'But the bass got broken in the church and I decided to mess around with the clarinet and other instruments,' he says. 'There was a Jewish guy who owned a music store in town and he gave me lessons. I moved to St Louis and joined McKinney's Cotton Pickers and eventually came to New York to play.'[8] Barefield also played with Benny Moten's band before joining Ella.

With Barefield, a superb soloist, the orchestra did a spate of recordings, many of them tunes they played at the Roseland Ballroom where they played for several weeks in February and March. Between February 15 and late March, they recorded a total of thirty-eight cuts, including a greater number of instrumentals than usual.

They went on another tour after that. In Barefield's recollection, while there were inconveniences associated with being black and on the road, there was also much camaraderie.

I miss the road now. Young musicians don't know what it was like back then. Integration really brought about a decline of black clubs and intimate jazz places where black people could go and play. Even touring in the South was not so bad to me because I enjoyed

Back home at the Savoy Ballroom, the Webb organization quickly regrouped, although inevitably there were changes in personnel. Trumpets: Taft Jordan, Irving Randolph, Dick Vance, Francis Williams. Trombones: John McConnell, Earl Hardy, George Matthews. Tenor Sax: Elmer Williams. Alto Sax: Chauncey Haughton. Drums: Bill Beason. Ken Whitten Collection

interacting with the black people down South, and everybody knew everybody, and black musicians had a kind of status in the black community. Those people looked forward to us coming down there to do those tours, year in and year out. We had friends and girlfriends down there. Some of the musicians had children down there, and those tours were the only time they could really see them. Now, with the advent of integration, we play in huge places like Madison Square Garden and places way out by the airport, and we don't see the black community anymore and black people don't come to see us. Black people have lost control of their own music now. In the old days the only things whites controlled were the recording studios, but they did black stuff.[9]

Barefield did not stay with the Ella band long. By early May he had left for a job as a studio musician with ABC's Blue network, one of the first black musicians to play regularly on radio. Later, he played with Calloway and with Sidney Bechet. Like most of the musicians who played with Ella in those years, he never really got to know her: 'She showed up on time for rehearsal and then after rehearsal she left. None of the guys knew what she did in between.'[10]

Barefield was replaced on clarinet by Pete Clark. Three other musicians left also, perhaps because of Barefield's leaving but also perhaps because another extended tour was in the offing for the group and the trombone section didn't want to go. George Matthews, Chauncey Haughton, and Sandy Williams were replaced by James Archey, Floyd Brady, and John McConnell.

With the new trombone section, Ella and the orchestra went into Decca's New York studios in early May and cut four sides, including 'Gulf Coast Blues', written by Clarence Williams and first recorded seventeen years earlier by Bessie Smith. Milt Gabler's attempt to give the band a new sound, it was Ella's first real foray into blues singing, and it caused some critics to sit up and take note. Wrote Edgar Jackson in *Melody Maker*, 'Those who remember Clarence Williams' tuneful "Gulf Coast Blues" will not be the only ones who will enjoy this latest record of it by Ella Fitzgerald. The version may not have the primitive guts (forgive the word but it's so right for the occasion) of the old Bessie Smith waxing, but Ella sings better than she has for a couple of years or more, and the improved musicianship of her band makes the accompaniment worthy of her work.'[11]

The record, which was released in June, quickly climbed to the top of the race record charts, and was a hit at just the right time for a summer tour of black clubs and theatres.

Moe Gale decided that the orchestra was becoming an albatross around Ella's neck and tried to persuade her to disband it and join Benny Carter's. Gale went so far as to put out a few leaks to the press, but Ella refused to go along with the plan. The Gale agency released a statement that the Ella Fitzgerald and Benny Carter bands would continue as separate organisations, 'for the time being'.

With the big band's popularity waning in New York, Moe Gale decided to send Ella and Her Famous Orchestra on tour. There were still eager audiences in other parts of the country, as Lionel Hampton knew when he left Benny Goodman and struck out with his own big band in the autumn of 1940.

Trumpet player Irving Randolph joined the band about that time. From St Louis, he'd first played with Andy Kirk: 'He was scuffling around, not doing much. We tried to make a little money. We were in Iowa or someplace, and Fletcher Henderson passed through there, and I was jamming someplace and he heard me. He said, "Gee, I like the way you play," but it went right in one ear and out the other, because I said to myself, "Here's a guy that knows everybody in New York and knows all the trumpet players. Why does he want me?" But believe it or not, he wrote a letter, and here I come.'[12]

Later, Randolph played with Cab Calloway. Not long after he joined Ella's band, the band went on the planned tour, and Randolph couldn't help comparing the travelling styles of the two orchestras: 'With Cab, we always travelled on the train. With Ella we only used the train for a long trip, like going to the West Coast. With Ella, each musician was responsible for his own clothes. With Cab, we didn't have to worry about that, because they had a man to do all those things.'[13] In keeping with the comparative success of her band and Calloway's, Ella's tours were of the shoestring variety. As her maid, dresser, and general factotum she had just one woman, Georgia (Georgianna), her cousin. The road manager sometimes doubled as bus driver.

The tour that summer included engagements in the South. The Gale Agency did not pay much attention to anything but playing dates. It was up to Ella and the musicians to find their own accommodations in boarding houses or private homes. Says Roger Ramirez, 'I don't remember where Ella stayed because I was so busy trying to find a place for myself. Nobody went ahead to do those kinds of things for you. If you had connections, you'd be all right. If you didn't have any connections, you'd be in trouble.'[14]

Recalls Beverly Peer, 'We stayed in black folks' homes, and every musician had to have his own contacts in the South, because the bandleader was not responsible and the booker and the road manager were not responsible. Most of the musicians stayed with people they already had contacts with, either through other musicians or through having been down there before with other bands. Ella had her own contacts. We never saw her when we weren't playing or on the bus. On the bus she was "one of the boys" – she'd sing and dance and scat on the bus. But when we got off the bus, she kept to herself.'[15]

For Ella, as for the others, there were redeeming elements to that tour. Wherever she went Ella was mobbed. In New Orleans, she tried to leave the stage of the New Rhythm Club and was set upon by four thousand screaming fans who tore at her clothes and shoved autograph books in her face. Many fans were knocked down, and several others were trampled. Police were called in an attempt to maintain order.

From the South, the band moved into the Midwest, and by the time they reached Detroit in September, they had covered some twenty thousand miles and thirty-six states. Ella, never sylphlike to begin with, had ballooned. In addition to the hardships of a road tour particular to black entertainers, she had fallen victim to the musician's disease: excess. Depending on their personalities, and the times, musicians found their own ways to wind down after a performance. Some drank, some took drugs (although drug use was a comparative rarity among jazz musicians in those days), some ate. Ella ate, and ate, and ate.

A casualty of that tour was John Trueheart, Chick Webb's childhood friend from Baltimore. He too had become debilitated by tuberculosis and would never rejoin the band.

Back in New York, Ella and the band recorded three sides for Decca in late September, one of which, 'Five O'Clock Whistle', was a minor hit. The following month they returned to the Savoy for a brief engagement. In November, they performed at the Tropicana Club and recorded three more sides for Decca. But while they had worked fairly steadily and continued to record, the orchestra was clearly in decline. A *Down Beat* readers' poll, the results of which were published in January 1941, listed twenty-three bands, but not Ella Fitzgerald and Her Famous Orchestra. Nor was Ella included among the favourite female vocalists, despite the popularity of her recording of 'Gulf Coast Blues'. The only distinction she earned for 1940 was that her record was number one on *Esquire* writer Carlton Smith's 'Ten Outstanding Platters for 1940'.

Through the early part of 1941, Ella and the band played on the East Coast and recorded another eight sides for Decca. One of the cuts, 'Muffin Man', was something of a hit, especially in England. The Gale Agency issued a press handout announcing that Ella had 'responded to requests for phonograph records to be used in London bomb shelters, sending the first hundred recordings of her newest hit "The Muffin Man" to the Drury Lane section of the wartorn city'.

The war in Europe had begun to touch Ella and her group. She was denied the opportunity to tour in Europe. A peaceful England would have welcomed her, for her records had, from the first, sold well there. But once Hitler had invaded Poland in September 1939, and England had gone to war two days later, all opportunities for overseas touring were dashed. The Selective Training and Service Act of 1940 also hung over the heads of Ella's young musicians.

In June 1941, the band headed west. The Gale Agency had got Ella a part in an Abbott and Costello film for Universal Studios called *Ride 'Em Cowboy*. In it, she was to play a singing maid, which was par for black singers-turned-actresses, not to mention straight black actresses, in Hollywood. Actress Hattie McDaniel had recently become the first black to win an Academy Award for her portrayal of Mammy in the 1939 film *Gone With the Wind*. Just as black musicians played in front of watermelon backdrops without public complaint, so did blacks in Hollywood take roles as servants if they wanted to work. Even as Ella filmed her bit part, Walter White of the National Association for the Advancement of Colored People (NAACP) was launching a crusade against 'Mammyism', but blacks in Hollywood would resist joining the assault on the Hollywood system for years.

In *Ride 'Em Cowboy* Ella sang 'A-Tisket, A-Tasket' and 'Rockin' and Reelin' with a popular close harmony group called The Merry Macs. From all accounts, Ella enjoyed her brief stint as an actress and did well at it, showing a flair for comedy that led Universal to enlarge her role. But given the unwritten rules for black appearances in white Hollywood films, her role could not have been augmented appreciably, subject as it was to being 'excised' by southern censors. As long as she was playing a humble maid, southern audiences would probably get to see her, but if the footage in which she appeared seemed in any way to grant her humanity, it would be cut out immediately.

With the band, meanwhile, Ella had an engagement at Los Angeles's Orpheum Theater. They also recorded for Decca in Los Angeles at the end of July. When they were not recording or working at the Orpheum, some members of the band got a chance to jam with other musicians for $6 a night at a club session organised by a young white jazz buff named Norman Granz.

Granz, who had worked his way through the University of California at Los Angeles by clerking at a brokerage house, had started collecting jazz records in college. A chance meeting with Nat King Cole had helped him get closer to the world of jazz musicians, whose work he admired so much that he felt they should do it for him.

'Black musicians were playing all over Los Angeles in the early '40s,' said Granz in 1979, 'but almost entirely to white audiences. This was because there were very few places that welcomed blacks as patrons. I was particularly aware of this because in addition to my day job as a film editor at MGM I had been putting on occasional jam sessions at the Trouville Club in the Beverly Fairfax area. One day Billie Holiday came to me and complained that Billy Berg, who owned the club, wouldn't admit some of her black friends.'[16]

A new musicians' union rule guaranteeing regularly employed musicians one night off a week provided Granz with the opportunity to stage jam sessions one night a week. He approached Billy Berg with the idea of turning Sunday nights, when the club was ordinarily dark, into jam session nights. While Billy Berg's usually had dancing, for jam session nights the bandstand would be enlarged and the dance floor filled with tables. These gigs were for serious listening, not for dancing.

Furthermore, Granz wanted the club open to integrated audiences not only for Sunday night jam sessions but during the rest of the week as well. Using economic arguments, Granz talked Berg into accepting his proposition, and for the first time a Los Angeles club was integrated.

Musicians were delighted to play for serious audiences, as well as with the $6 a night Granz paid them. Soon, Sunday nights were the most popular nights at the club, and other club owners were approaching Granz about playing at their places.

At the time, Granz was interested solely in musicians and instru-

As Ella gained confidence, her position as orchestra leader became more believable. By the time the band played the Roseland State Ballroom in Boston in 1940, new instrument stands and the bass drum sported yellow baskets and the initials E.F.
Frank Driggs Collection

mental sessions. He had no truck with singers, including Ella Fitzgerald. He was interested in real jazz.

Returning to New York, the band played a few more dates and was joined briefly by a young trumpet player from South Carolina named Dizzy Gillespie, who had recently left Cab Calloway. 'I played a couple of weeks with them at Lavarge's [Levaggi's] in Boston, and then came back to New York,' Gillespie recalls. 'That stint with Ella Fitzgerald was pretty funny too, because at first Teddy McRae was the leader who took charge of everything. Ella just sang. It was Ella's band, and the money went to the Gale Agency, which paid Ella, but the musical directorship of the band was in the hands of Teddy McRae and he hired me for those two weeks.'[17]

Unwittingly, Gillespie witnessed the demise of Ella Fitzgerald and Her Famous Orchestra. By early October the Gale Agency had decided that Ella would appear as a single, backed by a four-piece combo. The band, under the direction of Eddie Barefield, would be booked separately. The band lasted just a few months.

All the musicians found other jobs, and the breakup of the band was no great tragedy. Some thirty years later, a number of the old band members reunited for a time under Eddie Barefield. Those members of the band who are still alive are still working. Beverly Peer often performs with Bobby Short at the Carlyle Hotel in Manhattan and at the time of writing has been with Short 'going on thirty years'. Roger Ramirez, Irving Randolph and Teddy McRae are still working too. But few if any have worked with Ella since the breakup of the old band.

Says Peer:

When Ella comes to New York she doesn't call any of the old boys. She pretends she doesn't even know who we are. Around 1980, she came to New York for some event at Lord & Taylor. Somebody who was interviewing her asked her about the old guys who played with her who were still in New York. Ella said she didn't remember anyone because she was 'just a little girl' at the time. The interviewer even called my name, but she said she didn't remember me. That was a lie. Ella didn't want to let on how old she was, and she didn't want to give any credit to any of the old musicians or even work with them when she came to New York. She'd rather work with new people. That's not so much her doing as it is Norman Granz, but nobody should forget who they started with.[18]

Teddy McRae was in the first combo with whom Ella recorded in October. Others were Tommy Fulford on piano, Ulysses Livingstone on guitar, Beverly Peer on bass, and Kenny Clarke on drums. Three weeks later, Eddie Barefield on alto sax and Bill Beason on drums replaced McRae and Clarke for five additional sides. With one combination or another, Ella played small clubs in and around New York.

On December 7, 1941, the Japanese air force bombed the US naval base at Pearl Harbor, Hawaii, and the United States entered World War II. Several of the band personnel either enlisted or were drafted into the service. Among those who were drafted was Tommy Fulford, who subsequently died in the service. Roger Ramirez again stepped in to take over from Fulford. Other bands experienced similar losses of personnel. The music world was in turmoil, and so was the world of Ella Fitzgerald.

The Chick Webb band had been like an umbilical cord to her memory of Webb and the security she had felt with him. It is probably no coincidence that around the same time as she was severed from the band, she got married.

A lot of young people fell in love and got married in those war years – not all of them because the fellow faced being drafted and shipped overseas. There was a desperate feeling in the air, and Ella may well have got caught up in it. She had her own sense of desperation with which to contend. She needed a protector.

Her husband was named Benny Kornegay. According to Beverly Peer, 'Everyone called him Cigarette. I don't know why they called him that – he wasn't real tall and thin. He was a very quiet, private guy.' Some sources describe him as a dancer, others as a dock worker. Musicians who were with Ella at the time say he was 'in the sporting life'. 'That's who she went off with in between shows,' says Peer. 'She was always with some man. All the good-looking guys hung around her because she could sing and they thought she had money.'[19]

At first, Kornegay apparently functioned as a protector for Ella. Recalls Irving Randolph, 'He travelled with us. He picked up the checks.'[20] But by the end of 1942, she was travelling without him. Perhaps Kornegay did not enjoy the travelling, or feeling superfluous. Columnist Sidney Fields reported that while Ella was away on the road, Benny played her records at home, then went out to listen to more of his wife's singing on a jukebox. 'He understands when people like to do something,' Ella told Fields, 'it's better not to try and stop them. But I have to learn to cook. We just started our apartment and I want to get into the kitchen. We've been eating in restaurants, and he's getting tired of it.'[21]

Apart more than they were together, emotionally as well as geo-graphically, the couple had separated within a short time, and Ella got an annulment. Reportedly, the judge who granted the annulment said to her, 'You just keep singing "A-Tisket, A-Tasket" and leave these men alone,' which sounds like a flippant remark that Ella created in order to make her listener laugh and stop asking questions. She later insisted that she had got married on a dare and refused to discuss the marriage or the annulment in any detail. In fact, she professed to have trouble remembering Kornegay's name.

5 On Her Own

Ella's wasn't the only big band to suffer in the early 1940s. Many white big bands underwent changes when their leaders – among them Bob Crosby, Glenn Miller and Artie Shaw – voluntarily enlisted in the armed forces. Other bandleaders saw their ranks depleted by the draft. The upheaval caused by the war, together with wartime gas rationing, which curtailed bus and auto travel, contributed to the change in popular taste and band size from big band to small combo. The big black bands like Calloway's, Ellington's, Basie's, and Lionel Hampton's continued, as did Fletcher Henderson's and that of Earl Hines, but according to some music historians Ella's band had started to sound too much like a white band to survive.

Ella went out first as a single without musicians, relying on the house band wherever she was booked. For any young singer, the change from a big band backing to being backed up by small combos of musicians she didn't even know would have been difficult. For timid Ella, accustomed to and needing the familiar cocoon of the Webb band, the new arrangement was a real challenge. Her nervousness about performing increased manyfold. The late Mel Lewis, whose big band was in Monday-night residence at New York's Village Vanguard for many years, remembered that Ella was having a hard time adjusting to work with a small combo!

My father, Sam Sokolow, was bandleader and house drummer at a place called McVan's in Buffalo. It was owned by an old white woman named Lillian McVan, and her specialty was bringing in people who were great but who were nobody. She brought in Bill Robinson, Coleman Hawkins, Nat King Cole. The place was packed all the time, and she was getting them cheap because they weren't known yet. Buffalo was a good music town in those days, and the musicians and everyone in town always went to McVan's because the performers were so good.

Ella came into Buffalo as a single, and she brought all these arrangements from Chick Webb's band. My father's band at McVan's was only four pieces, and of course they couldn't do much with the arrangements done for a fourteen-piece band. All they could do was play one part from each section, and that meant she hit places where there were only three pieces. The piano player used a solo box in those days. They weren't modern players, but neither was Chick Webb's band. It was the style of the day.

But she was a pain in the ass about it. My father came home and said to me, 'She's so good but she's such a pain. She doesn't realize it's only four of us and we can only do what we can.' These guys were some of the best show musicians in town, and they were playing for everybody, including Bill Robinson. My father kept saying, 'I don't know why this woman complains because she's so good she has no reason to complain.'

I used to go down there every night to hear her and watch her, and I didn't think it sounded so bad. You could see that she was lonely. There was an older woman with her – I don't know who she was. [This was probably Ella's cousin, Georgianna Henry.] But Ella just sat in her room between shows. She never really sat with the musicians and talked to them. She probably got $300–$400 a week, but in those days that wasn't terrible money.

Years later, around 1959–60, I worked with her, and I said, 'You know, I remember you from McVan's in Buffalo.' She said, 'McVan's . . . McVan's . . .' I think she didn't want to remember it.[1]

In March 1942, Ella was teamed up with a group called the Four Keys, featuring three brothers – Bill Furness on piano, Slim Furness on guitar, and Peck Furness on bass – and Ernie Hatfield on drums and vocals. They played small clubs in and around New York and recorded four sides for Decca in March and April, producing one hit, 'All I Need Is You'. Then, as rumblings from the musician's union grew ominous, they went back into the recording studios on July 31 to cut three more sides, Ella's last for more than fifteen months.

James Cesar Petrillo of the American Federation of Musicians wanted his members to receive royalties for the records they made. The recording companies adamantly refused, preferring the long-standing arrangement in which only featured artists and bandleaders received royalties. Petrillo argued that with the record business thriving, the record companies were making large enough profits to spread some of them around. He called a strike for August 1, 1942, and there was little question that the rank-and-file members of the AFM would follow his orders.

Big-name singers, and their recording companies, scrambled to cut as many pre-strike discs as they could. The fact that Ella went into the Decca studios at the eleventh hour to cut only three sides attests to her declining popularity.

As the strike wore on, record companies used some ingenious methods to keep the juke boxes supplied. Artists recorded *a capella* or backed by instrumental tracks recorded in England. Ella was not called in to record *a capella* or any other way, and with no new records to keep her name out before the public, she found herself less and less in demand. Fortunately, *Ride 'Em Cowboy*, the Abbott and Costello film, was released that year, giving her some much needed exposure.

The Gale Agency still managed to find bookings for her. She played the Savoy Ballroom occasionally, her appearances bringing back fond memories of the Chick Webb days both to Ella and to Savoy old-timers. In September 1942 she made her first appearance with the Four Keys at the Aquarium Theater in Times Square. The amplification system broke down and she had to sing without it, but she captured the attention of the audience just the same. 'What more can be said of any singer?' reported *Variety*.

In *Down Beat*'s annual readers' poll, published in January 1943, Ella was placed thirteenth on the list of most popular female vocalists, largely by virtue of her recording with the Four Keys: 'All I Need Is You'. Billie Holiday was fourth. The top three spots went to Helen Forrest, Helen O'Connell and Anita O'Day, all three of them white singers with white big bands, which had fared much better than black bands in terms of both live performances and recordings.

Ella appeared with some frequency at the Apollo Theater which, almost alone among Harlem clubs and theatres, had continued to

Backstage at the Apollo Theater, Ella's dressing room reflects the history of the famous theatre. The names of singer Wini Johnson and orchestra leader Les Hite are scratched into the dressing table's surface. Ella snacks on milk and donuts surrounded by makeup, good luck telegrams, and a photograph of an admirer.
Ken Whitten Collection

draw crowds. As a former Apollo Amateur Night winner, Ella was a favourite at the Apollo, always greeted as a 'hometown girl made good'. In her Apollo dressing room, one of thirteen on four floors, she liked to set out a spread of fried chicken, cold drinks and cut watermelon.

Early in 1943, while playing at the Apollo, Ella heard a voice that astounded her. It was that of a skinny young girl named Sarah Vaughan, winner of an Apollo Amateur Night contest. Seeing herself in the youngster, who had also entered the Apollo contests on a friend's dare, Ella offered her help, as did singer Billy Eckstine. Soon, Sarah Vaughan had joined Eckstine as a vocalist with Earl Hines' band.

Ella appeared at the Apollo again in June, and the following month opened at a new club on Broadway called the Club Zanzibar. She was not the headliner; that distinction went to Peg-Leg Bates, who had headlined at the Cotton Club downtown in 1938 and who by the time of his appearance at Club Zanzibar had thirteen different peg legs, 'one to fit every suit, all colors'. The site had seen the rise and demise of any number of nightclubs, and Ella was worried about repeating her experience at the Famous Door on West 52nd Street. But Club Zanzibar remained open, and she was so well received that she was held over for fifteen weeks.

The Four Keys having been drafted, later that year the Gale Agency decided to try pairing Ella with the Ink Spots, a group of five young men who specialised in vocal harmony and who'd already had hits with 'It's a Sin To Tell a Lie' and 'Whispering Grass'. Ella enjoyed working with the group.

Pianist Bill Doggett was an accompanist for the Ink Spots at the time. 'Those were the original Ink Spots – Ivory Watson, Happy Jones, Charles Fuqua, and Bill Kenny,' says Doggett. 'They're all dead now.'

Doggett, who has his own band now, is from Philadelphia and so, he feels, came by his interest in music naturally. 'Philadelphia was a cheap town, and when bands would be coming from the South, that's one of the first places they would stop. The Strand Ballroom was there, run by a fella named Rich Dupree. Bands used to be able to play there two times a week – we used to have dances on Tuesdays and Saturdays – and go get a room and board for maybe $5–$6 a week. Philadelphia had those big houses that could take a whole band. In fact, a lot of them used to stay right on my block on Vantoff Street.'

According to Doggett, Ella was very easy to work with: 'Playing with Ella was beautiful. She was not difficult in the least. I can't ever remember Ella being difficult.'[2] In spite of the fact that she hadn't had a hit in some years, the record ban notwithstanding, this period seems to have been a relatively happy one for Ella. She had matured considerably since the Webb band had broken up. Forced to adjust to new musicians and new arrangements, she'd risen to the challenge. Sobered by the experience of being out of the record-hit limelight, she had learned to appreciate the opportunities she had to perform before live audiences.

With the Ink Spots, Ella returned to the Decca recording studios in November 1943, shortly after James C. Petrillo lifted the recording ban. The record companies had at last capitulated to his demand that musicians receive record royalties, although they would soon take the matter to the courts and win a decision in their favour. It would take another musicians' union strike several years later to win lasting rights for sidemen.

In that first recording session, in which Ella and the Ink Spots were accompanied by John McGee on trumpet, Bill Doggett on piano, Bernie McKay on guitar, and Bob Haggart on drums, Ella cut only one side, 'Cow Cow Boogie'. The exigencies of the war precluded a great number of cuts, for wartime shellac shortages had drastically reduced the number of records produced (some major recording companies bought up old discs and ground them up to recycle into new records).

In March, she recorded two more sides with an orchestra whose identity has been lost, and without the Ink Spots: 'Once Too Often' and 'Time Alone Will Tell'. None of these sides was especially memorable, and none was a hit.

The Ella–Ink Spots team was, however, proving to be popular in clubs and theatres. Gene Ramey, a bassist, recalls playing the Apollo with Ella and the Ink Spots three times. The Gale Agency booked another extended tour, this time in a package deal with Cootie Williams' band led by Duke Ellington's former lead trumpeter. 'We did a tour with Ella, playing theatres around the country,' says Doggett. There were the Ink Spots, and Ella, and Cootie Williams's band, a tap dancer named Ralph Brown, and another act called Red and Curly. The Ink Spots always closed the show.

'We toured in the South with that show. We travelled by train and by chartered bus. The bus driver knew exactly where to go to the black neighbourhood. Now, when the big–time acts come into town you don't even know they're in town. It was wartime, and we did some shows at army camps.'3

Much of Ella's work in those years was for the US armed forces. She sang for Armed Forces Radio, went on USO tours, and did whatever she could to help the morale of America's fighting men. The Gale Agency was happy to arrange for her to make such patriotic appearances, fully aware that while they might not garner much profit they did function to keep Ella's name before the public.

The war had changed some of the aspects of road touring – gas rationing either precluded or made more difficult long trips by bus or car – but it hadn't changed the mind of the South. If anything, southern white attitudes had hardened, primarily out of concern that returning black soldiers might start getting uppity. This road tour was especially hard for Ella, who met up with John Hammond in New Orleans, where the tour had just arrrived from Atlanta. Hammond was in the army at the time, serving as a talent scout for armed forces entertainment. In his autobiography, he recalled that Ella's troupe was 'tired and unhappy with the accommodations in New Orleans. I lunched with Ella in a miserable black hotel while she told me her troubles.'4

If New Orleans, with a substantial black population, had so few suitable accommodations for Ella and the others, there is little to imagine about the facilities available to Ella and her troupe in smaller southern cities and towns in the 1940s.

Later on, the tour headed west, where they were booked for an engagement at Billy Berg's, the Los Angeles club with mob connections where Norman Granz had first started staging his jazz jam sessions. Ella was singing when a man came staggering on to the stage, a knife protruding from his chest. Barely missing a note, Ella finished her song.

For all her seeming nervousness on stage, Ella was remarkably good at dealing with distractions. Many people have favourite stories about how she could put down a loudmouth without ever dropping a note. One couple recall an appearance of Ella's at the Crane Estate in Ipswich, Massachusetts, an 'elegant baronial estate with formal gardens where famous bands and singers appeared in outdoor concerts. Unfortunately, one night the bugs and mosquitoes did not respect Ella's eminence and, attracted by the spotlights as she was in the midst of one of her scat numbers, one hovered around her face. With perfect aplomb and cool as always, she kept waving it off, but it came attacking back. Then, nonchalantly she interposed into her rendition, "These bugs are bugging me", and brought down the house.'5

Back in New York, Ella and the Ink Spots recorded two more sides on August 30, 1944: 'Into Each Life Some Rain Must Fall' and 'I'm Making Believe'. Says Bill Doggett, '"Into Each Life Some Rain Must Fall" was, I think, one that sold over a million copies. I was on that one.'6

Ella was delighted to be back on the charts again, although she realised that the popularity of the Ink Spots was a major reason for the record's success. Pairing her with the group had been a clever move on Moe Gale's part.

'Also around that time, we did some broadcasts for NBC Radio,' says Doggett. 'We would use some of the studio musicians for those radio broadcasts.'7 It was important for Ella's career to get that twice-weekly radio show on NBC. Every Monday and Wednesday night for fifteen minutes, Ella, backed mostly by studio musicians, sang her old hits and new songs. The show lasted a few months, about par for 'sustainers', shows without sponsors, sustained by the network. Radio sponsors would not back black shows, pleading that their southern product buyers might be offended.

Wartime had brought about a change in American musical tastes. With loved ones far from home, Americans wanted to hear ballads; and ballads meant singers. Since the early 1940s singers had so increased in importance that in their way they helped to eclipse the popularity of the big bands. Ella, who had once been kept from singing ballads by Chick Webb, now sang them almost exclusively. In 1945, the year following her hit, 'Into Each Life Some Rain Must Fall' with the Ink Spots, she had another major hit with the Ink Spots, 'I'm Beginning to See the Light'. That February 1945 session was the last she did with the group.

Decca kept trying her out with different vocal and instrumental accompaniments. In March 1945 she recorded with the Delta Rhythm Boys on vocals, Renee de Knight on piano, Hy White on guitar, Haig Stephens on bass, and George Wettling on drums; in August 1945, with Randy Brooks and His Orchestra. Each time, the cuts were almost all ballads. Finally, in October, she departed from her standard ballad fare. On the fourth of the month, accompanied by Vic Schoen and his Orchestra, she recorded a song written by Lionel Hampton which had already become his theme song.

'Flying Home' was an instrumental number, and Ella scat-sang.

Also known by then as bop singing, scatting was a form that had been originated by Louis Armstrong back in 1926 when, in the process of recording 'Heebie Jeebies', he had accidentally dropped his sheet music and scatted the lyrics rather than stop the session. From then on, Armstrong had occasionally scatted as had other singers, especially those with instruments for voices. Ella had been scatting in jam sessions ever since Chick Webb had suggested that she improvise with her voice while the instrumentalists improvised on their tools of the trade. By the mid 1940s, however, with the introduction of bebop by its originators Dizzy Gillespie and Charlie Parker, scat singing was becoming a popular way to vocalise jazz. Ella tried it with some success on 'Flying Home' and enjoyed the musical departure.

On October 8, Ella had another chance for a change of pace when she recorded with Louis Jordan and His Tympany Five. Jordan had played with Chick Webb for about a year in 1937–8, and had backed her on 'A-Tisket, A-Tasket'. Ella decided that Jordan would provide the right accompaniment for a novelty tune based on a West Indian folk song. 'I got tired of singing about lost love,' Ella explained, 'so when I came across a number called "Stone Cold Dead in De Market", I asked . . . if I could record it.'[8]

The calypso rage had not yet arrived – its heyday was about 1949 to the early 1950s – but Ella was ready to chance recording a calypso song, so sure was she that the humorous lyrics about a woman who flattens her good-for-nothing husband with a frying pan would strike the funnybone of the public. Jordan duly augmented his regular small combo – Aaron Izenhall on trumpet, Josh Jackson on tenor sax, Bill Davies on piano, Carl Hogan on guitar, Jesse Simpkins on bass, and Eddie Byrd on drums – with Latin instrumentation: Harry Dial on maraccas and Vic Lourie on claves. 'Stone Cold Dead in De Market' was backed by another novelty, 'Petootie Pie'.

Ella wanted to have another hit record of her own, and so she turned to the novelty form that had brought her initial success. She hoped that the humorous lyric would overcome the reluctance of the public to listen to foreign-sounding music. Happily, 'Stone Cold Dead in De Market' sold several million copies and was requested by audiences wherever Ella performed. At the black Earle Theater in Philadelphia, a screaming audience demanded that she sing 'Stone Cold Dead in De Market' three times before they would let her continue her act.

Around this same time, John Hammond, recently discharged from the army, was working as recording director for the Majestic Radio and Phonograph Company's new music label, Keynote. One of the first artists he set out to sign was Ella Fitzgerald. Ella had been under contract to Decca since she'd recorded 'A-Tisket, A-Tasket' a decade earlier. Hammond felt, as he wrote in his autobiography, 'that she had not been receiving from Decca the sort of treatment I believed she deserved. I did my best to persuade Moe Gale, Ella's agent, and Gene Treacy [who ran Majestic's record division] to bring Ella to Majestic. Gale asked for an annual guarantee of $40,000 for Ella, more than three times the amount she was getting at Decca. I thought she was worth it, as did Treacy, yet for reasons I never understood Gale ended up re-signing her to Decca at the same $15,000 guarantee she'd been receiving all along. It was a hard blow.'9

Clearly, Gale had not negotiated in Ella's best interests but in his own, for he enjoyed a comfortable relationship with Decca. But Ella didn't even consider leaving the Gale Agency. In point of fact, she would not have been much better off with any of the other white booking agencies, all of which exploited their black stars. There were no black booking agencies to speak of. Even Lionel Hampton and his wife Gladys, who otherwise made every effort to be independent, were with Joe Glaser's Associated Booking Corporation, because most white theatre owners would not even consider negotiating with a black, and whites owned most theatres, no matter the complexion of their clientèle.

In 1947, Ella tried another experiment – scat-singing to bebop, urged on by one of its originators, Dizzy Gillespie, who had his own band and was busy making music history with a style that featured solos and was jazz for its own sake. A reaction to the big-band swing style, in which instrumental solos had been almost completely overshadowed by ensemble sections, the new music was started by a small creative group of musicians led by individuals like guitarist Charlie Christian, saxophonist Charlie Parker, pianist Thelonious Monk, and trumpeter Gillespie. It first took shape in Harlem, then moved downtown to West 52nd Street where for a time it was called 'Fifty-second Street Jazz' because no one knew how to describe it.

Bop melodies and harmonies were more complex, and the tempo was faster than in classic jazz. There was less emphasis on arrangements and more on improvisation. Soloists reigned supreme, and their improvisations were aggressive and hard-hitting, with many

dissimilar themes and key changes. To many musicians, it sounded like nonsense, and the name by which it was eventually called, bebop, was a nonsense name.

Now considered the first modern jazz style, bebop took a long time to catch on. Many classic jazz musicians, critics, and knowledgeable jazz fans were actively hostile to it, distinguishing it from what they called 'true jazz'. The general public did not understand it at all, and were put off by its almost total lack of danceability. Nevertheless, Gillespie was determined to bring it to the larger public with a big band.

Organising a big band in the postwar period was a gamble, especially considering the fact that Gillespie was too poor even to buy arrangements. But Billy Eckstine, whose own band folded that same year, let Gillespie use whatever material of his he wanted, and Diz considered himself all set.

Gillespie and a small group – Milt Jackson, Ray Brown, Sonny Stitt, Stan Levey and Al Haig – debuted at the Spotlite, owned by a black man named Clark Monroe, on West 52nd Street in 1946. Monroe had suggested that Gillespie play eight weeks with the small group, build up to big-band size, and play another eight weeks with the larger group, which he did.

The larger group included a twenty-one-year-old tenor sax player named James Moody, fresh from the Air Force, where he'd played in his first band. 'The Air Force was segregated then,' says Moody, who was born in Georgia and raised in Reading, Pennsylvania, and Newark, New Jersey.

> We were in a black unit, and it was an unauthorized band. I had a saxophone and I just knew a couple fingers on it. I couldn't play. That was the beginning of my musical career because I'd wanted to be a musician, but I'd never studied. They had a white Air Force band come over and give us lessons, and I learned more about how to read music.
>
> Linton Garner, Erroll Garner's brother, was in the same band. He asked me to play my scales, and I played a C-scale for him. He

After the orchestra broke up and Ella went out on her own, the Gale Agency continued to represent her, but with little imagination in the view of John Hammond and others.
Author's Collection

looked at me and said, 'Is that it?' I said, 'Yeah.' He said, 'Boy, you're in for a rude awakening.'[10]

Dizzy Gillespie visited the base with his first big band, heard Moody's group, and told them to get in touch with him when they got out of the Air Force. After their discharge, Moody, tenor sax player Joe Gayles, and trumpet player Dave Burns joined Gillespie at the Spotlite. Following that second, eight-week stint, Gillespie took his big band on the road.

By the time Gillespie was ready for his second try at touring with a big band, the Gale Agency, which represented him, wanted him on a bill with Ella as headliner. Ella was popular with both black and white audiences in the South, where most of the group's engagements were scheduled, and the agency felt she would help Dizzy with southern audiences. Ella was familiar; people in the South would come just to hear her sing her greatest hits. Once there, they would have little choice but to listen to Gillespie's bebop. Gillespie agreed, and that decision proved to be a wise one. Recalled James Moody, 'It was funny to see the reaction of the people to the band. Down there it was a little different because the people weren't quite aware of bebop, and they didn't know how to dance to the music at that time. So they would stand and look up at the band as if we were nuts, you know. One time, down South, this guy was looking up and he said, "Where's Ella Fitzgerald?" He was mad because he didn't see Ella Fitzgerald yet, you know.'[11]

Accompanied only by her piano player, Ray McTooney, and cousin Georgianna, Ella went with the band to Indianapolis, where the tour opened in a large black theatre. Moody recalls that after the engagement he and his two friends Joe Gayles and Dave Burns gave Ella their salary to hold for them. Unfortunately, her pocketbook was snatched. 'It was later found in the commode,' says Moody, 'but the money was gone. Ella made good on it for us. She didn't have to do that.'[12]

Touring was fraught with unexpected events, although purse-snatchings were rare. After that incident, Ella learned to be more careful.

Ella and the Gillespie big band next headed South, which was just as difficult for touring black performers as ever. Moody recalls that they stayed primarily in rooming houses. 'They'd charge $2 a room, but when we'd get there, the price would go up to $4. Georgie was a great cook; she'd cook greens, corn bread, wonderful things, and she'd invite us all in to eat. She must have had a hot plate or something, because she cooked in the rooming houses, backstage, everywhere.'[13]

Most of their performances were in large auditoriums or theatres for dances. Most nightclubs could not afford to pay a big band to perform. 'We'd play separate dances,' says Moody. 'One night we'd play a white dance and then the next night it would be a black one. The funny thing about it was that when it was a black dance the whites would be upstairs as spectators, but when it was a white dance there were no spectators.'

Moody recalls only one unpleasant incident, which was in essence a compliment to Ella, albeit a back-handed one: 'One time we got into a town late and the sheriff and his wife were there waiting for us. The wife said, "You know, Ella, I just love the way you sing," and the sheriff said, "Yeah, my wife loves the way you sing. Would you sing something for us?" I mean, Ella's on the bus! Ella was saying, "I'm tired. My voice is tired. I can't do it." They wound up leaving us alone, but they were pretty persistent.'[14]

It took courage for Ella to refuse to sing for a white sheriff in the South, no matter how much she was within her rights to do so. Another white sheriff might have decided that her singing was a condition for entry into the town.

Musically, that six-week tour was one of the happiest times of Ella's life. Bebop was a revelation to her, and she felt challenged as she had not been since her foray into calypso. 'I used to just get thrilled listening to them when he [Gillespie] would do his bebop,' she said years later. 'That's actually the way I feel I learned how to what you call bop. It was quite an experience, and he used to always tell me, "Come on up and do it with the fellas . . ." That to me was my education in learning how to really bop.'[15]

While Ella's primary material was her greatest hits, she enjoyed the opportunity to try out new forms. Milt Jackson, who was the vibraharpist in Gillespie's eighteen-piece band on that tour, recalls that Ella sang all kinds of material: 'Mostly ballads. Scat singing was something we all did; it's something that just goes along with our music. She was the headliner, she closed the show. She'd do anywhere from five, six, seven numbers, depending on the encores. She was a very hard worker in that sense – as long as the people showed their appreciation, she would perform for them.'[16]

That tour with Gillespie's band was also satisfying for Ella personally. There was a great camaraderie in the Gillespie group. Ella recalls that Dizzy always wanted his wife, Lorraine, to cook him eggs: 'At a lotta the theaters we played, my cousin [Georgianna Henry] and his wife used to do the cooking for everybody backstage, and everybody in the audience would be getting up because the food smell would be coming from backstage.'[17]

Also, it was during that tour that she came to know Ray Brown, Gillespie's bass player. Known as one of the best bass players of the Jimmy Blanton school, Brown was born in Pittsburgh on October 13, 1926. He had studied piano and bass in high school and played eight months with Jimmy Hinsley and Snookum Russell before going to New York when he was just eighteen years old. On the day he arrived, he met Dizzy Gillespie and joined his small group. The following year, he toured with Ella. Eight years Ella's junior, Brown was at first enamoured of Ella, the star, and at first she simply responded to him as a good-looking young man whose attentions were flattering. But soon there was something more. When Ella started getting jealous of the girl groupies who hung around Ray, there was no question that she was getting serious. Photographs from that time show that she had slimmed down considerably and was an attractive woman. While after the tour was over it was hard for Ella and Ray to see each other, they made a point of meeting whenever their schedules permitted.

Touring and performing with Dizzy Gillespie marked a turning point in Ella's career in more ways than one. She loved singing bebop and almost immediately recorded her first side in the style. It was 'Lady Be Good' by George and Ira Gershwin. She first sang it with Gillespie on WNEW radio's 'Make Believe Ballroom' show, where the two appeared after the tour returned to New York. It was a radio jam session, and they were just noodling around, but Ella liked the song. The A&R man at Decca records liked it, too, and on March 19, 1947, it was one of three sides that Ella recorded with Bob Haggart and His Orchestra (the other sides were 'A Sunday Kind of Love' and 'That's My Desire'). It was an immediate hit. Dave Garroway, host of a popular radio show in Chicago, played it, and soon Ella had been invited to perform at the State-Lake, Orpheum, and Chicago Theaters.

Ella made bebop accessible by vocalising it, and thus she brought it to an audience that might otherwise not have heard it. Its full acceptance dates to the night of September 29, 1947, when Ella and the Gillespie Orchestra played a concert at the venerable Carnegie Hall. Ella sang 'Stairway to the Stars' and 'How High the Moon'.

While Ella did a lot for bebop, bebop also did a lot for Ella. It was in

A comparatively svelte Ella with Louis Jordan at the Decca recording studios in 1947. Ella's introduction to bebop opened up a whole new musical world for her.
Frank Driggs Collection

this period that she was dubbed 'The First Lady of Song', a moniker that would remain with her from then on.

Ella was eager to record more bebop songs, but Decca may have decided to let 'Lady Be Good' enjoy its run before releasing another song to compete with it. It wasn't until December 20, 1947, that Ella did another – and she hadn't recorded since July 11. The main reason for the late December recording session was probably the threat of another musicians' strike. This time James Petrillo's concern was the proliferation of music shows on radio, which, he charged, were depriving musicians of work. He called for a strike on January 1, 1948, insisting that there would never, 'ever, ever, ever', be any recording of any kind.

As record companies scrambled to get as much new material recorded as possible, they tended to concern themselves with their white singers and musicians, since 'race records' were a secondary market. As a black, Ella's recordings were still considered to be primarily in that market. Among white singers, there was considerable secrecy and intrigue involve in getting new songs on to wax without letting other singers find out about them. Peggy Lee had written 'Mañana', and thought she had the only orchestra-accompanied version of it, only to find out that another recording of the song with instruments had been made before January 1.

Still, Ella was a big enough star to warrant some pre-strike attention. For that December 20 recording session, Ella was accompanied by a pick-up group that included Ray Brown on bass and Leonard Graham on trumpet. They did three sides – 'My Baby Likes to Re-Bop', 'No Sense', and 'How High the Moon'. Three days later, Ella returned to the Decca studios with Illinois Jacquet on tenor sax, Sir Charles Thompson (Lester Young gave him the nickname 'Sir Charles') on organ, Hank Jones on piano, Hy White on guitar, John Simmons on bass, and J. C. Heard on drums. The four sides they recorded on that date were 'I've Got a Feeling I'm Falling', 'You Turned the Tables on Me', 'I Cried and Cried and Cried', and 'Robbins Nest'.

She wrote lyrics for her rendition of 'Robbins Nest', which, according to Sir Charles Thompson, started out as the background of an arrangement and was elevated to the status of instrumental during a May 1947 recording session with Jacquet. Fred Robbins was a popular disc jockey at the time, so they named it after him. 'Later on,' according to Thompson, 'after Ella Fitzgerald had made her record of it, they brought in someone else to write words, so now there are three names on the song and it is no longer called "Robbins Nest" but "Why Have a Falling Out Just When We're Falling in Love".'

As the strike wore on, popular singers began recording without instrumental accompaniment, as they had during the previous strike. This time, Ella was among them. In late April 1948, she recorded two sides accompanied only by a vocal group called The Song Spinners. She was not keen on doing so, but Milt Gabler at Decca and Tim Gale were insistent, and Ella would sing *anything* if her advisers insisted.

Nor was she at all happy with one of the songs, 'My Happiness'. According to Tim Gale, 'She cut it under protest; I brought the dub backstage to her at the Paramount, and she said, "It's a shame. A corny performance of a corny song." It turned out to be one of her biggest sellers.'[19]

That song was even more popular in England than it was in the United States, as Ella would discover with surprise some months later while on her first tour abroad.

6 Settled

Ella and Ray Brown had continued to see each other whenever their schedules permitted. Marian Logan, who at the time was singing under the name Marian Bruce, recalls that when she met Ella, Ella and Brown were dating. By late 1947–early 1948 Brown had made the decision not to accompany Dizzy Gillespie's band on their first European tour. 'At that time I was in a bit of a curl between her wanting me to travel with her as well,' Brown recalled. 'She wanted me to travel with the trio; she had Hank Jones playing piano. So finally I just decided that I was gonna stay in New York.'[1]

Soon, Ray had moved out of the Harlem YMCA and they began living together. It was a good relationship, both personally and professionally. Despite the eight-year age difference, they had much in common. Each appreciated the other's art and understood the pressures and pleasures of entertaining. At recording sessions, they held hands between sets, and in live performances, Ella enjoyed being backed by Ray's trio. It seemed an ideal situation.

The trio, now called Ray Brown's Rhythm Group, included Harry Smith on drums as well as Brown and Hank Jones. Jones was an exceptionally talented musician, and he continues to perform on occasion. He'll appear at Indigo Blues in Manhattan with his trio or backed only by a bassist at Fat Tuesday's, also in Manhattan. 'He's a star,' said the late Mel Lewis in 1989. 'He demands so much bread for a gig – and if he gets it he works. If he doesn't get it, he stays on his farm. He's a gentleman farmer – puts on the overalls, gets on his tractor. Once in a while I still work with him.'[2]

Born in 1918 (the same year as Ella) in Detroit, Jones had absorbed the styling of the major thirties pianists like Art Tatum, Teddy Wilson, and Fats Waller by the time he arrived in New York in 1944. In New York, he came under the tutelage of Bud Powell and Al Haig.

He and Ray Brown first met in Buffalo, where both were playing. Later, both stayed at the Harlem YMCA. 'There was a piano downstairs in the lounge,' Jones recalls, 'and we used to go down there and play almost every day, he with his bass and I on the piano. He introduced me to Ella, who needed a pianist at the time. I think the one she had before had a drinking problem. I was with her about four years.'

Jones enjoyed the time he worked with Ella. There were few pressures aside from those that were a normal part of touring. By this time, Moe Gale was booking Ella into high-class venues, and the group was able to perform primarily in big cities in the northern states. In Jones's recollection, the hotels they stayed in were first-class. Nor can he recall any racial incidents.

The group had a cohesiveness both personally and professionally. 'When it was just the trio backing her, we did our own arrangements,' he said. 'We called them "head arrangements" [not written down]. We would all do it together. Ray Brown was an excellent arranger as far as his musical thinking was concerned. Some things I would do, some things he would do. And Ella had a very musical mind herself, a lot of ideas, a lot of input into anything that happened on the stage. Of course, much of the improvisation came right on the stage when she was playing – singing. I say "playing" because Ella thought like an instrument. Her voice was her instrument, and she actually could improvise as a horn player, like a Lester Young would or as a Slam Stewart would on bass. As a matter of fact, on "Lady Be Good" she used to do a section in which she imitated something that Slam would have played, and she almost got the same sound that he got. The arrangements themselves were not improvised; they were set. Only the variations on the melody were improvised. That's what jazz is.'[3]

A stylist in his own right, Jones was a great asset to the Ray Brown trio, which played frequent dates, but did no recording because of the record ban.

On occasion, Brown and Jones left the group to go on tour with

Norman Granz's Jazz at the Philharmonic. Granz had come a long way from his pickup concerts at Billy Berg's in Los Angeles in 1940. He'd gone into the army in 1941, where he served in Army Special Services, and received a medical discharge in 1943. Meanwhile, he had maintained his ties with jazz musicians and continued to organise jam sessions.

In 1944, twenty-one Chicanos were arrested during rioting in Los Angeles and subsequently convicted of murder. They were called the 'Zoot Suiters', and their defence became a *cause célèbre* for West Coast liberals. Granz was among them. He decided to stage a jazz concert for the benefit of the Chicanos and booked the largest auditorium in LA at the time. The concert was first titled 'Jazz Concert at the Philharmonic'. When the type-size Granz chose did not allow for so many letters, he dropped the word 'Concert'; thus, Jazz at the Philharmonic was born. The concert was so successful that Granz decided to present such events monthly.

Two days after that first concert, Granz listened to a transcription of it and realised that live recording could capture a level of spontaneity and improvisation that was not possible in studio recordings. He had also recognised the potential of the new LPs to record long performances of jazz. However, he was unable to persuade the major record companies. Mannie Sachs and RCA listened to the demo and commented that all he could hear were 'clunkers and crowd noises'. Granz received the same response from Columbia and Decca. But he would not be dissuaded. He finally found a sympathetic ear at Mercury, which agreed to distribute records on Granz's own new record label, Clef. Early in 1945 'Jazz at the Philharmonic I' came out. 'How High the Moon' became the first commercially issued live record. 'This is it,' proclaimed Granz in his programme note. 'In this album we've got it.'

A year later, Granz started taking JATP on tour. The structure of the concerts was usually the same. There was no star. Each musician was featured for five choruses. Granz used a core group of musicians and augmented the group with local talent in the cities where they played. He had given a nod to popular taste and included singer Helen Humes. The first tour, up the West Coast and into Canada, was unsuccessful, so Granz returned to LA and his monthly concerts at the Philharmonic, which continued to attract good crowds.

Granz recorded these concerts and issued them on Clef through Mercury. The records sold well and brought JATP a national audience which, once established, provided the basis for Granz's next try at national touring.

According to John McDonough in the *Wall Street Journal*,

> What he didn't realize was that he had also stumbled upon the keys to a jazz empire. Jazz at the Philharmonic (JATP) jump-started a selling reciprocity between box-office and record sales no one had imagined possible. The albums leveraged the concerts. The concerts generated more live records. And within a couple of years, JATP was a national phenomenon . . . By the early '50s Mr Granz had virtually cornered the market (and most of the talent) in mainstream American jazz. Some called him a monopolist. He probably was. He managed talent, produced records and packaged concerts. By controlling his product from raw material to distribution, he built the closest thing America has ever seen to a vertically integrated jazz conglomerate.[4]

When asked, Granz would simply explain that he had identified a need; nobody was bringing together the great musicians. For Granz, the term 'great musician' often meant black musician, and from the first he made it clear that they were going to travel first-class and get first-class treatment. In 1947, Spencer's Department Store in Dayton, Ohio, invited Granz to autograph albums but when he showed up with some of his musicians, didn't want them in the store. Granz responded by ordering that every one of his albums be taken off the shelves of the store and yanking the entire inventory. He also ordered his distributor, Mercury, to quit selling his albums to that store.

That same year, in Jackson, Michigan, Granz and his group entered a local restaurant to have lunch and were patently ignored. They then staged one of the first lunch-counter sit-ins, occupying each stool as it became empty. They were never served, and they were thirty minutes late for their concert, but they had caused enough of a disruption to make their point.

Ray Brown once said that Granz was obsessed with integrating previously segregated facilities: 'That was as important to him as the concert. We used to plan our strategy on the airplanes. He'd wire all these big hotels and send two or three of us to each one.'[5]

Granz insisted that all JATP shows be open to mixed audiences, and made sure all his contracts included clauses barring discrimination in ticket sales and seating. Further, in each set of programme notes for the shows, he included this statement: 'Jazz is America's own . . . deriving much of its inspiration and creation from the Negro people. Jazz holds up no superficial bars . . . As in genuine democracy, only performance counts . . . It is an ideal medium for bringing about a better understanding among all peoples.'[6]

Naturally, the first Jazz at the Philharmonic tours went nowhere near the South, and there were some northern and western theatre owners who refused to agree to Granz's terms and so did not get Granz's show. But the tours were successful, and for the next decade JATP did two ten-week tours a year. 'I gave to people in Des Moines and El Paso the kind of jazz they could otherwise never see or hear,' said Granz in 1953, adding that he had learned a great deal about scaling a house, or deciding how many seats to price at which rate. 'You can't be piggish,' he explained. 'On the other hand, you can't be easy. I've got a sixth sense about it.'[7]

The core group of musicians on the early tours included Coleman Hawkins, Lester Young, and Ray Brown, and Ella made it her business to catch as many of the JATP concerts as her schedule permitted.

Ella was in Akron, Ohio, to attend a JATP concert and see Brown when she was recognised by the audience. They called for her to sing, and Granz, who was perfectly happy with Helen Humes who was already on stage, reluctantly consented. Ella sang one song, and her performance brought down the house, whereupon Granz reconsidered his anti-Ella bias. Ella's speciality was ballads, not jazz, and jazz was Granz's chief interest; but he realised how popular she was with audiences, and given her relationship with Ray Brown, it made sense to have her work with the group. He offered her a contract with JATP, and she immediately accepted.

Thus began a personal and professional relationship that survives to this day and that deserves major credit for the continued viability of Ella's career. The personal relationship with Granz would develop later. The professional shot in the arm represented by the opportunity to perform with the finest jazz musicians took effect immediately. The native instrumentality of Ella's voice and her abilities as a mimic could have had no greater milieu in which to develop and flourish.

In taking on Ella, Granz was also taking on a considerable burden, for she was still under recording contract with Decca and so could not record for him. Any live concert recordings he did could not include Ella. This infuriated him, and he determined to do something about it. But there was nothing he could do as long as Ella's Decca contract was still in force.

When they were not touring with Granz, Ella and Ray Brown's Rhythm Group played individual dates, including the World's Fair of Music at Grand Central Palace in July. Wrote a newspaper reviewer, 'Miss Fitzgerald's inimitable style is too familiar to warrant detailing at this time. Her bag of tricks – hearing a note and gently slipping to the exact pitch, humming and bouncing her way through a melody – have not diminished in effectiveness since she first appeared with Chick Webb, the drummer, who introduced Miss Fitzgerald to the music world. Her method of distorting a chorus, poking fun at it, and vocalizing around it in meaningless syllables still has the strong flavor of originality.' As was her custom, Ella sang old favourites like 'A-Tisket, A-Tasket', 'Cow Cow Boogie' and 'Lady Be Good'. She also included some current hits, including the novelty song, 'The Woody Woodpecker Song', and 'Nature Boy', the number one record in the country.

What distinguished 'Nature Boy' from other number one records in the past was that it was a recording by a black singer, Nat King Cole, and represented one of the first times that a record by a black performer made the crossover to the white audience. The time was right for such a crossover, because the migration of blacks to the North during and after World War II had been reflected in an increase in 'race programming' on urban radio stations. The stations that played this type of music tended to be low-frequency stations at the extreme ends of the dial, but determined listeners could find them. They included a growing number of white listeners, mostly young, whose ears were more open to the realistic, earthy lyrics of black songs that were those of their parents. Still, it would be several years before black music approached the mainstream. 'Nature Boy' was a white song in every way except for the complexion of the man who sang it. Also, it was released at a time when there was a paucity of good new recordings.

'Nature Boy' had been recorded by Capitol just before the Petrillo record ban. Written by a Brooklyn-born, bearded, long-haired, self-described 'yogi' named Eden Ahbez, the song expressed the 'universal truth' that the greatest thing one can learn is to love and be loved. Had word of the song leaked out before January 1, other singers might have recorded it as well, but somehow Cole and Capitol had managed to keep the song a secret. First broadcast on the WNEW radio 'Music Hall' show on March 22, it was the number one song in the country within one week. In no time, other singers, white and black, were recording 'covers' of it, record ban or no: Frank Sinatra recorded it *a capella* for Columbia, Sarah Vaughan for Musicraft, and Dick Haymes for Decca. But Cole had a commanding market lead. Except for Billy Eckstine, he would continue to enjoy the distinction of being the one black singer to have achieved a nearly complete crossover to the white market until about 1954, when the advent of rock 'n' roll, so undeniably black influenced, really began to make the music world more fluid between black and white.

Nineteen forty-eight also saw greater fluidity between America and Europe in the music world. Now that the war was over, Europeans, who had begun to associate jazz with freedom after World War I, were eager again to hear American jazz in live performance, which naturally had been forestalled for nearly a decade. A parade of jazz musicians began crossing the Atlantic to bring this needed sustenance.

The Gale Agency, which had by this time merged with Joe Glaser's Associated Booking Corporation, booked Ella for a European tour in the autumn, a tour heralded by *Melody Maker* in July with an effusive announcement:

> Swing enthusiasts will be thrilled to learn that Ella Fitzgerald – America's 'First Lady of Song' – is the latest addition to the US personality parade visiting Britain this year . . . Although Ella has long been eminent in the field of swing singing, there is no doubt that she now stands at the zenith of her career. Today she is generally accepted by musicians and fans alike as one of the outstanding singers in jazz.[8]

In the late summer of 1948, amidst preparations for that first tour abroad, Ella Fitzgerald and Ray Brown got married. While some writers on Ella have suggested that it was Ella's contract with JATP that prompted their tying the knot, it is more likely that the impending trip to Europe was the catalyst. Ella needed a passport. The two may well have decided, or it may have been suggested to them, that decorum would be best served by their making their 'liaison', as Granz put it, legal. Anyway, a trip to Europe would be a fine honeymoon. They were married in a small private ceremony in Manhattan not long before the trip.

The newlyweds arrived in Southampton on the *Queen Mary* on September 15, 1948, with a small group that included Georgianna

Henry and Hank Jones. They were scheduled to open at the London Palladium on the 27th. Betty Hutton, the American 'Platinum Screwball', had preceded Ella at the Palladium, however, and proved so popular that she was held over. The Palladium management hastily arranged for Ella to begin her tour in Great Britain at the Empire Theatre in Glasgow, Scotland, instead.

On the opening night, she was nervous and the audience picked up on that, but she was always nervous onstage and it didn't usually affect her singing. She was also suffering from a head cold, brought on by the damp weather in the British Isles, but Ella was a professional and never let illness stop her if she could help it. Her repertoire was almost the same as she had performed at the World's Fair of Music in July. She had not planned to include 'My Happiness', the song she had recorded with only vocal accompaniment by The Song Spinners back in April. But to her surprise, that's what the audience wanted. So, she sang what she still considered a corny song as best she could, and the following day she went out and bought a copy of the record to refresh her memory of what she also considered a corny arrangement.

Following that concert, the group did another in Scotland, at an Odeon Theatre, as Hank Jones recalls. 'At that time, Great Britain and the US didn't have a reciprocal agreement concerning musicians,' says Jones.

An American musician couldn't play there unless he was part of an act. Ray Brown, Ella, and I were considered an act, so that's how we were able to play. But we couldn't bring a drummer. So we had to rely on local rhythm sections, and at this theatre we had a local drummer and a local conductor who usually conducted a high school band. Ella launched into 'Lady Be Good', and she sang it very fast. About halfway through, the drummer dropped out. Then the score – it was a long, 15–16 page score, fell off the conductor's stand. He didn't have time to stop and pick it up, so he got down on the floor on all fours and was trying to read the score. This is the only time I ever saw Ella completely stop singing and just start laughing. Ray Brown and I just kept playing.[9]

Fresh from a triumph in Glasgow, where the crowd had called for encore after encore, Ella opened at the London Palladium the following week. She was not the headliner there – that distinction was enjoyed by Britain's own Gracie Fields – and her reception was lukewarm at best. Even *Melody Maker*, so effusive back in July, commented, 'We who know her voice so well and admire it so much felt, however, that for some reason, we were not seeing Ella at her best. Although she sang as impeccably as ever, with style and phrasing that are unsurpassed, she seemed to lack stage personality, and was obviously labouring under great nervous tension at the opening show Monday night.'[10]

For Ella, that show, and that review, were sobering experiences. Insecure under normal circumstances, she was mortified by the comment about her lack of 'stage personality', for although she was always initially nervous it was onstage where she felt the most whole, and the most loved.

Sid Colin, a London musician and writer on music, suggests that the comment revealed as much about the British personality as it did about Ella's:

> That remark about her lack of stage personality may have been a typically British reaction, polite and euphemistic, to seeing for the first time, in the flesh, the 'skinny kid' (Ella's own description of herself) who had won their hearts with 'A-Tisket' and 'Mr Paganini' back in the thirties. Ever since her film appearance in *Ride 'Em Cowboy*, Ella had been putting on weight in quite an alarming fashion. Now, at the age of thirty, she must have appeared almost matronly. To the British, who were wont to think of American entertainers as resembling the frenetic Betty Hutton, it must have come as a profound shock. In many ways it must have been a cruel ordeal, in those days before her audience had completely accepted her, for Ella to appear in public at all.[11]

It was British jazz aficionados who really appreciated Ella, which fortunately she learned after the end of her week's engagement on the Palladium's regular bill. The following Sunday night she was invited to appear at bandleader Ted Heath's London Palladium Swing Session, and the minute she walked onstage she was greeted by a thunderous ovation.

Ella was astonished, and nonplussed at the difference in the reaction of this crowd. But she soon realised that this was a different kind of crowd. No calls for 'My Happiness' from them. They wanted to hear the new bebop sound, and called for encores of 'Lady Be Good', and 'How High the Moon' and 'Flying Home'. Ella soon relaxed and began to enjoy the evening, singing as long as the crowd wanted her to, until the show had to end or face big overtime bills from the Palladium management.

When Ella and her small entourage reboarded the *Queen Mary* on October 30 and headed for home, she was generally pleased with her first tour abroad, although what stayed with her longest was the reaction of the general Palladium audience, not that of Ted Heath's special Swing Session. But being in Europe had been exciting for her; moreover she was in love.

In 1949, Mr and Mrs Ray Brown bought a two-storey, six-room house in St Albans, Queens, which was fast becoming the residence area of choice for well-to-do blacks. Many, like Duke Ellington, Dinah Washington, and Gladys and Lionel Hampton, remained in Harlem, occupying apartments or houses in fashionable sections like Sugar Hill. But Harlem in the years after World War II became a community in decline, and by 1951 a national black magazine reported that St Albans was becoming the 'suburban Sugar Hill', and ran photographs of the homes of Count Basie, Ella, Mercer Ellington, Billie Holiday and others who had chosen the outer borough.

For Ella, whose own home life had been disrupted as a child, a house was essential to her vision of a normal married life. So was a child. Once they had established their home, the Browns adopted an infant son whom they named Ray, Jr. Ella, who had always loved babies, was overjoyed to have one of her own. In fact, she told many acquaintances that Ray, Jr was her biological child. But it never occurred to her to give up her career. While New York bookings became more important to her, and she was grateful for the annual three-week stint at the Paramount Theater, she continued to tour often, for her first love would always be the stage. A nurse cared for Ray, Jr, both at home and when he was taken along on tour.

During the spring of 1949, Ella and Ray performed at the Royal Roost and Bop City in New York, during both of which engagements they were recorded. At Bop City, Ella introduced 'In a Mellotone', the music for which had been written by Duke Ellington, but for which she had written lyrics. Her lyric-writing career had been stalled for some time, and that worried her. She wanted to write songs for others to sing, but publishers were not willing to take a chance on one of her songs unless she herself recorded it.

Later that same month, April, she recorded two sides with Louis

Although Ray Brown was considerably younger than Ella, the two enjoyed a deep romantic attachment. They are shown here with Billie Holiday, Ella's idol, and Illinois Jacquet. The couple in the foreground are not identified.
Ken Whitten Collection

Jordan and His Tympany Five: 'Baby It's Cold Outside' and 'Don't Cry, Cry Baby'. They went on tour in the summer, recording in Los Angeles with Sonny Burke and His Orchestra 'Crying' and 'A New Shade of Blue'. While the titles of the songs she sang were mournful, Ella was anything but. She felt settled in her personal life at last, and with her husband travelling with her, road tours also seemed more fun. She and her sidemen and her cousin and personal maid, Georgie, played pinochle between shows, and Ella clowned whenever the mood struck her.

They were on the West Coast twice, in July and November, and recorded there. Ella also recorded several times in New York in 1949, usually accompanied by guest orchestras, including Sy Oliver's.

During a September 20 session with Oliver's orchestra, Ella recorded a novelty song that was her own idea to do and that would become a classic: she sang 'Basin Street Blues' in a near-perfect imitation of the gravelly-voiced Louis Armstrong. After the record was released, one fan actually asked her, 'How did you and Louis Armstrong come to make a record together?' That tickled Ella. On the other hand, she would have occasion to regret ever having imitated Armstrong, for she was often asked to do so again in her live dates, and it wreaked havoc with her vocal chords. But for Ella, what the audience wanted, it got, and she gamely risked those precious organs on request.

Not for Ella the 'star act'. She remained remarkably untouched by her fame. She did not even have copies of many of her early record hits, having feared that people would think her egotistical if she had gone into a record store and asked for her own discs. Her reason for being, aside from her husband and child, was singing and making audiences happy.

Ella was always willing to sign autographs, to sing the additional song requested, to go the extra mile for her fans. One fan, Norman Matuleff, recalls how easy it was for him to get her to visit his fraternity house after a concert with JATP at the University of Iowa in Iowa City in 1951:

One day at dinner, one of my fraternity brothers at Phi Epsilon Pi house said that since I was on the committee why didn't I ask my 'friend' Ella over for dinner when she was in town. Everyone laughed. I thought about this and decided it wasn't such a bad idea. Ella was my favorite singer and probably most favorite entertainer, and I glibly said I'd write her to come to our fraternity house for refreshments and perhaps a few special songs after the concerts. My fraternity brothers began to tease and say things like, 'When Ella comes here, be sure she sings this song or that.' No one believed she would come.

I called New York and spoke to Norman Granz. He immediately said that since my name was Norman, we would be friends. When I asked him about Ella coming for dinner he didn't laugh at all. He said he'd talk to her and call me back. He called back in a few days and said Ella and Ray Brown – I believe he was married to her at the time – would be delighted. He added that it would be after the second show so that it probably would be late.

Both concerts at the Memorial Union were sell-outs, with several thousand students and faculty in attendance. Matuleff and Ella chatted during the breaks:

She was an extremely friendly and gracious lady from the beginning. There was never any suggestion of a fee for coming to the house. And she asked me if we had a piano and if we would like her to sing some tunes for us. She even asked me if we had any favorites and I asked her if she would sing my roommate's favorite, 'Dream a Little Dream of Me,' and also maybe for me, 'The Man I Love.'

After the concerts, Ella changed into a long, black dress and furs and I met her backstage, where she and Ray and I got into her limo and drove to the house about a mile from the Student Union. In the car we talked about her heavy concert schedule and how responsive college students were to jazz. I asked if Granz would be with us and she said he had to go on ahead.

When the limo pulled up in front of the house, it was like something in New York or LA. All the men rushed out and formed a kind of path for her. Inside, we all went to the dining room for cake and coffee and chatted in an informal way for about half an hour. Then Ella turned to me and said, 'Norm, would you like me to sing for you?'

We all went upstairs to the music room, where Ella stood at our piano, with all the men sitting around the floor in that room and one behind her. I'm not quite sure now whether Ray played the piano or whether there was somebody else that came along in the limo. She sang about six or eight songs, including the ones we had talked about, and she dedicated the ones we had selected. The audience was enthralled, and even after two concerts, and at almost midnight, she was absolutely sensational.

When the singing was over, there wasn't a sound at first. And then all the men stood up and cheered. We escorted her to the door and then to the car. I can remember many of us sitting up later that evening, talking about the experience. And still today, when we get together, people remember when Ella came to the house.[12]

Even in the material she recorded, Ella saw no reason not to give people what they wanted. Of ballads, she once told a reporter, 'They sell better.' Moreover, ballads were still her favourite genre. 'Despite all of the things I've done, despite the different kinds of songs I sing, I still consider myself basically a ballad singer,' she told a reporter for *Ebony* in the spring of 1949. 'I suppose I'll always be that way. I love ballads. Despite what they'll say, that will never change.'[13]

Changes in the music business around that time helped Ella sing the songs she liked best. Nineteen forty-nine was a watershed year in many ways. *Billboard* inaugurated its rhythm and blues chart that year. Rhythm and blues still meant black, but at least that euphemism sounded better than 'race records'. The *Billboard* move reflected the increasing popularity of ballads sung by black male singers, especially Billy Eckstine and Nat King Cole. The *Los Angeles Mirror* reported in January 1949, 'Negro vocalists, long tops in the jazz field, have seldom been top contenders in the singing of sweet ballads. Eckstine is giving the Crosbys and Comos a run for the money now.'[14]

While Ella enjoyed the new popularity of ballads, she bemoaned the fact that 'people didn't seem to want to dance anymore'. She'd always enjoyed dancing and missed the 'swing' element in music. But she bowed to the trend and did a great deal of recording in 1950, including a session in September with the Jazz at the Philharmonic All Stars (Harry Edison on trumpet, Charlie Parker on alto sax, Coleman Hawkins and Flip Phillips on tenor sax, Hank Jones on piano, Ray Brown on bass, and Buddy Rich on drums). By this time Granz had managed to negotiate an agreement with Decca that would allow him to record Ella.

She also did a lot of live performing. When in New York, she played the Apollo at least once a year, enjoying the feeling of 'coming home' to the unique Apollo craziness. One of the keys to the success of the

105

Apollo, aside from the abundant talent it featured, was that its managers retained what had worked in the past. There were still Apollo amateur nights, and on those nights stagehand Norman 'Puerto Rico' Miller, dressed in a yellow and pink garden dress, picture hat, and orange and magenta feather boa, or in some similarly outlandish costume, was still on hand to brandish his fake pistol and chase unsuccessful amateurs offstage. Ella enjoyed stepping out on to the Apollo stage after the amateur contests, and receiving the thunderous applause due her for having won such a contest once and, unlike most of the other winners, gone on to major stardom.

The following week, she would go into the Paramount, or some air-conditioned, palm frond-bedecked club and be received with similar enthusiasm, though never equal to that of the Apollo. The next week she might go on one of Norman Granz's JATP tours, or set off for Europe to play Great Britain and the Scandinavian countries. Through it all, she never lost her stage fright, or her insecurity.

During a European tour in 1950, Ella met up again with Marian Logan, who was then spending most of her time abroad. Logan had found herself on the wrong side of a powerful West Coast club owner after she had refused to 'entertain' Howard Hughes; assured that she would 'never work again' in the United States, she had gone to Europe.

'We became good friends,' says Logan,

> She had a marvelous sense of humor. She was shy, and she was very insecure about her looks. She used to tell me, 'You're so beautiful.' It was hard on Ella. Everyone around her was so young and slim and she was young and fat, and she thought of herself, I guess, as kind of ordinary. Nobody ever made her realize that she had a beauty that was a lot different and a lot more lasting than the beauty of those 'look pretty today and the next day look like raggedy-bose-of-yacka-may'. Nobody ever made her feel valuable even for her talents. Nobody made much over her. She was always a very lonely person.[15]

Norman Granz was not one to make much over anybody. But he recognised Ella's talents and strongly believed that she was being mismanaged. He became an unofficial adviser to her. He criticised Decca for expecting her to do so much inferior material and suggested that Ella push to do more material that suited her. He believed that her voice and diction were perfect for American classics like the music of George and Ira Gershwin. Ella took his advice. Happily, Milt Gabler at Decca was willing to listen, and on September 11 and 12, 1950, she went into the Decca recording studio in New York, with only the piano accompaniment of Ellis Larkins to record eight Gershwin songs.

Larkins was classically trained and a 'singer's pianist' who had an ear for what a singer could do. Ella, of course, was a singer who could do a great deal, and both enjoyed the sessions, which produced the material for Ella's first long-playing record, 'Ella Sings Gershwin'.

It was a marvellous foray into the new format, which Decca and other record companies had scrambled to adopt after Columbia had introduced it the previous year. Among the songs were 'I've Got a Crush On You', 'But Not For Me', and 'Someone to Watch Over Me'. Ella performed each with her customary sense of the nuances of the music and with a real understanding and appreciation of the lyrics, which were intelligent and sophisticated and told a story. So much of the material she was accustomed to singing, whether novelty songs, blues, or jazz, consisted primarily of choruses.

The album was destined to be a classic, although once record companies discovered that there was no future in ten-inch discs, Decca added four songs (by other writers!) and reissued it as a twelve-inch LP. But those mid-September, 1950, recording sessions set no different stylistic course for Ella. Two weeks later she was back in the studio recording 'Santa Claus Got Stuck in My Chimney'.

While Ella legend blames Decca for the corny material she recorded during her twenty years under contract with the company, in truth Ella liked doing a range of material, including novelty tunes. In 1951 Rosemary Clooney recorded a novelty titled 'Come On A-My House' which, with its suggestion of what her listener would be given at her house (which was in fact candy, although more was implied) was quite racy by the period's standards. By this time, the recording industry was less inclined to do 'covers' of songs already made popular by other singers. But according to Arthur Josephson, nephew of Barney Josephson, founder of the famous Café Society Downtown at Sheridan Square in Manhattan, Ella wanted very much to do a 'cover' of the Clooney song:

It was a warm evening in June or July. The musicians who were playing at the club at that time were Cliff Jackson, the club intermission pianist, who played great stride and blues, Edmond Hall, one of the all-time great jazz clarinettists, Jimmy Crawford, superb drummer who had played with the Lunceford Band for years, Cecil Scott, J. Williams, and several others. They were out in front of Café Society Downtown enjoying an evening break between the dinner music time and the first show. They were standing about chatting and laughing when a cab pulled up in front of the club and out came Ella. She obviously knew that they would be there and had come to visit. She hugged all of them and was full of such camaraderie and joy. Everyone was laughing and talking and kidding, and she was the one that lit up that spot. It was quite evident that she and they held each other in great esteem.

She was wearing a black sequined gown (probably for a performance somewhere), and I was surprised to see how short she was. Her vitality was really something.

She said she'd been introduced to what she called 'a cute little tune' and that she hoped to record it soon. Then she began to sing it while tapping her foot and snapping her fingers and swinging without background music. The tune was 'Come On A-My House', which Rosemary Clooney made famous a short time later (and it made her famous as well).

Then, just as suddenly as she came, Ella looked at her watch, said she had to go, and full of the same bounce and sparkle got back into the cab and off she went, leaving everyone full of warmth and good feelings. The men watched her cab drive away, and the smiles and expressions in their eyes were so revealing as to how they felt about her. I've never forgotten that.[16]

Ella did indeed record 'Come On-A My House' on June 26, 1951, accompanied by Bill Doggett on organ (he'd accompanied her on piano when she had toured with the Ink Spots back in the early 1940s), Hank Jones on piano, Everett Barksdale on guitar, Arnold Fishkin on bass, Johnny Blowers on drums, and the Charles Singers.

That autumn, while on a tour that included dates on the West Coast, Ella did three recording sessions for Decca in Los Angeles, among them her first session with Louis Armstrong. On November 23, she and Armstrong, backed by Jones, Brown, and Dave Barbour's Orchestra, recorded 'Necessary Evil', 'Oops!', 'Would You Like to Take a Walk', and 'Who Walks in When I Walk Out'.

Armstrong by this time was a bona fide star, not just a popular jazz musician. Two years earlier, he'd been featured on the cover of *Time* magazine. During the 1950s, he would appear in nine feature-length films and be a guest on six or eight television shows a year. Ella was delighted to record with such a big star, but having admired Armstrong for years, she would have been pleased to sing with him under any circumstances.

'As far as I know, this was their first session together,' says Hank Jones, 'but they worked together as if they'd been working together for twenty years. It went very smoothly – no rehearsing, just boom. The normal recording time in those days was about three hours, but I think the session took less than three hours.'[17]

Four days later, the two teamed up with Bing Crosby and recorded three sides with J. S. Trotter's Orchestra. A month after that, Ella recorded another four sides with Sonny Burke's Orchestra.

Hank Jones left around that time. His place in the Ray Brown Trio was taken by Oscar Peterson, who would soon break out of the accompanist orb to become a headliner with JATP. Born in Montreal in 1925, Peterson had carved out a niche for himself, and a good living, in the province of his birth, and saw no reason to go elsewhere. More than one bandleader had tried to lure him away, but Oscar was after quality in jazz, and he did not believe that most big bands represented that, being, of necessity, concerned with commercial success, or pleasing the public. He had, however, been following with interest the progress of Jazz at the Philharmonic. Thus, when Norman Granz went to hear him at the Alberta Lounge in Montreal, and later offered him the opportunity to do a JATP concert at Carnegie Hall, Peterson decided to venture south.

With JATP, he found great musicians, and he became an important part of JATP for many years, creating, with Ray Brown and guitarist Irving Ashby, the first of the Oscar Peterson Trios that would be a fixture on the classical jazz scene for a quarter of a century.

Ashby, born in Boston, had played with Lionel Hampton and was lately of the King Cole Trio. He stayed with the Oscar Peterson Trio and was replaced with Barney Kessel, who was later replaced with Herb Ellis. Ray Brown stayed around, however. He and Peterson enjoyed a mutual love of music that did not quit. Said Brown of Peterson once, 'Oscar wrote some hard music, but he didn't write it down. We had to memorize all of it . . . And Oscar would play a tune in one key one night and walk in and play the whole arrangement in another key a week later.'[18]

For Ray, it was the most challenging job he'd ever had. He and Oscar would noodle around all through an intermission, trying to get a single phrase right, and if they didn't like it, they would continue to noodle long after the last show was over.

For Granz, who had broken off from Mercury in 1951 and gone independent, a whole new set of recording possibilities opened up. He began to issue Oscar Peterson sides on Clef.

He also started featuring Ella with the Oscar Peterson Trio at JATP concerts, and Ella enjoyed this time in her career more than many. Peterson has a great sense of humour and a penchant for dubbing his friends and acquaintances with nicknames. His nickname for Ella was Madam Queen, which she loved. Over the years, according to some observers, Oscar got Ella to loosen up on stage, which made her live performances far more enjoyable. In addition to having a good personal relationship with Peterson, Ella blossomed in front of his musicianship. Like the sidemen with whom he played, she was consistently challenged, and delighted to be. The Canadian music critic, Bob Smith, wrote that he once asked Ella to recall her accompanists over the years, and she reeled off a list of names. Smith listened, then said triumphantly, 'You've forgotten one. Oscar Peterson!' Ella responded immediately, 'No, no, Bob. Oscar's an artist, not an accompanist. Don't ever make that mistake again.'[19]

Ella and the Oscar Peterson Trio were part of JATP's first European tour in 1952, a tour that Granz undertook not for financial reasons, since he was doing very well in the US market, but as a way of establishing JATP internationally.

In 1952, JATP could not perform in England, whose Musicians' Union was locked in battle with the American Federation of Musicians. Not long after World War II had ended, the AFM had refused to allow British musicians to work in the United States. The Brits, led by bandleader Johnny Dankworth, had retaliated by pushing through similar rules in England. However, there was a lot more to Europe than England, and the first European JATP tour visited fourteen countries.

Barney Kessel, white, and a native of Oklahoma, who had done studio work with Charlie Barnet's and Artie Shaw's bands, was the guitarist in the Oscar Peterson Trio for this tour. Recalls Peterson, 'Barney Kessel was really the first guitarist in the group. He was fresh out of the studios, and you know what that means. He never got to play any solos, only whatever was on that [music] sheet. So Barney was jazz-starved, he came in like an enraged panther . . . Ray [Brown] was in seventh heaven. "Ah," he said, "this is gonna be a different group now." [20]

Kessel remembered that JATP tour of Europe as being music all the way – onstage and off – for music was the lifeblood of the musicians. Ella was no exception. As Kessel told author Kitty Grime,

> I remember once in Genoa, Italy, we sat down to eat and the restaurant was empty except for Lester Young and his wife and Ella and me. So while we waited to give our breakfast order, I pulled out my guitar and she and Lester started making up fabulous things on the blues. Another time, when we were touring Switzerland, instead of gossiping with the rest of the troupe on the bus, she and I would get together and she'd take some tune like 'Blue Lou' and sing it every way in the world. She would try to exhaust every possibility, as if she was trying to develop improvization to a new point by ad-libbing lyrically, too, the way calypso singers do.' [21]

For Ella, the JATP group became like a family, and it provided an important note of stability as her marriage to Ray Brown broke up. After an initial separation, Ella and Ray divorced in 1952. According to one acquaintance of Ella's, 'It was probably more on Ella's side than Ray's. She always had a problem with men.'

Had they not both been in the entertainment business, their marriage might have lasted longer. Says Hank Jones, 'When you're caught up in this business, you're subject to all sorts of stresses and strains that are certainly different than for somebody who goes to an eight-to-five job every day. You're travelling a good bit of the time. You're living under adverse conditions as far as food and lodging, travelling, packing, and unpacking. All these things create a number of stresses and strains.' [22] At the same time, Ella and Ray were trying to maintain a so-called normal life, with a house and a child. The age difference put pressure on the relationship, too, for Ella, in her early thirties, was more ready to settle down than her much younger husband. Given the difference in their ages, it is unlikely that they would have got together in the first place if it had not been for their shared interest in music. This mutual interest they managed to maintain. While Ray moved out of the house in Queens and Ella received custody of Ray, Jr, the ex-spouses remained good friends and continued to work together for many years.

7 On the Granzwagon

In 1952, the same year that she and Ray Brown were divorced, Ella experienced serious problems with her throat, possibly because of the great popularity of her Louis Armstrong imitation, which audiences requested again and again. Phil Schapp, owner of the club Storyville in Boston, recalls that her throat was bothering her when she debuted at his club that year.

> She was the star of the show, but she was a little nervous – you know, what's she gonna sing, what's she gonna do, should she open with this song, should she open with that song. I said, 'Do whatever you want, it doesn't make a difference. Whatever you do, it's gonna be great.' She was always asking for little bits of advice, but she knew what she was going to do. She had a voice problem that year and that week was very difficult for her. She went into the hospital and had an operation after that. She was worried that she might not be able to continue, but she recovered and went on to greater things.[1]

For any singer, the prospect of losing one's voice is frightening. For Ella, it was more than that. She lived to sing, and now that her marriage to Ray Brown was over, she needed more than ever the love that she got from live audiences. Those weeks after the operation were among the hardest she ever lived through.

When she recovered, and rejoined JATP, Ella leaned ever more heavily on Norman Granz for advice and guidance.

In March 1953, JATP went on its second European tour – a ten-week one that featured Ella and drummer Gene Krupa. In Stockholm, two thousand fans turned out, and were so enthusiastic that it took the performers forty-five minutes to fight their way out. The group received similar adulation in Oslo, Brussels, Paris, Geneva, Zurich, Milan and Turin.

Taking a sidetrip from the continent during that tour, Jazz at the Philharmonic became the first American group in sixteen years to play in England. US groups were still effectively banned for commercial performances by the British Musicians' Union; but Granz saw a way to get around that prohibition after North Devon was hit by floods in the spring. Granz asked permission to perform two charity concerts in aid of the flood victims, and the Musicians' Union was hard-pressed to refuse such a request.

The concerts were staged at the Gaumont State Theatre in London. Ella was a stunning success in the audience's opinion, but not in her own. It was reported that she was in tears after the performance because she thought she had sung badly. But then, that was Ella. Not even winning first place in *Down Beat*'s new Critics' Poll that year would give her a sense of security about her ability to meet her own high standards of performance.

And then there were the changes in the entertainment business to worry about. Whether Ella herself identified trends, or whether she simply picked up on the gloom-and-doom forecasts of others, the 1950s were hard on someone who constantly worried about a premature ending to her career.

By 1954, the big concern in the entertainment world was the impact of television. First introduced to the general audience at the New York World's Fair in 1939, television had now become a fixture in many American homes, and its impact on live entertainment, particularly in clubs and theatres, seemed ominous. That year, the British music publication *Melody Maker* carried a comical piece written about New York by A. William Lovelock in which he elaborated on the threat posed by the 'evil eye' of American show business:

The bubble of night life had burst. Well-known night spots were closing down, old-established bars were on the real estate market, and not *one* movie theater throughout the length of Broadway was employing a house orchestra . . . And in two million rooms scattered across the island from Brooklyn Bridge to Harlem, the missing club clientele sat in the darkness, hushed and tongue-tied, hypnotized by the evil eye that put the hex on New York's famous night life . . . television!

Norman Granz wasn't worried about television. He was already going against the tide by featuring primarily older musicians. In his studied opinion, there was always a market for classic jazz. Ella need not worry. Besides, he was paying his stars, like Ella and Gene Krupa, around $50,000 a year. He once explained the comparatively large salaries he paid his musicians by saying, 'I figure you can live a lot longer with yourself if you share the gains with your people. I don't dig getting too hungry.'[3]

Granz had been serving as Ella's unofficial adviser ever since she had joined up with JATP. In 1954, the two made their business relationship official. As Granz recalled, it was during a JATP tour in Japan, on a flight from Tokyo to Osaka, that he finally broached the subject of becoming her manager, suggesting that while he might not be able to do any better than the Gales and Joe Glaser, with whose Associated Booking Corp. the Gales had merged their business, he certainly could do no worse. After nineteen years in the music business, Ella's career was still unfocused, her material haphazardly selected, in his opinion. Ella was not sure. Granz had a reputation as a genius, but also as a man who could fly off the handle at any moment. She preferred the sugary words of the Gales and Joe Glaser.

But she could not argue with Granz's suggestion that she should have had much more money to show for her years as a top performer and top-selling recording star. She was hardly alone among black stars, who'd historically been forced to seek white representation if they wanted to be in show business. No black agent had ever been able to get a toe in the door of entertainment management. Back in the 1930s, a young Reverend Adam Clayton Powell, Jr, who was gearing up to lead boycotts of Harlem stores, city buses and public utility companies to force hiring of blacks, had a weekly column in the New York *Amsterdam News* called 'Soap Box'. One such column addressed itself to the exploitation of black performers, especially black orchestras, by their white managers:

The truth of it is that they are only sharecropping. Duke Ellington is just a musical sharecropper. He has been a drawing account [money-maker for his manager] which has started to run around $300 per week. At the end of the year when Massa [Ellington's manager, Irving] Mills' cotton has been laid by, Duke is told that he owes them hundreds of thousands of dollars . . . When they finish totaling, there aren't any profits.[4]

Not much had changed in the twenty-odd years since Powell, who by the 1950s was a Congressman from Harlem, had written that column. It was common knowledge that Glaser, who represented Dinah Washington, Billie Holiday, Pearl Bailey, Louis Armstrong, Lionel Hampton and many other black stars, exploited them. The late Max Gordon, longtime owner of the Village Vanguard, reported that Glaser referred to his black clients as 'schwarzes', a Yiddish term for black that suggested inferiority. It was also common knowledge that Glaser routinely took as much as a fifty per cent commission from those stars, like Armstrong, who had no head for business and no proper advisers. Even Gladys Hampton, who was the business manager for her husband, Lionel, and who knew perfectly well what Glaser was doing, could do little but complain frequently. As a black woman, she had to rely on white agents and managers, and it was not until the 1960s that she found one who would not exploit her husband.

Ella knew she was being used by the Gales and Glaser. As Billy Eckstine had once put it in a radio interview, she was 'supposed to be the first lady of song, and she's getting the *seventy-fifth* lady of song's money, you know!'[5] But Ella was not good at making changes and preferred the known to the unknown under any circumstances.

What made her take the risk of leaving the Gales and Glaser was Granz's offer to represent her for one full year for free, without commission. She would not hear of his working for free; she would pay him his commission. Both agreed that if their new business relationship were to be worth anything, it should not involve a contract. Also, without a contract, they would not have to go through a lot of legal trouble if the relationship did not work out.

That relationship could be stormy at times. Ella and Granz frequently disagreed on musical matters, and they would not speak for days. Typical of their fights was one that Granz told about in 1965:

One time in Milan, she wouldn't sing 'April in Paris', even though it was her big record at the time; she let the audience shout her into 'Lady Be Good'. When she came offstage she yelled at me, and I yelled louder at her, and we didn't speak to one another for three days. Some nights I may tell her to do six songs, but she feels good and goes out there and stays for an hour and a half. It's part of her whole approach to life – the desire to sing and to please people by singing.[6]

But Granz filled the void left when Ella and Ray Brown divorced and functioned (as he still does) as a professional protector in a way that no one had done since Chick Webb. Granz attended to her business matters, ran interference with the press, and made the musical choices she found it difficult to make. More than anyone except Webb, he is responsible for Ella's success.

Granz had an irascible side. He could also be insufferably stubborn. But he did a lot for Ella Fitzgerald. For a man whom some in the world of jazz accused of pandering to 'lower-class swing enthusiasts' and of bald-faced commercialism, Granz was remarkably good at judging the direction in which Ella and her music should go.

It was not long before Ella relocated to Los Angeles, selling the house in St Albans, Queens, and taking young Ray Brown, Jr, to live closer to where Granz and JATP were based. Drummer Mel Lewis, who was also living in Los Angeles at the time, recalled, 'She moved to middle-class South LA, where Ben Webster and all of them lived. I went to her house and I remember seeing her son, who was a little kid. I went to Ben's house, too. It was a nice neighborhood, nothing to be ashamed of. It was also an integrated neighborhood.'[7]

By 1954 Ella had been in the music business eighteen years, and her friends threw her a party at her opening night at Basin Street in New York in early June. Eartha Kitt, Pearl Bailey, Dizzy Gillespie, Harry Belafonte and others were in attendance. Steve Allen acted as master of ceremonies and officiated over the reading of cables and telegrams from Lena Horne in Paris, Billy Eckstine in London, Benny Goodman, Fred Waring, Rosemary Clooney, Ray Anthony, Guy Lombardo, the Mills Brothers, Lionel Hampton, Louis Armstrong and others, and over the bestowal of awards and plaques by jazz publications and societies. Among these were Le Jazz Hot of France, Musica Jazz of Italy, Club Deritmo of Spain, Bladid Jazz of Iceland, Blue Rhythm of India, and Tempo of Australia. Decca Records gave her a plaque of appreciation; in the last eighteen years, Ella had sold twenty-two million records for Decca. Her first recording, 'Love and Kisses', was played, as well as her 237th, 'Who's Afraid?'

When Allen asked her to sing, Ella said she would prefer to speak first: 'I guess what everyone wants more than anything else is to be loved,' she said. 'And to know that you people love me and my singing is too much for me. Forgive me if I don't have all the words. Maybe I can sing it and you'll understand.'[8]

It is to be hoped that Ella held that evening to her bosom as, the following month, she was reminded that no matter how celebrated her talent, it could never shield her completely from racism. In mid-July, two months after the US Supreme Court had handed down its famous decision declaring 'separate but equal' education unconstitutional in *Brown v. Board of Education*, Ella suffered discrimination at the hands of Pan American World Airways. After performing in San Francisco, Ella, accompanied by Georgianna Henry and pianist John Lewis (who had joined JATP that year but who would leave soon after *Down Beat* announced that Lewis' Modern Jazz Quartet had won the award for best small group of the year), boarded a Pan-Am plane bound for Honolulu. There, they planned to meet up with Granz, who would join them for the continuation of the flight to Sydney, Australia, where Granz had lined up some concert bookings for Ella. The three were given the first-class seats they had requested, and even had seat assignments for the continuation of the flight to Sydney.

In Honolulu, there was some time before the continuation of the flight, so they got off the plane and met Granz. When they went to reboard, they were not allowed on. Nor were they allowed to retrieve the personal articles and luggage that they had left on the plane. Moreover, they were unable to get another plane to Sydney for three days, which forced the cancellation of several engagements in Australia.

All four sued the airline, alleging that their being denied the right to reboard had been 'maliciously motivated by prejudice against them because of their race and color'. The Pan-Am action, they claimed, had 'caused them humiliation and mental pain in addition to serious financial damage'. In the suit, which was not filed until January 1955, Ella and Norman Granz sued for $50,000, plus an additional $50,000 in punitive damages. Lewis and Henry sued for $10,000, plus an additional $50,000 in punitive damages. The suit was eventually settled out of court in February 1957 for an undisclosed sum, but which was reportedly about $7,000.

While engaged in this fight against discrimination, Granz continued his efforts to get Ella into exclusive clubs. In April 1955, reportedly with the help of Marilyn Monroe, who put pressure on the club's management, Ella made her debut at the Mocambo in Hollywood and packed the club. Among the stars that night in the usually star-studded club audience were Monroe, Eartha Kitt, Frank Sinatra, and Judy Garland and her husband Sid Luft. Ella was such a hit that she was held over at the Mocambo, after which she became the first jazz performer ever to entertain in the Venetian Room of the Fairmont Hotel in San Francisco.

Not long afterward, Ella appeared in her second Hollywood film, the Jack Webb-directed *Pete Kelly's Blues* (Warner Bros, 1955). She played herself and sang 'Hard-Hearted Hannah' and the original title song. *The New York Times* critic said, 'the wonderful Ella Fitzgerald . . . fills the screen and sound track with her strong mobile features and voice'.[9]

From Hollywood, Ella went on another JATP tour. This one included Dizzy Gillespie, who'd had to give up his big band because of financial problems and changing musical tastes. Also on that tour, or joining it for various engagements, were Illinois Jacquet, Lester Young, Roy Eldridge, Flip Phillips, Buddy Rich and Gene Krupa, along with Oscar Peterson, Ray Brown and other veterans of JATP tours.

The tour was scheduled to go the farthest South of any previous JATP tour. Ordinarily, the release of *Pete Kelly's Blues* would have helped attract audiences to see Ella, but it was unlikely that any in Ella's southern audiences got a chance to see her in the film, given the southern censors' penchant for cutting all scenes in which blacks appeared as equal to whites.

The Supreme Court ruling two years earlier had done nothing to change the attitude of most southern whites towards segregation. In fact, it had only hardened their attitudes. So had the Montgomery bus boycott, which had started in December 1955 after Rosa Parks had refused to give up her seat to a white man, and which still continued in spite of all efforts by the white power structure in Alabama to stop it. Norman Granz and his integrated group of musicians knew very well that they would encounter hostility below the Mason-Dixon Line.

To forestall at least some of the unpleasantness, Granz chartered an airplane for the southern parts of the tour. He also insisted on his standard non-discrimination clause. But there was only so much i-dotting and t-crossing he could do. The tour ran into serious trouble twice.

The first time was in Charleston, South Carolina, where the manager of the concert hall where JATP was scheduled to play had signed Granz's contract, only to learn later that by doing so he had apparently violated a city ordinance prohibiting mixed audiences. Aware that the police could descend at any moment, Granz persuaded Georgianna Henry to smuggle the night's proceeds out to the waiting charter plane. Fortunately, the authorities chose to exercise forbearance that night, and the move proved unnecessary.

In Houston, Texas, which Granz described as 'a tough city, a very, very prejudiced city', they ran into greater problems. According to Granz, 'Of course the first thing I'd do was rent the auditorium myself. Then I'd hire the ticket seller to sell tickets to my concert and tell him that there was to be no segregation whatsoever. Well, that was new for Houston. I removed the signs that said "White toilets" and "Negro toilets". That was new.'[10] Granz even hired local police, who were of course white, to keep order. Having done as much as he could to avoid trouble, he put on the concert.

There were two shows. After the first show, Granz sent out for food and some of the musicians retired to Ella's dressing room to shoot dice and play cards. Lester Young, Illinois Jacquet and Gillespie were on the floor of the room, along with, according to Gillespie, about $185, when three plainclothes policemen barged in and arrested two of the gamblers (somehow, they failed to collar Lester Young). Gillespie recalls, 'They asked everybody their names, and I told them my name was "Louis Armstrong".' Ella herself was not gambling – she and Georgianna were eating pie and watching – but the police arrested her anyway, because the gambling was going on in her dressing room. They also arrested Georgianna. Gillespie recalls that Ella ' had on a pretty blue taffeta gown and a mink stole and she was crying'.[11] Granz protested and was himself arrested.

But Granz kept his wits about him. He told the manager of the hall that he would cancel the second show. It was his show, and the money was his to lose. But the manager didn't want a show in his hall cancelled. The manager persuaded the police to book the JATP musicians between shows. They trooped to the police station where, coincidentally, press photographers were waiting. Ella was

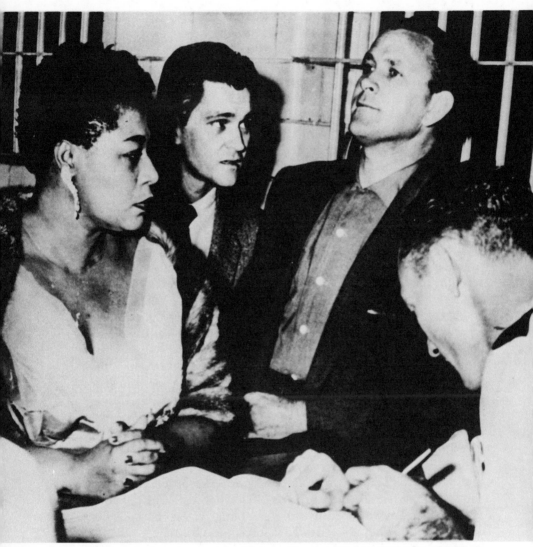

Caught up in a police raid in Houston, Ella was mortified to be booked on a misdemeanor charge of shooting dice in her dressing room at Houston's Music Hall in 1955. She protested she wasn't part of the game. She was released on a ten dollar bond, and Norman Granz later succeeded in having the charges dropped.
AP/Wide World Photos

indignant that they had the nerve to ask for an autograph.

Granz posted fifty dollars bail for himself, Gillespie, Jacquet, Henry and Fitzgerald and the five returned to the hall for the second show. The following morning, Granz called a press conference and told all, charging that the whole incident had been a set-up because the Houston authorities could not put up with the thought of a mixed audience. They left town soon after.

When the case came up for hearing in October, Granz paid a Houston attorney to represent them. The charges were not difficult to beat, since the police had entered Ella's dressing room without a warrant. All charges were dropped and Police Chief Jack Heard admitted that the arresting officers had been 'a little bit over-zealous'. Granz got back the fifty dollars he had shelled out for bail. Edward (Sonny) Murrain, a columnist for the black newspaper *New York Age*, reported in his 'Front and Center' column of November 12, 1955, 'Although there was hardly a whisper in the national press, jazz impresario Norman Granz spent $2,000 to clear himself, Ella Fitzgerald, and her secretary, Georgianna Henry of gambling charges filed against them in Houston, Tex., on Oct. 7. Granz was so provoked that he retained a Fort Worth lawyer to fight the case in court on Oct. 25. The defendants were all vindicated.'

Moreover, Granz saw to it that the arrests were expunged from the records.

While Ella was in Hollywood to film *Pete Kelly's Blues*, she had recorded the songs she sang in the movie, as well as 'Ella Hums the Blues' for Decca. She also did 'Necessity' with Frank Sinatra for Chairman Records, a never-released cartoon soundtrack. Back in New York, on August 1 and 9, she recorded twice with Toots Camarata and His Orchestra. The four sides she did on August 9 were her last for Decca. Norman Granz finally succeeded in buying her contract from the company with which she had been for twenty years.

Granz got Ella's recording contract by using a clever ploy. Decca had recently been acquired by Universal Pictures. Universal was in the process of filming *The Benny Goodman Story*, in which many musicians who had been with Goodman, among them Gene Krupa, Stan Getz and Lionel Hampton, played themselves. Gene Krupa and Stan Getz were then under exclusive recording contracts with Norman Granz, but Granz said nothing until the picture was completed and Universal was making plans to release the movie's soundtrack album on Decca. Only then did he politely remind

Universal and Decca that the playing of Getz and Krupa could not be included on the album unless he gave his permission. He would grant that permission, he said, if Decca released Ella Fitzgerald from her contract.

Granz immediately formed a new label, Verve, because he felt he needed a broader, 'pop' label for Ella. This was his fourth record label: Clef was for classic jazz; Norgram was for modern jazz – Lester Young, Dizzy Gillespie – and Down Home was for traditional musicians like Kid Ory and Red Allen.

The next time Ella entered a studio in Los Angeles in January 1956, was for Granz's Verve label. The first sides, for which she was accompanied by Buddy Bregman's Orchestra, were 'Stay Here', 'The Sun Forgot to Shine', 'Too Young for the Blues', and 'It's Only a Man'. She did four more sides accompanied by Harry Edison on trumpet, and others, in February. But for the balance of February and into March, she recorded the songs that Norman Granz had long known she could do best: the songs of Cole Porter.

While Granz was devoted to classic jazz, his tastes were far from parochial. From an early age, he had enjoyed the songs written in the heyday of American musical comedy in the 1920s and 1930s, particularly liking the lyrics. As he once said, simply, 'I felt at the time the tunes ought to be done and that the best person to do them was Ella.'[12]

With the development of the LP, such a thing as an album devoted to the work of a single composer was possible. Moreover, in Granz's opinion, it made sense. A trail-blazer in many areas of music, Granz became the first producer ever to give star billing to a composer.

He chose Ella to sing the songs of the great composers not just for the clarity and trueness of her voice, but also for her lack of ego. Or, by contrast, the fact that she had a vocal personality strong enough to avoid imposing it on the material. According to Benny Green,

Here Ella was in the identical position of a great soloist trying to make a song sound like itself instead of like *herself*. Only a singer for whom the conventional problems of intonation and diction had long ago ceased to exist could begin to tackle a task as demanding . . . But the prime attribute of the songbooks in toto resides in Ella's ability to put a tight rein on her instincts as an improviser and to give the material readings of classical serenity that are faithful to the intent of the composer.[13]

For her part, Ella was eager to try a new direction. In fact, she was certain that her career depended on it. 'Basin Street and Birdland had closed down,' she explained, 'and I was wondering where I was going to work.'[14]

A Cole Porter songbook was an enormous undertaking, primarily because there was such a large body of Porter works. He'd written hundreds of songs, and most of them contained witty, sophisticated and memorable lyrics. To choose ten or twelve for an LP was a daunting task in itself. Ella and Granz, along with Buddy Bregman, who served as musical director on the project, spent weeks culling Porter songs. Eventually, they realised they could not release a single album; only a double album would do. Altogether, Ella taped thirty-two Porter songs.

Then Granz took the tapes to Cole Porter himself, for Porter was notorious for hating the way most singers rendered his songs. Brick-top, the legendary international nightclub hostess, got away with singing them in the 1920s, provided that she taught Porter and his friends in Paris the Charleston. They became such good friends that Porter actually wrote 'Miss Otis Regrets' with her in mind, a signal honour. He also favoured Mabel Mercer, who achieved her first real popularity in Bricktop's Montmartre clubs in the 1920s, and considered her rendition of 'Love For Sale' the finest he had ever heard. But he was known to walk out of a club when a singer launched into one of his songs. Norman Granz respected that, and wanted Porter's sanction for the Ella album.

Granz visited Porter at his apartment in New York's Waldorf Towers. Porter, who was in his mid-sixties, had been an invalid for nearly twenty years by then, having in 1937 suffered a riding accident at the Piping Rock Club in Long Island. His horse had been frightened by something, reared up, thrown him, and then fallen upon him, crushing both his legs. Some twenty operations later, Porter still had only limited use of his legs, but he had continued to write memorable songs and to object to just any singer singing them.

Together, Granz and Porter listened to the tapes. When the last song was over, Porter said, 'What diction she has,' and gave his okay.[15]

Released on Verve in June 1956, 'The Cole Porter Song Book' was a double album with twenty-six Porter hits from stage shows. By the end of the third week in July, the album was second on *Down Beat*'s list of top best-selling jazz albums. By the end of 1956, it was the eleventh biggest LP of the year. It was Ella's first top-selling album.

It was also the biggest-selling album that Norman Granz had ever produced.

Earlier that same month, Ella had appeared at the third Newport Jazz Festival, which no doubt had contributed to the great sales of her new album. The brainchild of Louis Lorillard, one of the heirs of the Lorillard tobacco fortune, and his wife, Elaine, a jazz festival in Newport, Rhode Island, was practically a contradiction in terms. By definition, jazz meant black people, and Newport was not accustomed to black people except as maids and chauffeurs. Nor was Newport used to an influx of outsiders of the kind that could be expected for such a festival. In the past, the Newport community had imported members of the New York Philharmonic to play concerts each summer, but that was another thing entirely.

The Lorillards were determined, however, and they hired jazz pianist and Boston nightclub owner George Wein, whom Elaine Lorillard knew, to be the first impresario. Wein chose the talent carefully for the two-day festival on the grounds of the Newport Casino. It included Ella, the Oscar Peterson Trio (Ray Brown on bass and Barney Kessel on guitar), and Eddie Condon's Orchestra. There was no budget for a big band, but Wein did get Stan Kenton to act as emcee. The weather was terrible, but the audience of about ten thousand had a good time nevertheless. There were no racial incidents, the audience was fairly well-behaved, and the festival generated world-wide publicity.

However, the board of the Newport Casino complained that the ten thousand folding chairs had wreaked havoc on the carefully-tended lawns and refused to host another festival.

The second festival was held at Freebody Park, which was owned by the town. Count Basie, Woody Herman, the Dave Brubeck Quartet and Louis Armstrong's All-Stars were among the star-studded list of talent. The weather was good, the crowds larger, and the sound system was terrible, but there was no stopping the Newport Jazz Festival by that time.

By 1956 the festival had a track record and an international reputation; and it would spawn a series of imitations world-wide, all of which were good for jazz people. It functioned to keep jazz in the spotlight at a time when other forms were seriously competing for a share. Folk music was one, spawning the first Newport Folk Festival in 1957. Rock 'n' roll was another.

In June 1956, Ella appeared at the Starlight Roof of the Waldorf-

Astoria with Count Basie. Neither black musician had performed often in such posh surroundings – especially in New York – and New York reviewer Gene Knight made reference to that fact several times in his account of the engagement. But, according to Knight, Ella especially won the audience over just the same. It was 1956, and racial lines were starkly drawn; the June 5 review is a period piece and is quoted here quite extensively for that reason:

> The joint was jumpin' last night. Pardon me, I meant to write the performers were received graciously last evening and with considerable enthusiasm. After all, you don't call the Starlight Roof of the Waldorf-Astoria a joint. What would vice-president Claude Philippe think? But when Ella Fitzgerald sings and Count Basie plays his hot piano, the joint jumps, that's all. I don't care whether it's Birdland or the Waldorf. 'Cause when Ella throbs those blues and the Count picks his way among those eighty-eight keys, something's gotta give.
>
> And it's the audience. They give out with wild handclapping and shouts of approval. Doesn't make any difference whether the patrons are wearing minks and orchids or black ties and ordering champagne. Or wearing beads and dark glasses and ordering gin. Jazz is jazz and the beat is the beat . . .
>
> Miss Fitzgerald opened with 'It's Delovely', followed by 'I've Grown Accustomed to His Face', 'Cheek to Cheek' and 'Lady Be Good', which was sluggish. This was a slow start and Ella knew it . . . But like the fine trouper she is, Miss Fitzgerald swung into 'Black Magic' . . . 'Caravan', 'Witchcraft'. At this point, Ella got 'em – meaning the audience.
>
> I think she would have gotten 'em sooner with newer songs, but the fact remains that she got 'em finally. She got 'em some more with 'I Love You Porgy'. Had 'em groggy with 'Angel Eyes' (her best number on my score card). Swung 'em for a loop with her scat-talk in 'How High the Moon'. Knocked 'em out with her final blues routine, backed by Basie's band . . .
>
> And the beg-off sedate patrons of the Starlight Roof were clapping hands in rhythm with that sinful syncopation. Ella Fitzgerald was singing out and Count Basie was playing in – all in. Call it mob psychology (if you can call Waldorf patrons a mob), but the fact remains that – whatever it is – Ella has it, the Count has it. And the customers love it.

To give you an idea of the effect Ella and the Count have on their listeners, as I was leaving the Starlight Roof, Louis, the dignified maitre d', snapped his fingers and snorted: 'Yeah man! Cool-eh wot?' And I retorted, as I bounded toward the elevator, 'You said it, boy. Solid – but solid!'[16]

At the time, the Montgomery Bus Boycott was in its sixth month, and white northerners like the patrons of the Waldorf-Astoria Starlight Room were sending contributions to the Montgomery Improvement Association, headed by a young Reverend Martin Luther King, Jr. While blacks in Montgomery were demonstrating for the right to enjoy equal accommodations with lower- and middle-class whites (upper- and upper-middle-class white Montgomeryites had cars and didn't ride the buses) Ella Fitzgerald and Count Basie were showing upper-class whites in New York that there were no colour bars to the enjoyment of good music – at least as long as the dividing line between entertainers and audiences was clear. When the show was over, the black entertainers left by way of the service door.

In August 1956 Ella recorded two major albums. Accompanied by Buddy Bregman and his orchestra, she did thirty-four cuts of Rodgers and Hart music. All the cuts were on the resulting double album, which became Ella's second best-seller. 'The second album is more relaxed than the first,' she told a reporter, referring to the Cole Porter album. 'On the Rodgers and Hart songs, we had time to feel the melodies.'[17] As William Simon pointed out in the album's liner notes, the Rodgers and Hart album completed a cycle for Ella: 'It has taken twenty years, during which time Ella Fitzgerald merely has outgrown, outlasted – and outsung – what few young ladies have challenged her absolute supremacy among popular and jazz vocalists.'

Norman Granz realised that in a time of change there was still a place for standards. Audiences of all ages could identify with the music Ella sang, and with Ella herself. Having found a winning combination of Ella and quality show music, Granz wasted no time in planning an album of Duke Ellington's songs. In the meantime, Granz put Ella and Louis Armstrong together for an ambitious session accompanied by Oscar Peterson, Buddy Rich, Herb Ellis and Ray Brown. The resulting album, 'Ella and Louis', became another classic, although Norman Granz was not pleased with it. Armstrong, whose agent, Joe Glaser, booked him and all his other acts without

The Jazz at the Philharmonic All-Stars boarding a Scandinavian Airlines plane at New York's LaGuardia Airport for the start of a 1956 European tour. Clockwise from right: Flip Phillips, Gene Krupa, Ella, Herb Ellis, Illinois Jacquet, Dizzy Gillespie.
Popsie Randolph photo, Frank Driggs Collection

respect for the fact that his clients were human and needed a rest between concerts or between concerts and recording sessions, was not at top form. Nevertheless, the album with Armstrong only solidified Ella's position in the pantheon of musical legends.

Another result of the success of that album was Granz's decision that it was silly to have four record labels. That year, 1957, he consolidated all his recordings under the Verve label and brought in new producers who were familiar with the commercial music market.

8 The Songbooks

In the late 1950s, when Granz started issuing the song books, Ella was approaching forty. In society's view, forty was old. Rosa Parks was forty-two when she refused to give up her seat on the Montgomery bus and launched the famous boycott, but she was then and would be known thereafter as the little old woman who took a stand. Young veterans and their wives, and the baby boom they had generated, occupied centre stage in American demographics.

Thus, to be enjoying a career renewal at that time in her life was important to Ella. Under Granz's representation, she was singing in new venues, reaching new audiences, and recording the best work she had ever done. 'It was like beginning all over again,' she said. 'People who had never heard me suddenly heard songs which surprised them because they didn't think I could sing them. People always figure you could only do one thing. It was like another education . . . We just went from one songwriter to another, all the great ones, and it opened up another whole level of audience for me. People started saying, "You know, no matter what this lady sings, she's still singing a pretty tune."'[1]

Moreover, Ella could take heart in the fact that the black press, at least, did not consider her too old to be the subject of rumoured love affairs. Never comfortable with her looks when she was young, Ella had not become secure about them as she approached middle age. Thus, to be the subject of romantic rumours must have given her some satisfaction, although she was far too uncomfortable with publicity to exploit them as she could have. Fans loved reading about these rumours. Says one, 'I thought of her particularly when I'd chub up a few pounds and comfort myself with the thought that Ella's life was not over simply because she was not a size six.'[2]

In 1956, the rumours were that she had married a Philip Roten of Los Angeles. In 1957, the story circulated that she had a younger lover in Denmark with whom she had enjoyed an 'intercontinental romance' for several years.

There was considerable substance to the rumours about the younger lover from Denmark, although by most accounts he was from Norway. During a JATP tour in Scandinavia in the early 1950s, Ella had met Thor Einar Larsen, an assistant producer ten years her junior. They had either become good friends, or lovers, depending on the source, and had arranged to meet in Paris, London, Rome, New York, and wherever else they could in the following years. Ella took a flat in Denmark in the early fifties, and one reason may have been that she wanted a place where she and Larsen could spend time together in private.

In late July, Ella 'revealed' that she and Larsen had been secretly married for two years, or so *Jet* magazine reported. According to *Jet*, 'The marriage announcement was made when reporters visited the pair at a suburban house in Oslo, Norway, where the singer displayed a photograph of herself she said she had given Larsen some time ago. It was inscribed: "To my beloved Thor, my love and my husband." In addition, the two were wearing identical rings on the third finger left hand. [*Jet* provided a photograph of the two, with arrows pointing to the rings] It was also reported that Larsen had written his father a letter, telling him that he had married Miss Fitzgerald.'

The wedding was supposed to have taken place in Oslo, Norway. The following week *Jet* reported that the two denied a secret marriage and that Larsen had dismissed the story as 'pure nonsense'.

The plot thickened in August when the *Chicago Defender* reported that Larsen had been jailed in Sweden for exploiting a purported fiancée:

JAIL ELLA'S 'MATE' IN LOVE SWINDLE
GOTHENBURG, Sweden – Thor Einar Larsen was sentenced to five months at hard labor here last Monday and banned from the country until Jan. 1, 1963, for operating a marriage swindle.

> Larsen, a 28-year-old Norwegian, is the man to whom singer Ella Fitzgerald is reportedly secretly married. Both have denied the rumor.
>
> But officials here discount their denials as being customary in the case of a secret marriage and especially in this case where Miss Fitzgerald might have found it professionally unwise to admit to being a party to an interracial union.
>
> Since the exposure and conviction of Larsen, the concern here is whether Larsen swindled the American singer or went through a fake marriage with her in order to exploit her.
>
> His conviction was based on a charge that he stole money from a young woman to whom he was engaged.
>
> Ella, en route to Nice last week, stopped over in Oslo reportedly to visit Larsen. At Nice she appeared as the star attraction at the Monte Carlo casino gala given to aid the polio fund.[3]

While the word on the street is that Ella was never actually married to Larsen, the possibility exists that they were married and that the sudden denial just one week after the story broke was a result of the suit against Larsen in Sweden. Neither Ella, nor Larsen if he really cared about her, would have wanted her to be mixed up in that unfortunate affair.

Ella has always been reluctant to discuss her romantic life. When asked that year about the men in her life, she told a reporter for the *Los Angeles Times Mirror*, 'I guess I pick them wrong. But I want to get married again. I'm still looking. Everybody wants companionship.'[4] But Ella was never to marry again. Her assessment of her taste in men is shared by her friends and fans. 'She always had a problem with men,' says one friend. According to an Ella fan, 'I've hung on gossip from assorted of her sidemen I've met who would cut through their own cynicism when it came to Ella; their brows would furrow and they'd say, "She has terrible taste in men. I don't think she's really *happy*."'[5]

In 1986, an interviewer for the *Essence* television show asked Ella how she had managed to avoid the pitfalls that had befallen people like Billie Holiday, Dinah Washington, and Judy Garland. Problems with men came to Ella's mind. 'Well,' she answered, 'I think all women have some kind of pitfalls. We all have some kind of skeleton in the closet. I used to be a little too romantic. Sometimes you learn from it, and sometimes it comes out in our songs.'[6]

Two other unpleasant incidents marred a year that was a difficult one for Ella as far as her personal life was concerned. While performing in Atlantic City, she was attacked onstage by an escaped mental patient whose last name also happened to be Fitzgerald. And while performing at the Paramount in New York, she had to be rushed to the hospital for an emergency operation on an abdominal abscess, which she did not even know she had, although she later admitted that she had felt ill during her performance.

But professionally, 1957 was a landmark year for Ella. In June, she recorded a four-record album titled 'Ella Fitzgerald Sings The Duke Ellington Song Book' and containing thirty-seven Ellington or Ellington-associated songs. Norman Granz had done another clever bit of engineering to get Ellington, who was under contract with Columbia Records. When Johnny Hodges, Ellington's lead alto sax player, left the band, Granz had signed him to a contract with JATP and to a contract with Verve. When Hodges rejoined Ellington, Granz still had him under recording contract and was thus able to 'force a few concessions', as he put it: 'I would have Duke for one LP or two if I used Ella. We planned far in advance, but in the end Duke failed to do a single arrangement. Ella had to use the band's regular arrangements. She'd do a vocal where an instrumental chorus would normally go. To stretch it to four LPs, we padded it with various small group things with Hodges, Ben Webster and so on.'[7]

Ella and Duke enjoyed the sessions, although she, too, wished he had written some arrangements. For his part, Duke was moved to write, with his long-time collaborator Billy Strayhorn, and record an album titled 'Portrait of Ella Fitzgerald', a four-movement work which included 'Royal Ancestry', 'Beyond Category', 'All Heart', and 'Total Jazz'. In his spoken introductions to each section, Ellington talked of browsing through Ella's 'family album': 'As we turn the pages, we observe that she is of "Royal Ancestry", and in our first movement we try to capture and convey some of the majesty of Her Majesty . . . and the more we leaf through the pages the more we realize that this is a personality of wonderful warmth, and that she is "All Heart" . . . In terms of musicianship, Ella Fitzgerald is "Beyond Category". In our musical search for a tonal portrait of Ella Fitzgerald, we find a melodic parallel in which royal ancestry, greatness of heart, and talent beyond category are the principal components in the quest for "Total Jazz".'[8] The suite became part of the four-album package.

Wrote Irving Kolodin in *Saturday Review* in April 1958,

If there is any doubt, after her volumes devoted to the songs of George Gershwin, Rodgers and Hart, and Cole Porter, whether Ella Fitzgerald is the greatest jazz vocalist of the day, her mammoth collaboration with Duke Ellington and band . . . should resolve the statement permanently. Indeed, there is some doubt, after hearing two or three of the LP's eight sides, whether Miss Fitzgerald isn't the greatest jazz singer known to history. By the time one has completed the grand tour of the eight sides (one is devoted mostly to an instrumental suite written in her honor) all doubts are dissipated: Ella is undisputed Queen of the Realm, mistress of the Empire and lands across the seas.[9]

While Granz continued to feel that the album would have been more of a groundbreaker if Ellington had written arrangements for himself and Ella, he was none the less very interested in having Duke with JATP. The following year, Ellington and his orchestra went to Europe for Granz for the first time, and would return several times thereafter. 'The representation he gave me was great,' said Duke. 'It makes a lot of difference when the man who is doing the talking for you is a millionaire.'[10]

The Ella and Duke album also sold well, as did the next pairing that Granz arranged: Ella and Louis Armstrong singing *Porgy and Bess*, accompanied by a fifty-piece orchestra led by Russell Garcia. The two were supposed to sing a duet at the Newport Jazz Festival in July, 1957, but Armstrong – or his advisers – decided to emphasise his commercial hits at the expense of his jazz reputation. The duet did not take place, and listeners had to be content with the *Porgy and Bess* album. It was no surprise when Decca decided to take advantage of Ella's popularity by reissuing the one songbook she had recorded in her twenty years with them, 'Ella Sings Gershwin'. Ella was on a roll. That year, she won all the major music polls. Her counterpart as best male singer was Frank Sinatra.

In March 1958, Ella recorded 'The Irving Berlin Song Book', accompanied by Paul Weston's Orchestra, and that autumn Ella's song book work earned her at last the highest honour that the music business bestows. She won not just her first Grammy but a second that year, both of them for song books. She won Best Solo Vocal Performance – Female for 'The Irving Berlin Song Book' and Best Jazz Performance – Individual for 'The Duke Ellington Song Book'.

Due to the stomach abscess she had suffered, and the emergency operation she'd had to undergo as a result, Ella had gone on a diet. By February 1958 she was forty pounds thinner than she had been in the autumn of 1957. 'I have to laugh at how I looked – a great big blown-up balloon,'[11] she told reporters, referring to her 300-pound plus weight before the diet. When she opened at the Mocambo in Hollywood that month, she looked comparatively svelte in a brown satin dress. As had become her custom, she was a great sucess at the Mocambo. But then, in the late 1950s, Ella was a success wherever she performed.

In public statements, Ella gave the credit to her audiences. 'Most singers, myself included, always seemed to prefer European audiences,' she said in early 1958,

> because over there people knew how to listen. I think it was because all of them, even the young ones, knew more about music than Americans. They didn't come simply to listen. They came to learn and study music as well as to be entertained. But Europeans aren't in this class all by themselves any more. Americans now go to song recitals and concerts for the same reason . . . I notice they don't yak and stir in their seats so much anymore . . . The kids listen to you now and seem to appreciate it when they hear something good. But a couple of years ago, when I used to sing a ballad at a jazz concert, the audience would start getting restless, waiting for me to get going on a jump tune. Now I can sing three or four ballads in a row and they'll listen quietly.[12]

While she was making those statements, the phenomenon of rock 'n' roll was in its ascendancy. So much for Ella's analysis of musical trends, although she was hardly alone in failing to foresee the impact of rock 'n' roll.

This form of music constituted a serious threat to popular singers like Ella. Eventually, it would send into shadow, at least for a time, the careers of such major stars as Frank Sinatra, Bing Crosby, and even Ella Fitzgerald herself.

The brash new form was a far greater threat than bebop had ever been; although Nat King Cole was assaulted on a stage in Birmingham, Alabama, in 1956 by members of the local White Citizens Council who said they were campaigning against 'bop and Negro music', Cole's music was obviously not the real problem. What rock 'n' roll did was to assault the popular market, which bebop had never tried to do.

That it was based on black forms, with particular obeisance to Chuck Berry and Bo Diddley, and that it signalled another step forward in the emotional maturation of Americans – accepting music based on black forms boded well for accepting blacks into other areas of American life – was small comfort to black entertainers, including Chuck Berry and Bo Diddley. It was whites like Bill Haley and His Comets and Elvis Presley who would reap the rewards, both in financial terms and in terms of popular success.

For black singers, it was quite a reversal to observe, from 1952 on, that white singers were recording 'covers' of black songs. At first these white versions seemed to satisfy the white teenage audiences. A turning point of sorts occurred in 1956, however, when Little Richard's 'Long Tall Sally' outsold Pat Boone's version. Obviously, the kids wanted the real thing, which meant both a little more work for black singers and a lot more for white singers like Elvis Presley who could deliver the requisite raunchiness.

Rock 'n' roll was the musical expression of the emerging generation gap. Prior to its onset, there was no difference between young and old in musical tastes. But the products of the postwar baby boom that had begun in the 1940s were reaching their adolescence, and given the prosperity of the 1950s, were enjoying not only numerical clout but financial clout as well. Accordingly, commercial record companies rushed to market the products that they thought would appeal to the new, young audience, much to the consternation of older singers of more mass market songs. As the popularity of rock 'n' roll burgeoned, Frank Sinatra's career went into decline for a while. Club singers like the legendary Mabel Mercer, whose diction and storytelling ability had influenced Ella a great deal, went into temporary retirement.

Frank Sinatra, Nat King Cole, and many others criticised the new music. Cole wrote a song titled 'Mr Cole Won't Rock 'n' Roll'. Ella predicted the early demise of rock 'n' roll. In early April 1958, she said in an interview:

Rock 'n' roll is losing popularity, and is simmering down to where it started from – just plain everyday jazz. Not that there's anything plain about jazz. But that's where rock 'n' roll is going back to . . .
I think [the kids] have just had enough of extreme rock 'n' roll stuff. Even when they do rock 'n' roll now they don't throw themselves around like they used to, and I think that's a good sign.

> Personally, I don't care for rock 'n' roll. At first, I think, the songs and gestures were too suggestive. The kids got wild when they heard them. It was a natural reaction of mass psychology. One girl starts yelling when she heard Elvis and another one thinks she should, too. Pretty soon it's a riot. I just don't like it, and I think a lot of other people don't either.[13]

The 'suggestiveness' of rock was to grow, of course, and to become even more extreme in the performances of the Rolling Stones, the Grateful Dead, with the advent of heavy metal, and so on.

Rock 'n' roll had not seriously affected Ella yet. She continued to perform and record, although she was a worrier who could not help being concerned that her career would suffer. Musicians who worked with her in the late 1950s mention a certain unease about her performances, an unease that sometimes caused her to blame them when she didn't sing up to her own high standards and then, feeling guilty, to suspect that they were expressing resentment behind her back.

Drummer Gus Johnson had joined Ella in 1956, after playing for Lena Horne for several years, and remained with her for nine years, until 1965. 'She had her little ways, too, you know,' he says. 'She's self-conscious, which she shouldn't be at all, because she's so great. But she knew she wasn't as pretty as Lena, although she sounded better. Nobody's going to sound like Ella! Still, she's very sensitive, and if she saw you talking she might think you were talking bad things about her. I used to tell her all the time, "Go ahead and sing. Nobody's talking bad about you."'[14]

There was plenty of work, for there was always a market for the classics – good songs, with meaningful lyrics. She continued to cut records and sing songs in live performance that had appeal to young and old, although in the era of rock 'n' roll they were more old than young.

She also had an opportunity early in 1958 to appear in another Hollywood film, *St Louis Woman*, a highly fictionalised biography of the late black jazz composer, W. C. Handy. Nat King Cole played Handy. Ella played herself and sang W. C. Handy's 'Beale Street Blues'. While the cast was packed with musicians and singers, few managed to act convincingly. Those who came off best, like Ella, played themselves.

In April, she joined Duke Ellington for a concert at Carnegie Hall.

The reviewer for *The New York Times* wrote, 'In her two special areas, the ballad – "Sophisticated Lady" – and the scatted rhythm tune – "Cotton Tail" – her singing was a model of considered ease and grace. Between times, however, she seemed unable to disentangle herself from the special rhythm section that provided her accompaniment.'[15]

Also while in New York, Ella participated in a televised 'jam session' with Benny Goodman, Harry James, Jo Stafford, and others. So inspiring was the session, according to the *Chicago Defender*, that a Broadway agency proposed a package tour that winter, to consist of Ella, Johnny Mathis, Nat King Cole, and Count Basie's band. Nothing came of the idea, however, since all of the musicians involved already had their own 'packagers'.

From New York, Ella set off on another tour with Jazz at the Philharmonic. Granz launched this one in Brussels with 'An Evening with Ella Fitzgerald and the Oscar Peterson Trio'. Following that special evening, Dizzy Gillespie, Stan Getz, Roy Eldridge, Sonny Stitt and Coleman Hawkins came on board, and the tour became Jazz at the Philharmonic again. They played several dates in France before heading for the British Isles and the first tour ever of Jazz at the Philharmonic in England.

Unpleasantness awaited them there. Arriving at London Airport from France, the JATP group found that it had been singled out for 'the treatment' at Customs Hall. Customs officials searched everything, from instrument cases to cigarette packages. Ella's entire wardrobe was gone through – even the lining of one of her coats was unstitched. Writer Sid Colin suggests that the country was afraid of rock 'n' roll infiltrators: 'The country was still in shock over a film called *Rock Around the Clock*, in which Bill Haley and his Comets had so aroused its adolescent audience (they had yet to be yclept "teenagers"), that they had leapt to their feet, uttered hoarse cries and danced in the aisles! Who knows what alien substances were coursing through their veins to provoke such manic behaviour?'

Ella didn't care why she had been subjected to such humiliation, she only knew she didn't like it. 'I've been in a million places,' she told a reporter after leaving Customs Hall. 'But I've never, never been put through anything like that. I wouldn't like to say at the moment that I'm glad to be here.'

She calmed down after a time. A London reporter remarked that she looked slimmer than when he'd last seen her, and Ella responded,

'Oh, thank you, thank you. That's the sweetest thing you've said today.'[16]

Ella left the tour after that, while JATP, including Lou Levy, Gus Johnson, and Max Bennett, who were functioning as Ella's usual combo at the time, continued on to the continent.

Mel Lewis sometimes filled in for Gus Johnson.

It was back in the days when Gus Johnson was her regular drummer, and I worked with her with Lou Levy, Jim Hall and Wilfred Middlebrooks. I was based in California, but Gus wasn't, and there were a lot of times when they wouldn't want to fly Gus out to California just for two or three concerts, so they would call me to do it. I am on two albums with her – 'Ella Swings Lightly' and 'Porgy and Bess'.

I was doing a lot of Norman Granz's record work out there. He would call me to do things as favors. It saved him bread at the time, and it saved a hassle, and I would just walk right in and take care of business.

Ella was friendly to me, she always had nice words to say. When I first worked with her, she made me welcome. She didn't act like, 'Who are you?' In fact, I think she knew who I was, and that's when I brought up to her that I had met her when I was a little redhead hanging around in back behind the drummer in the band at McVan's in Buffalo. (She was there before I was allowed to play. I probably would have played behind her at McVan's because when I finally joined the union, my father made me his substitute. But by the time I was sixteen years old and in the union, Ella had really become a star and gone on.)

Anyway, I found her to be a very sweet woman to work for, except at those times when she didn't feel she was reaching the audience. She would blame it on the band, and then she would turn into a bitch. Then she wasn't sweet Ella anymore, and I never did understand that. But after I worked for a few other singers around that time, I realised that was the routine – blame it on the band.

But I still enjoyed working with her because she was a consummate musician. She swung every time, and it was just interesting – good programming. But when things didn't go right, she would really scream about everything. Then she'd see us talking after the show, and she'd say, 'What are you talking about? If you're going to talk about me, tell me to my face.' But we wouldn't even be talking about her.[17]

Ella went back to New York for a stint at the Copacabana, the first black artist to headline there. Again complimented on her weight loss, she announced that she was determined to lose more. She'd not lost her ability to charm the six hundred-odd patrons of the nightclub with a varied repertoire that included a cool-jazz version of 'St Louis Blues', which meandered on so long that, sensing that the audience was getting restless, Ella interpolated, 'I guess these people wonder what I'm singing. Believe it or not, it's still "St Louis Blues".'[19]

She felt fortunate that she had been able to move into such venues as the Copa and the Mocambo, for she was no longer performing in as many theatres as she once had. After 1957, Norman Granz had stopped touring JATP in the United States.

Various reasons have been cited for Granz's decision, none of them by Norman Granz himself. Some suggest that changes in the American music business were the reason – that it was getting hard to compete with Elvis Presley and that he didn't like the cool jazz of Miles Davis and other newcomers to the jazz scene. There is also the suggestion that Granz got tired of fighting racism, which seemed to continue unabated in spite of some notable progress.

In Montgomery, Alabama, the bus boycott had, after nearly a year, been successful in establishing a more integrated seating arrangement. In various parts of the South, attempts were being made to integrate the public schools. Granz himself had effectively changed the whites-only admission policy of the Manhattan restaurant, Le Pavillon, by taking Oscar Peterson and Ella Fitzgerald to lunch there. But Nat King Cole had been attacked by White Citizens Council members in Birmingham, Ella and Granz and their group had been discriminated against by Pan-American World Airways, and in September 1957 Governor Orval Faubus of Arkansas prevented black students from integrating Central High School in Little Rock. Whether the reasons were musical, social or political, Granz decided he'd had enough of American touring. Henceforth, he would only organise JATP tours outside the United States.

This was a risky decision on his part, and had an impact on his record business, for the concerts had long subsidised the Verve label. Fortunately, Ella's records, among them at that time 'April in Paris', were selling so well that she alone took up a great deal of the slack.

Since Granz had become her manager, Ella had reached heights of popularity in live performance and recordings that she could only have dreamed of. In 1958 Granz celebrated her success with an 'Ella Fitzgerald Night at the Hollywood Bowl' at which she was backed by one hundred and eight musicians and entertained an audience of twenty-two thousand. The night was such a triumph that the following year she returned for another gala performance.

By contrast, the second half of the 1950s had been years of decline for Billie Holiday, who lost her battle with drug and alcohol addiction in July, 1959, when she died in a hospital in Harlem. She'd been barred from working in New York clubs because of her conviction for drug possession and was so erratic that she frequently missed the gigs she could get. Norman Granz had tried to help her – signing her up for JATP tours in Europe and recording her on Verve. According to John Hammond, 'To work for Norman was a full-time job for many who, like Billie, might not have worked at all without him.'[19] But Granz had been unable to exert over Billie the influence he had on Ella. It was probably too late anyway. Billie had spent her talent; Ella had saved hers.

Ironically, that same year, Ella played a washed-out, drug-addicted blues singer in *Let No Man Write My Epitaph*, starring Bernie Hamilton. She wasn't very convincing, and looked a bit too healthy to be a drug addict. Critics suggested that she stick to roles in which she played herself.

Musically, the high point of Ella's grandest decade came at its end, in 1958–59, when Ella and Granz recorded the culminating album of the songbook series, 'The George and Ira Gershwin Songbook', a two-record album. George Gershwin had died by then, but Ira Gershwin worked closely with Granz from the beginning, helping to select the fifty-three songs that were eventually recorded from his brother's vast repertoire.

Granz and the musical director he chose for the album, Nelson Riddle, spent more than a year on the research and orchestration, and the songbook became an instant classic, destined for reissue.

All in all, Granz and Ella had recorded two hundred and thirty-seven tracks of songs by the great composers in the history of American musical comedy, rendering immortal what many had considered clever but ephemeral show tunes.

If the songbooks helped to ensconce the works of these American composers in recorded history, they also helped to create the Ella legend. 'It took such a long time, you know, for people to kinda catch on to me,' she told Bob Smith of CBC Radio in 1972, 'even though I started a long time ago. [People] classing you as just jazz, you know . . . they don't understand it, so therefore they don't become attracted to what you're singing. Through the songbooks we gained so many fans, not only our jazz fans but people who understood show music.'[20]

9 Time Out

By the end of the 1950s, Norman Granz had become disenchanted with the United States. In 1959, he moved to Lugano, Switzerland, where he organised occasional JATP tours in Europe and began to amass an impressive collection of modern art. Ella was concerned that she would lose his counsel; she did not always get along with Granz, but she leaned on him heavily. Not to worry, said Granz, he would continue to represent her. Ella and Oscar Peterson were the only artists he now managed. He left an efficient office apparatus in Los Angeles, and he turned frequently to look after Ella's and Oscar's careers as well as the affairs of his record label.

Granz insisted that he did not feel that jazz was dead in the United States, only that it was easier to present jazz concerts in Europe. He was furious when Nat King Cole, during a European tour that Granz had arranged, told Hazel Guild of *Variety*, 'Jazz in the US is at the bottom of the commercial barrel. It doesn't draw enough business, and that's why rock and roll came into being.'[1]

The week following the appearance of that interview in *Variety*, the magazine printed a letter from Granz rebutting Cole, who, Granz

Two giants of jazz, Ella and Duke Ellington. They recorded and toured together with JATP several times in the 1960s. At his funeral in 1974 Ella sang "Just a Closer Walk With Thee" in honour of her longtime friend. Ken Whitten Collection

said, was 'talking through his hat'. Granz wrote, 'Nat should know better because jazz in every conceivable form is bigger than ever, being used not only in concerts but on films, on television, and obviously on records. Let him check the sales of Brubeck and Garner on Columbia and Ella Fitzgerald on Verve. And he need only to look at the jazz concert grosses to know how well they're doing.'[2]

Before long, however, Granz had decided to get out of the domestic record business as well as the American jazz concert business. Rock 'n' roll, soul, and folk music were now the order of the day. Classic jazz was pushed well into the background as cool jazz and other forms came to prevail. Unlike classic jazz, which had a common repertory and a set of techniques that allowed improvisation that made aesthetic sense, the accent was now so much on originality that different players' styles became strange to one another. Granz considered the new jazz 'deadly serious' and thus not much fun.

Granz had amassed an impressive catalogue of nearly one thousand albums worth more than $2 million and could have made a nice profit from it without issuing new recordings, but he had never been one to rest on his laurels. Frank Sinatra had expressed interest in buying Verve, but a condition of his purchase was that Granz remain to run the company. Granz had no desire to leave Switzerland and move back to LA. In 1960, Granz sold his Verve and Clef labels to MGM for $2.8 million.

While Ella may have considered moving to Europe as well – she had kept a flat in Klampenborg, a seaside resort near Copenhagen, Denmark, for a time – she did not want to uproot Ray, Jr, who was then an adolescent. Besides, in some ways it was an exciting time to be in the United States, where the youngest president in history had just been elected and where many of those who had felt alienated and disaffected hoped for a new freedom and more sympathetic leadership.

Ella was not political by nature, but she had experienced her share of discrimination and heartily endorsed President Kennedy's summons to freedom. She was proud to entertain at the January 1961 Kennedy inaugural gala, organised by Frank Sinatra, which featured the largest number of black artists ever gathered at a presidential fete – Mahalia Jackson, Sidney Poitier, Harry Belafonte and Nat King Cole also appeared, along with Leonard Bernstein, Jimmy Durante, and Peter Lawford.

One week later, the same celebrities, augmented by Sammy Davis, Jr, Dean Martin, Count Basie, Tony Bennett, Nipsey Russell and others, reassembled at Carnegie Hall in New York in a Sinatra-organised tribute to Martin Luther King, Jr, which raised $50,000 for King's Southern Christian Leadership Conference. Ella was delighted to be able to help out.

Around that same time, Ella moved to a larger home in the swank Beverly Hills area, which was still a white bastion that did not look kindly on the arrival of Jews or blacks. According to the late Mel Lewis, 'She had her problems when she moved, just like Norman had. I never understand any of that crap. Ella Fitzgerald moves into my neighborhood, I'd be proud as hell.'[3]

A two-storey, seven-room house with a large front lawn, another broad, grassy area in the back, and a swimming pool beyond it, the house was modest by Beverly Hills standards, but it was just the home that Ella had always dreamed of. She helped to decorate it with furniture imported from Denmark. The panelled living room contained a bar. On the wall above the stereo she placed a large colour picture of Norman Granz. Beneath that was a photograph of Marilyn Monroe, who had helped get Ella into exclusive Hollywood clubs some years earlier, flanked by photographs of Ella at a recording session. She devoted much of her time to the gleaming new kitchen, where she loved to cook for Ray, Jr, and whatever friends came by. 'I'm a homebody,' she told reporters happily, but she had little time to enjoy the house, so busy was she touring.

Ella was on the road fifty weeks of the year, mostly on JATP tours abroad. Ray, Jr, accompanied her during school vacations. In February, she began a tour in Berlin with the Oscar Peterson Trio and the Lou Levy Quartet. They moved on to Belgrade, Yugoslavia, where their programme at Belgrade's largest concert hall was televised throughout the nation and billed as the musical event of the year. Both Ella and the Oscar Peterson Trio were given standing ovations, and the crowd greeted with angry shouts the announcement that the concert was over.

They moved on to France, where Ella performed at the Olympia theatre in Paris on Edith Piaf's night off. The only French word she attempted was 'merci'. It had become Ella's custom to finish her planned set, and then wait expectantly for suggestions from the audience. The audience at the Olympia theatre obliged, having no trouble with the English titles of her songs. From Paris, the tour returned to Germany and from there continued on to Israel.

Returning to the United States in April, Ella recorded an album of

Harold Arlen's songs with Billy May's Orchestra and met Arlen for the first time. Wrote Ralph de Toledano in *National Review* around that time, 'What most amazes about [Ella's] albums is how well they wear, how you can listen to them right through without tiring. Billie Holiday was a greater artist who drew her water from a deeper well. But you can listen to Billie for just so long before the manner becomes oppressive. There is no tiring of Ella Fitzgerald. Perhaps that is her genius.'[4]

Two months later, Ella was on the domestic jazz festival circuit. In the summer there were a variety of festivals, such as those at Newport and at Monterey, California.

Most of them were huge affairs, usually outdoors. In August 1961 she performed at the West Side Tennis Club in Forest Hills, New York, before an audience of eleven thousand who cheered at every possible point and when it was over, kept on yelling for more. George T. Simon wrote in the *New York Herald Tribune,*

> The fact that Ella swung as high and handsomely as she did emphasizes her amazing rhythmic sense. It's not too difficult to swing when you have a well integrated rhythm section to support you. Ella didn't have this on Saturday because of two last-minute resolute but frighteningly uncertain substitutes. Still there's such a natural drive to her voice, such an assured sense of swing, that she swept all that came before her, while receiving, of course, noble assistance from the two regulars in her quartet, tasteful pianist Lou Levy and the continually amazing Herb Ellis on guitar . . .
>
> As the crowd called for more encores, she announced that since it was impossible for her to fulfill all requests, she couldn't be fair to everyone, 'so I'm going to sing something I don't even know.' Whereupon she ad libbed a whole new set of lyrics to 'Bill Bailey.'[5]

Gone were the days when touring in the United States was difficult for her because she was black. Her status, the special care taken by Granz's organisation, and changes in US race relations had all contributed to the change. But touring under even the best conditions is exhausting. The sense of rootlessness is profound, and the jet lag wreaks havoc on even the healthiest body.

Georgianna had finally tired of the road, and Ella now had a new travelling companion, a woman named Arlene, for whom touring was a new and exciting experience. 'They used to send me postcards from all over the world,' says Marian Logan. 'I have a picture of Ella and Arlene backstage someplace.'[6] While Ella's eyes may have been jaded, Arlene's were not, and Ella saw familiar places, especially abroad, with new eyes, thanks to her.

Still, after so many years on the road, Ella was familiar with a great many theatres and enjoyed returning again and again to some cities and towns, both in America and abroad. In the United States, she looked forward to her engagements at the Fairmont Hotels in New Orleans and Dallas (conditions had changed greatly in Texas). She was always pleased to return to Vancouver, BC, where she'd performed annually for many years and where a club called The Cave was like a second home. In December 1963 she performed at the Queen Elizabeth Theater in Vancouver and was interviewed backstage by Bob Smith, host of the show 'Hot Air' on CBC Radio. He'd interviewed her often for both that show and for the *Vancouver Sun* and was one of the few media people with whom she felt comfortable.

One of the first things she wanted to do was to correct something Smith had written in a newspaper column about her: 'You said we'd sold a million records. We sold some million records, but at that time they never gave you a gold record for them. We had "Into Each Life", we had "Paper Moon", we had "A-Tisket, A-Tasket". We had about two more. We had about five or six that really sold over a million, and in those days you really had to sell a million, and in those days the only recognition you got was the royalty check.'

Smith asked who she liked as a singer onstage, now that there was such a preponderance of stage singers. 'I'm very fond of Eydie Gormé and Steve Lawrence,' Ella replied. 'I think they're going to be around for quite a while. And I'm very fond of Nancy Wilson. And there's a girl called Terry Thornton, and a fella named Johnny Hartman who I just love, and he just can't get that break. I think something's happening. We're just crossing our fingers, because this to me is one of the greatest male singers we have.'

Johnny Hartman had been in the business a long time and had been with Dizzy Gillespie's band. He was now trying a career as a single. 'He and David Allen are, to my mind, two underrated singers,' said Ella. 'Underrated girl singers? Carmen McRae. Yes, yes, oh yes. Also Ernestine Anderson. I just love the way they sing. Same way with Mel Torme. Everybody has their own style. They're not singing like anyone else, and yet there's something in their voice . . . maybe I hear things different from other people. My ear isn't a commercial ear. My ear is what I like, and probably somebody else wouldn't like it.'

Smith's final question was, 'Are there any guideposts, any thoughts, that you might pass along to young singers that might be listening to the broadcast this evening?' Ella replied, 'We have so many of them who have come up. But with the exception of Brenda Lee, they come up and before you know it, they're gone. My advice would be to stay in school and work in the summer until you really know what you want to do because, that age . . . you know, nowadays things are getting so that you really have to have an education, and I just keep pounding on that to the boys and girls. This world might look easy to get into – any kind of world nowadays – and to be disappointed if you don't make it in show business and to have nothing else to turn to . . .'[7]

Thankfully, Ella did not have that problem. She kept growing in stature. In early 1962, she won the first International Jazz Critics' poll sponsored by *Down Beat* magazine, scoring more than a third as many votes as her nearest competitor. In the last ten years, she had consistently topped all the polls in the jazz and popular fields, and by this time she had won more first places in polls than any other female singer in history.

Ella continued to record regularly. Sometimes she was accompanied by large orchestras like Nelson Riddle's, other times by just her quartet – Lou Levy on piano, Jim Hall on guitar, Wilfred Middlebrooks on bass, and Gus Johnson on drums, and still other times only by pianist Paul Smith and rhythm accompaniment. Granz recorded her frequently in live concerts abroad, and his old record label, Verve, issued the albums in the USA. In the early sixties Ella won more music awards. The Grammy she received in 1962 as top female jazz vocalist of the year marked her seventh such award in a row. But musical tastes were changing again. Records by the Beatles reached the United States in 1963, and the following year the four mop heads themselves descended on America. Domestic record companies, Verve among them, rushed to follow the new trend. In so doing, Verve chose not to renew the contracts of most of Granz's artists; the only ones whose contracts they renewed were Johnny Hodges, Stan Getz, Oscar Peterson and Ella Fitzgerald. Granz was disappointed: 'For better or worse, the company stood for something when I left,' he said years later. 'But the new owners were lawyers and marketing people. I can't blame them for not caring as much as I did. It wasn't their work. And it would have been foolish of me to expect the company to have continued as before.'[8]

But as the decade wore on, Granz grew steadily more angry at what he considered the company's short-sightedness. Sarah Vaughan went for five years without recording a single album. Of the twenty-seven albums Granz had produced with Art Tatum for Verve, not a single one was available, nor even listed in Verve's catalogue.

Only Ella, thanks in large measure to Norman Granz, continued to record regularly. She also tried to stay current, recording a Beatles' song, 'Can't Buy Me Love', and writing a song of her own called 'Ringo' which, she complained, the disc jockeys wouldn't play. Fortunately she remained essentially true to the material that had stood her in good stead for the last decade. Pianist Tommy Flanagan, who accompanied her off and on from 1956 to 1978, calls that period her 'heyday'.

'When I first heard her, I was in school,' says Flanagan. 'She was already a star, though she was young herself. I listened to her records with Chick Webb. I was only eight or nine when I heard "A-Tisket, A-Tasket", but I knew it was jazz.'[9]

Flanagan made his debut in the middle 1940s with Dexter Gordon.

I arrived in New York in 1956. Her pianist had just left her and I filled in until she went on vacation. I was working with Dizzy's band, and I met her through some friends. I didn't audition for her; I already had established a reputation. Gus Johnson was her drummer at the time, and she had Billy Morton on bass. It was just about three weeks that I played with her in 1956. She sang all kinds of music, and she still sings today a lot of the things she was singing back then. Didn't work with her again until 1962.

From 1962 until about 1965 I played with her regularly. I had a chance to organize my own trio behind her. That was good. I had a chance to select my own musicians. Before, I had inherited the other trio and I worked with people who were already there.

She was great to work with. There were a lot of rehearsals. She had a large repertoire, and it took her a while to learn all that stuff. There was so much material because she worked with orchestras and big bands as well as concerts with the trio. When she did shows in Las Vegas, that was a different repertoire, and I had to learn all of that.[10]

Their working relationship was not always a smooth one. The

main problem, as usual, was Ella's insecurity and her desire for attention. Observed Mel Lewis,

> Tommy would make remarks like, he thought her unhappiness stemmed from her insecurities, because he was much younger than her, and also he was a good-looking cat who could score all over the place, and I think that's what bothered her because she knew that could happen.
>
>   But she probably dug him more than anybody. First of all, being black, he could have a better understanding than Paul [Smith] or Lou [Levy] because they were white, although they were excellent piano players. But he was probably one of Ella's very favorites.[11]

Musically, there was no question that the two respected one another highly. Says Flanagan, 'She has a method of reading music that is really uncanny. She's an improvising musician. When she did a song, she would improvise all the way through. It didn't matter who the composer was, she did a great job on everything she sang, but I think she's the most comfortable with ballads. That's the way I like to hear her. Of course, she's also comfortable singing rhythm tunes – up-tempo things.'[12]

Writer Frank Tirro described Ella's style in 1964 this way:

> Her 1964 recording of *You'd Be So Nice to Come Home To* (SCCJ, IV/8) is an excellent example of the way she transformed a romantic ballad into a moderately up-tempo, swinging jazz number. Ella considers herself a member of the jazz combo or band, albeit the lead instrument, for in standard format, she states the tune and proceeds with a series of choruses. After the first chorus, the melody of the pop song is discarded, and she improvises a melodic line, occasionally trading phrases with an instrumental soloist, by exploiting intervallic features, range, articulation, rhythmic construction, and so forth. The words of the popular song are entirely incidental to her performance, for they merely provide a vehicle for the articulation of vocal sounds. Other syllables could be substituted, and indeed, often are. If one compares her solo work with instrumental solos by well-known swing musicians, one cannot fail to see that her vocal lines could be played very successfully by a trumpet or alto saxophone without loss of authority, and that most instrumental solo lines could be scat sung by the amazing Miss Fitzgerald.[13]

Tommy Flanagan agrees: 'There's no difference between Ella and musicians. But she's the lead soloist. You played behind her as you would a horn or anybody else who had the lead. She had a fabulous range. The secret to her greatness, I think, is the energy that she can bring to a song – not just one song but all the songs she sings. She is capable of maintaining a start and a finish. Her whole program was high-energy.'[14]

Throughout the early sixties, Ella maintained an exhausting schedule of concert appearances, both at home and with JATP abroad. 'She didn't worry about her voice,' says Tommy Flanagan, 'and she was almost never sick. I can remember only once, in Vegas, she was out for one night. Most singers who work in Las Vegas complain of desert throat. But that wasn't what was wrong with Ella. She had a touch of the flu or something like that, which kept her out for one night.'[15]

According to Ella, there was another occasion around that time (late 1964–early 1965) when she couldn't sing. This time it was because of something Frank Sinatra had said about her in a magazine interview, during which he was asked his opinions of some of his contemporaries. His assessment of Ella was that she did not breathe correctly and that consequently her phrasing was poor. This was the same criticism that Chick Webb had expressed thirty years earlier. Sinatra's comments upset Ella, who found it difficult to sing for about a week. For someone as insecure as Ella, such criticism was enough to plunge her into a deep depression. She felt defeated and seriously wondered if she was good enough to continue her career.

If high-energy performances were her trademark, Ella tried even harder in late 1964–early 1965, attempting to overcome with show-manship what she feared was the cooling of American audiences to her and her style. She looked forward to the next European tour, for going overseas was always good for her ego. She was not disappointed. She received raves in Paris, and a standing ovation in Dublin that made her cry onstage. In Hamburg, the audience wouldn't let her off the stage and kept calling for encore after encore.

That early spring, 1965, tour with her trio and the Oscar Peterson Trio, however, was the occasion when the exhausting schedule of high-energy performing finally caught up with her forty-seven-year-old body. The troupe was performing in Munich when Ella suddenly stopped singing and looked ready to faint onstage. Gus Johnson had to lead her off. She recovered sufficiently to continue with the tour. But a doctor she consulted feared that she was on the verge of a nervous breakdown and advised Granz to cancel most of her remaining engagements for the year. When the tour ended, Ella returned to Los Angeles, the shouts of 'Long live Ella – long live Oscar – long live jazz' from fans at Warsaw airport and other European stops ringing in her ears.

'We go at such a pace,' she had told Margaret Laing of the *Sunday Times* of London.

> You run to eat dinner because in some hotels the restaurant closes at 11.30 p.m. I don't like to eat between shows, it makes me short-winded . . . On the Continent we were sometimes at the second concert until 3 a.m. – in Frankfurt it was 4.30 – and then had to get up early to catch a plane. In Amsterdam, we did a midnight show, then flew to Warsaw to appear that night. A concert artist would never agree to do as we do. I don't think it's fair. People are paying – so you should be able to do the show right . . . Some people get very angry when you're ill. But working every day on a voice, you can't expect it to be perfect. It's a God-given talent – you shouldn't abuse it. I don't think I want to anymore.[16]

For several months, Ella rested at home in Beverly Hills. She did not record or do concert appearances, although she did perform on a few television shows, among them 'The Bell Telephone Hour', 'The Andy Williams Show' and 'The Dean Martin Show'.

Music promoter, writer, and critic Leonard Feather visited her at home in the fall and wrote an article for *Down Beat* in which he remarked that even with an interviewer who was an old friend she was ill at ease and 'scared of talking for publication'. After a while, she did relax and open up, however, telling Feather that she had a huge stack of songs that people had sent her that she wanted to go through. She also planned to take guitar lessons and had bought chord books.

Ray Brown, Jr, arrived home from Hollywood High School while Feather was at the house. 'Raymond is sixteen,' said Ella.

> I've got a little problem trying to make up my mind what to do about his music. He had a fine teacher, Bill Douglass, who said he had a good feeling for drums. He's got that edge, and I would like him to take advantage of it, not just play that go-go beat, which is

what I call it because that's where it started. But he does these little weekend gigs for a few dollars, and it's very exciting to him; but I'd like for him to concentrate on learning to read music so that he can do more with his ability. It's a good thing that his father is coming to Los Angeles to live. He'll probably stay behind him and make him realize he's got to do more. I don't think Ray is in favor of his playing with these types of groups.[17]

During her layoff period, Ella accepted an invitation from President Lyndon B. Johnson to make appearances in aid of a campaign against school dropouts. She cherished the autographed picture the President gave her in appreciation.

By early September, Ella was back on the concert trail, appearing at Melodyland in Anaheim with the Tommy Flanagan Trio, the Wild Bill Davis Trio, and the Nelson Riddle Orchestra and sporting a becoming new blonde wig.

Also that autumn, she and Duke Ellington got together to record another album. Norman Granz flew in from Switzerland with his bride, Hanne, a former airline stewardess whom he had married in August. This session went much more smoothly than the last. Pianist-arranger Jimmy Jones had transmitted Ella's vocal keys to Duke on the road and written some of the arrangements.

Ella, who was as nervous at recording sessions as she was onstage, would finish a perfect vocal performance and then say, 'Are you sure that was all right, Duke?' Ellington would assure her that it was, but that wasn't enough for Ella, who would then turn to Granz, in the control booth, for his reassurance. Granz was not the sort to give effusive praise, or graceful assurance. Often, he would suggest another take, and Ella would do it without complaint. Overall, the sessions went well, and when it was all over, Ella had a party at her house to celebrate.

In early November, she and Ellington and his orchestra did a concert at the Front Amphitheater at Stanford where she was accompanied by a quartet consisting of Lou Levy on piano, Joe Comfort on bass (Comfort had recently left Nat King Cole's trio to join the Nelson Riddle Orchestra), Gus Johnson on drums, and Herb Ellis on guitar. 'Don't go!' she cried out to a couple who had to leave during her solo set. 'I'm gonna sing with Duke! You'll miss it!' She was in great spirits.

The following day, she checked into Hollywood's Mount Sinai

Hospital suffering from fatigue. But the months of enforced rest earlier in the year had been enough for her and she refused to stop going. The next week she appeared at the Riverboat in the basement of the Empire State Building with Earl (Fatha) Hines, for whom that engagement was a rare opportunity to put together a big band. (Business in clubs made a quartet more practical.) Among the musicians he hired for that date was Eddie Baresfield, who had played with Ella back in the days following Chick Webb's death.

In early December, she was in New York for a tribute to Louis Armstrong at Carnegie Hall, sponsored by the American Guild of Variety Artists.

Audience admiration for Ella remained undiminished, as did her control of audiences. Ella fan Victoria Secunda recalls,

> One Saturday night – as with *all* Saturday nights – I was with a date on Rush Street in Chicago, this time at Mr Kelly's, ringside so as better to be in the aura of my muse. Ella was not only in top form, she was also very much the doyenne of the elegant dive. When boozy members of the audience would laugh or chat, she'd simply stop singing. One inattentive drunk in particular wouldn't shut up. In her next song, 'Why Can't You Behave?' Ella substituted these words for the final line: 'Why can't you be *quiet*?'
>
> I sent a mash note backstage saying how much I admired her and something to the effect that fans who summarily shot anymore who failed to pay homage to Herself would not spend five seconds in jail for exercising what is, after all, the moral imperative of a Fitzgerald groupie.
>
> At the beginning of the next set, Ella asked who among the audience had sent her the note. My hand shot up, and she dedicated 'My Funny Valentine' to me. I nearly wept.[18]

In 1965, for the first time in many years, Ella Fitzgerald had no hit record.

There were other kinds of recognition, however. In 1966 she was chosen 'Woman of the Year' by the *Los Angeles Times*. The following year, she won the American Society of Composers, Authors and Publishers' Pied Piper Award. She was also placed on *Harper's Bazaar's* list of the 'Hundred Most Accomplished Women of the Twentieth Century'.

In the summer of 1966, Norman Granz arranged a JATP tour in

Europe featuring Ella and Duke Ellington and His Orchestra, the high point of which was the St Tropez Art Festival. Ella recorded with the Ellington Orchestra at the Juan-Les-Pins Jazz Festival in late July. Back in the United States, in September, they performed at the Greek Theatre in Los Angeles in a concert that was recorded live.

In 1967, Norman Granz decided to try one last JATP tour in the United States. He assembled all his favourite artists, including Benny Carter, Coleman Hawkins, Oscar Peterson, and Ella, and everyone enjoyed the tour. But for Granz it only affirmed his belief that touring in the United States was too much bother. 'Never again,' he said. 'I made a profit, but it's too much of a production, too much work, and above all, too much aggravation. It's no fun any more, at least not in the States.'[19]

But it was still fun for Ella. Music and performing – wherever and whenever she could – continued to be her life, as it had been for going on thirty-five years.

10 Fine and Mellow

The seventies began auspiciously for Ella. Once again, musical tastes were changing. The great social and political upheavals of the 1960s, and the assassinations of President Kennedy, Malcolm X, Martin Luther King, Jr, and Robert Kennedy, may have contributed to a nostalgia for earlier, simpler times. Intimate cabaret singing was coming back into style. The era of huge concert 'happenings' seemed to have exhausted itself. Even the big-band sound was enjoying renewed interest. Those large orchestras that had kept going in spite of the diminution of interest in their music – Ellington, Basie, Lionel Hampton – suddenly had more invitations than they could accept. The trend caused musicians who had been with big bands in the past to try forming big bands again, as was the case with the Chick Webb Orchestra, which Eddie Barefield, who had briefly been its leader after Chick Webb's death, re-formed in the early 1970s and which even performed with Ella on occasion.

In the view of some, rock 'n' roll had declined into self-indulgence and amateurism and there was a renewed yearning on the part of sophisticated listeners for professionalism and craft. Ella had been asserting that she'd seen evidence of this trend for several years; now, at last, it was becoming evident to other people as well. Moreover, Ella, having now reached her fiftieth year, and her thirty-fifth year in show business, was approaching venerability, which had its disadvantages but also its advantages.

Professionally, there were mostly advantages. She now enjoyed entrée into the more rarefied regions of American music. In 1972, she made her debut with the Boston Pops, and by three years later she had appeared with more than forty symphony orchestras around the country.

In the United States, she was now the perfect subject for testimonials. Abroad, she was accustomed to being greeted by dignitaries at airports, as she was in Bergen, Norway, by the mayor and a crowd of five thousand in early 1970. But back home – especially in New York, which was not ordinarily impressed by celebrities – one had to have reached venerability before the mayor would pay attention. When Ella made an appearance in New York in early 1970, that city's mayor, John Lindsay, proclaimed 'Ella's Day'.

On March 30, 1970, Ella opened for the first time at the Empire Room of the Waldorf-Astoria – a milestone to Waldorf-Astoria denizens and aficionados, if not to anyone else. It was a testament to changing social mores that the Waldorf's publicity release mentioned that Ella's latest composition was a song written in memory of Martin Luther King, who had been assassinated two years earlier. She'd lived to see the racial barriers come down, at least for celebrity blacks. No longer did she have to rely on Norman Granz to assure her first-class treatment on the road. That made life much easier for Ella, who still spent more than forty weeks a year touring.

Frank Sinatra announced his retirement in 1971, although he would soon reconsider that decision. For Ella, there was no thought of retiring. 'I expect to sing as long as the public likes it,' she told reporters in Sao Paulo, Brazil, in June 1971, 'or until I'm too old or get married.'

That was the downside of venerability – the older she got, the more legendary, the less likely she was to find a husband or have a personal life. Clearly, she still cherished the dream of settling down and having a normal family life. How she would have fared as a 'homebody' after so many years on the road was not an issue she had to face. Realistically, it was too late for Ella to give up a satisfying professional life for the promise of a satisfying personal life. And when her professional life faced risk, Ella probably figured out herself where her priorities really lay.

Ella's eyes had been bothering her for years. Onstage, bright lights made her blink. Offstage, she was bothered by the flashbulbs of news cameramen. Dr Arthur Logan, who practised in Harlem and was physician to Duke Ellington, among other celebrities, had spotted the potential for eye problems. Ella's friend Marian Bruce had since become Mrs Arthur Logan: 'I remember Arthur telling her many times, "You've got to stop wearing that mascara." She would perspire so, when she was singing onstage, and then she would wipe her eyes, and her eyes would keep getting all that stuff in them. Arthur got on to her about that all the time: "Between the makeup and the perspiration, you are infecting your eyes." But she wouldn't stop wearing makeup.'[1]

In 1971, Ella's problems with her eyes were so severe that she finally had them examined. Doctors found a cataract on her right eye. Ella underwent an operation for its removal, which was deemed completely successful. She was subsequently fitted with contact lenses. But these hurt her, and she was too vain to wear eyeglasses onstage or in public. 'She memorized everything,' says Marian Logan. 'She wouldn't wear glasses.'

As if it were not frightening enough to experience her own body deteriorating, Ella had to face the deaths of more friends and colleagues. Especially difficult for her was the death of Louis Armstrong on July 6, 1971, of kidney failure brought on by heart failure. Ella was an honorary pall bearer at the funeral on July 9 in New York, which, in accordance with the wishes of Lucille Armstrong, Louis's widow, contained no music aside from the singing of the Lord's Prayer.

Jazz musician and historian Phil Schapp recalls, 'Ella worshiped Louis. I mean she just worshiped him. She came all the way from California for the funeral. She came and mourned Louis Armstrong because he was such an influence on her . . . she understood his timing and phrasing like few other singers.'[2]

And George Wein remembers, 'Ella flew in, sat in a pew dressed as a mourner in front of me, and flew back out right away. She wasn't looking for publicity. She's just that kind of person.'[3]

Keter Betts rejoined Ella's trio that December, this time to stay. A bassist, his given name was William Thomas Betts but his mother had called him a 'little mosquito' as a child, and eventually everyone called him Keter. In the early 1950s, Betts had been a member of Dinah Washington's original trio. Ray Brown, with whom he still plays golf, had recommended him to Ella: 'I first played with her in 1964 – we did a record called "Ella in Hamburg". I joined her around September 1964 and stayed with her until July or August 1965. I think I replaced Bill Yancey. I went back with her in sixty-six to do a month

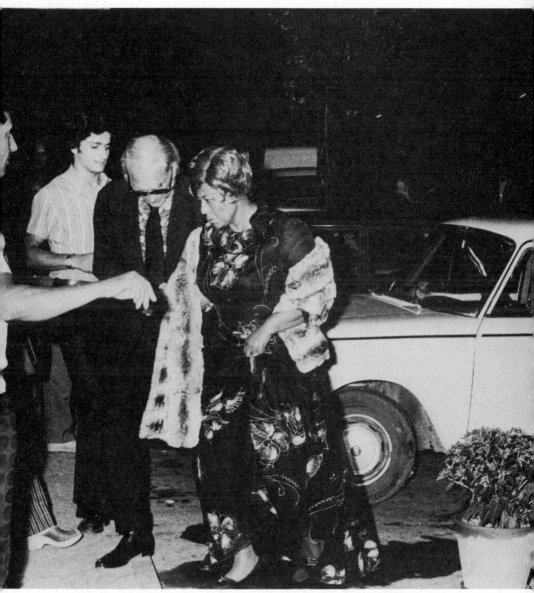

Norman Granz helps Ella from a theater in Pescara, Italy, where she performed in spite of a severe infection in her right eye. She was later forced to cancel the remaining concerts on that 1971 European tour. AP/Wide World Photos

in New York, and then I went back in sixty-eight to do five weeks in Europe and ended up doing about four more months with her.'[4] In 1971 he replaced Frank De Rosa. The Tommy Flanagan Trio now comprised Flanagan, Betts, and Ed Thigpen on drums. The star was still Ella.

On April 25, 1972, Ella celebrated her fifty-fourth birthday at home in Los Angeles. Because of a mix-up, she had no birthday cake. 'Do you believe it?' she said a few days later. 'All my family – everybody thought the other one was going to bring the cake, so nobody brought a cake.'[5]

By this time, 'family' meant more than relatives to Ella. She accorded that distinction to the small entourage who travelled with her regularly – her secretary/companion Arlene, her road manager Pete Cavallo, and her trio. Keter Betts refers to the group as 'the family': 'We rehearse at her house. She cooks for us – she's a good cook. She's very nice to the family – to us. Gives us nice gifts at Christmas. In my case I've gotten everything from golf bags to coats.'[6]

Said Ella of her trio, 'I'd be so lost without these fellas. They know every move that I make.'[7] The occasion for that comment was an interview Ella gave while appearing at The Cave in downtown Vancouver with the trio. Bob Smith interviewed her again on 'Hot Air', telling his audience that Ella was 'so innately shy and modest and yet so sweet above all, who looks so great onstage and moves so gracefully now, and is over the shyness of just being a great vocal talent [and] able to give it a modicum of show business, which of course is needed in a nightclub'. When he spoke to her, he began by complimenting her on, 'your coiffeur, your dress, your movements onstage – everything about you, you're like a teenager again'.

Ella responded, 'Oh, thank you, dear. Well, you know, I'm just so happy, Bob, that the eye operation, you know . . . it's such a great thrill when I'm working, I can look and see the people's faces and the expressions on their faces, you know. We tried to make our program this time instead of everything just "mod" or everything just one style, I tried to mix it up with something from the yesteryear and something from the day, because we find that there's so many people who were so thrilled when we did songs like "Indian Summer" and "Begin the Beguine". And with the bands coming back, it seems like something the people want to hear again.'

The arrangement for 'Begin the Beguine' was done by Marty Paich, a pianist and arranger who had worked with Ella for some years.

Quite by accident, Ella and others had once ad-libbed a list of bandleaders and dance halls from days gone by, and the audience had responded so well with names and places of their own that it had since become a part of her act. She recalled, 'I started saying, "Benny Goodman", "Tommy Dorsey" – and the people started applauding as soon as I mentioned the names, so we kept it in. Some of the names of dance halls were Sweet's Ballroom, when we were playing around California, the Trianon Ballroom, the Greystone Ballroom in Detroit, the Savoy Ballroom. We started thinking of different places that we'd played where there were famous ballrooms, and people from the different cities would applaud, so it's like a fun thing.'

But Ella always kept current. On her repertoire in Vancouver was the theme from 'The Mod Squad', a popular TV show about three hippie undercover cops. 'I always catch the program,' Ella explained to Bob Smith, 'and that's a beautiful song. Every time I heard it, I just said to myself, "there must be some lyrics to it," and I had the office search around and find out who wrote it, and we found out the fella had *one* copy of the lyrics. I thought the lyrics were so beautiful that I just started trying to sing it. I really would love to record it, you know, with a big band; it's such a beautiful thing.'[8]

In the late 1970s, Tommy Flanagan explained how he and Ella continually added to her vast repertoire:

Sometimes, Ella comes up with a tune she's heard somewhere, or I may send her a song that I feel is especially for her. Then we get together to find the key she's comfortable in. She tells me how she feels this piece should be done – seriously, or playful and humorous – whatever the kind of mood the song communicates to her. I then work up an orchestration that embodies her ideas and my own and we try it together.

But an arrangement for Ella is only a framework within which to move. She will still do all kinds of things within that framework, since there are moments when she feels that the song should be allowed to interpret the composer. Often, she'll add a new twist or improvisation, even when we're actually on stage performing. She may lag behind the beat a bit or move ahead of it, but she always knows exactly what she is doing.[9]

Ella soon had the opportunity to record a greater variety of songs, for Norman Granz had decided to get back into the recording business.

The impetus had been an Ella/Basie concert that he had staged in Santa Monica early in 1972. 'I don't know what possessed me to do it, but I decided to record it,' he said in 1979.

While I was at it I decided to add a few surprise guests. Oscar was in town, and I brought in Stan Getz, Roy Eldridge, Harry Edison, Ray Brown and some others. It was a lot of fun and went well, so afterwards I thought I'd see how it might go as a record. I put out a small mail order thing and it was a disaster. Sold about one hundred and fifty. But a few got over to Europe and I got a call from Polydor saying they would give me world-wide distribution if I went back in the record business. It was too good to refuse.[10]

Granz founded Pablo records, named after his favourite artist, Pablo Picasso, whose works he had spent a considerable portion of his fortune to acquire and some of which he sold in order to finance the new label. The motive behind Pablo was not profit – or at least not a primary motive. Granz had made all the money he felt he needed to make (Nat Hentoff once referred to Granz as driven by a kind of Old Testament need to be just). His motive now was to make people who found happiness in jazz happy.

Some three years later, Hentoff wrote, 'I remember seeing Granz a few years ago coming out of a meeting with sales executives at the major record label that was distributing Pablo in this country. There had been concern by the sales manager that pianist Tommy Flanagan had sold only 3,000 copies of a particular album. "So what?" Granz roared. "If there are 3,000 people who get pleasure from Tommy Flanagan's music, why shouldn't they have it?"'[11]

In June 1972, Ella went into a recording studio in Hollywood with a group of old JATP stock company members, plus some new musicians: Charles Turner, Al Aarons, Carroll Lewis, and Shorty Sherock on trumpet; J. J. Johnson, Bill Watrous, and Dick Noel on trombone; Christopher Riddle on bass; Wilbur Schwartz and Harry Klee on flugelhorn; Bill Green and Mahlon Clark on clarinet; Gordon Schoenberg and Norman Benno on oboe; Bobby Tricarico and Don Christlieb on baritone sax; Paul Smith on piano; Ralph Grasso on guitar; John Heard on bass; and Louie Bellson on drums. Together, Ella and the musicians did a group of Cole Porter songs arranged by Nelson Riddle.

Two months later in Palo Alto, California, she recorded an album with the Count Basie Orchestra and the Tommy Flanagan Trio whose cuts ranged from a Cole Porter medley to the theme from the TV show 'Sanford and Son'.

While Ella was still under contract with Columbia, Granz had negotiated terms with Columbia under which he could record her for Pablo. She was delighted with the arrangement, and Columbia realised that Granz's decision to return to the record business signalled a reawakening that they ought to exploit.

Not long after the Basie recording session, while she was appearing in Verona, Italy, Ella's left eye began to haemorrhage. She went to Monte Carlo, where an eminent eye specialist, Dr Miller Berliner, was staying. After examining her, he advised that she would lose her sight completely if she did not take a very long rest. She insisted, however, on going on to Nice for a concert in tribute to Louis Armstrong. (The concert was recorded but not issued in album form until 1983). She wore dark glasses onstage, and the lights were dimmed, but she still had to cut short her engagement there. She flew to Paris where Dr Berliner was then staying, and he ordered her home to Beverly Hills for complete rest. Norman Granz wasted no time in cancelling Ella's engagements until the late autumn.

While at home, Ella encouraged her family to come to her, and before long she had not only her son, Ray Jr, living with her, but also a niece and her niece's two children, aged ten and three. She collected recipes, she redecorated her house. She also got in touch with the Retina Foundation and other charities concerned with vision problems, and after she recovered she did occasional benefits for them. 'People don't realize the importance of their eyesight,' she often says.

After her long layoff, Ella was tired of being a homebody and eager to get back onstage. 'When that doctor said okay,' she said, 'I just grinned and went ahead. We rehearsed at home with the fellows and then performed in public. It seemed to me my voice had changed and was pitched way up somewhere, it was a strange feeling. But the fellows laughed and said the voice was all right.'[12]

Her schedule was not as hectic as it had been previously. 'We don't do it like we did before,' she explained.

We work much less than we have been. 'Course last year, we had seven weeks in Europe, then we went to South America for four, then we went back to Europe and that's where I became ill. I think we were just going a little too fast, and I have cut down very much.

Now we do like three weeks somewhere and then come back home for two, and then go out for three or four more and then come back home. No more rat race.[13]

In late November, Ella appeared at an 'All-Star Swing Festival' at Philharmonic Hall in New York City, which brought together Duke Ellington, Benny Goodman, Bobby Hackett, Count Basie, Teddy Wilson and others in a celebration of the renewed interest in swing music. It was Ella who was chosen to lead the salute to Louis Armstrong with a rendition of 'Hello Dolly!' in which she soon changed the lyric to 'Hello, Louis!' as a huge picture of Armstrong appeared high above the stage.

In early December 1972, Ella made her first appearance in northern California in over two years. Fred Wyatt, reviewing the five-day engagement for *Down Beat*, made no mention of any change in her voice. He did, however, note that 'the extent of her impaired vision was poignantly apparent as she was assisted on and off stage by men holding each of her arms. At times, a concerned Basie was one of the guides. Onstage, she capered and sang her up-tempo numbers with her famed ebullience to repeated applause and standing ovations by the audience.'[14]

There was nothing wrong with Ella's voice at all. In fact, a vocal transcription of a song – 'Lemon Drop' – that Ella recorded in the summer of 1973 is still being used to teach improvisation.

The occasion was the Newport Jazz Festival, which by this time had got so big that it was annually held in New York City, not Newport, Rhode Island. Ella was accorded a 'Salute' at Carnegie Hall. She appeared with the resuscitated Chick Webb Orchestra – a seventeen-piece band led by Eddie Barefield that included Taft Jordan, Dick Vance, Francis Williams and Frank Lo Pinto on trumpet; George Matthews, Al Cobb, Garnett Brown and Jack Jeffers on trombone; Chauncey Haughton, Pete Clark, Arthur Clarke, Bob Ashton and Haywood Henry on reeds; Cliff Smalls on piano; Lawrence Lucy on guitar, and Beverly Peer on bass – and with Roy Eldridge, Eddie (Lockjaw) Davis, and Al Grey, who were charged with reviving memories of Jazz at the Philharmonic. But a poor sound system made it difficult for the musicians, who appeared in the first part of the evening, to play at their best. Ella did the second half of the show.

Segments of that concert, and others at Carnegie Hall, were recorded and issued as 'Newport Jazz Festival: Live at Carnegie Hall', a two-record set. Wrote Dan Gailey in *Jazz Educator's Journal* in 1987: 'The serious student of improvisation stands to gain much from Ella's improvisations, as a closer look will reveal how similar her solos are to the great be-bop instrumental soloists. The relatively simple start of her solo that gradually blossoms into a furious stream of notes closely parallels many horn players.' There followed a detailed transcription – to the extent a detailed transcription of scat syllables is possible – and notations as to 'her incredible mastery of sequences . . . her use of fragments . . . her treatment of single pitch phrases'.[15] Ella, who has no formal training in how to read music, would be delighted at how seriously her improvisation is taken, although, like a lot of lay people, she would have trouble figuring out what the transcription was all about.

By this time, she had finally started wearing glasses onstage occasionally, when her eyes were bothering her. It was either that, or act like a cripple, which was an even greater blow to her vanity.

The following January, at Avery Fisher Hall in New York City, Ella became the first pop singer and first woman to receive the Lincoln Center Medallion, which had previously been bestowed on Dmitri Shostakovitch and Andres Segovia. The audience for her concert that night filled the hall as well as all the available space onstage. It was a night to remember for Ella, who never failed to feel humble when accorded high awards.

The album she recorded that month, 'Fine and Mellow', seemed a fitting expression of her mood. Another cut on that album, which she recorded for Pablo with Clark Terry, Zoot Sims, Eddie 'Lockjaw' Davis, Harry Edison, Tommy Flanagan, Joe Pass, Ray Brown and Louie Bellson, was 'I'm Just a Lucky So and So'.

Less than four months later, Duke Ellington died. Ella attended the funeral at New York's cathedral church of St John the Divine and sang a dirge-like version of his composition 'In My Solitude' as well as the moving spiritual, 'Just a Closer Walk with Thee'.

She later sadly admitted,

I don't really remember what I was singing. I have the feeling I was singing the wrong words, but all I knew was that from where I was standing I could look right across the body and I was sort of frozen. I knew his death had to come sometime, but I'd known him ever since I was a girl. He used to tell me things that made a lot of sense.

Once I had a big problem with a love affair when he and I were working in the same theater and I turned to him for advice. He told me, 'Ella, it's like a toothache. If it hurts bad enough, you get rid of it. You miss it for a while, but you feel better afterwards.'[16]

Two years before that, while appearing in Vancouver, BC, she had told Bob Smith, 'He told me that he was going to write a show for me, and I'm still waiting on that, because I know it would just be too much with his songs.'[17] Doing a show on Broadway had long been a dream of Ella's, but Ellington had not gotten around to making it happen for her.

It seemed to her that such funerals were getting to be a habit. She loved working with Count Basie, but she realised that, more and more, the two were paired because they were among the only big names left from the heyday of swing and jazz.

That December, Ella was the honoured guest at the dedication of the Ella Fitzgerald Center for the Performing Arts at the Princess Anne Campus of the University of Maryland. A $1.6 million building that served over twelve hundred students, it was the first such structure in the United States to be named after a black artist.

'Every night when I say my prayers, I just thank God for that beautiful honor, and that I am here to see it functioning,' she said a few years later. 'You know, so many things like that happen only after the person has passed on, but here I am alive to see it happening.'[18]

By 1975, Ella and Basie were being paired with Frank Sinatra, yet another legend and survivor from days gone by. Ticket prices for their concert at the Uris Theater in New York City were definitely 1975, however – $40 for the entire orchestra and loge, with the mezzanine scaled from $35 to $15. There was some grumbling about the high prices, but the three enjoyed sold-out audiences for their two-week run, which, in that youth-oriented era, was not bad for three senior citizens (Sinatra was fifty-eight, Ella fifty-seven, and Basie seventy-one). Of course, the majority of the audience were their peers, and could afford the tickets.

The show was primarily Ella's and Sinatra's. She had the first half, he the second, and Basie's group played three short numbers to open the programme and then faded into the background. Oddly, Ella, whose forte was usually her ballads, this time skimmed through the ballads and devoted more attention than usual to the up-tempo tunes.

John S. Wilson wrote that on 'T'ain't Nobody's Business If I Do' she 'projected a strong comic presence that was a far cry from the preoccupied façade she usually wears'.[19]

And if the Basie band did not get to share the spotlight as much as they were accustomed to, they always enjoyed the opportunity to work with Ella. Wrote a critic in *Stereo Review* around that time, 'Those who take pleasure in minimizing Fitzgerald's achievements should study the faces of musicians, like those in Count Basie's band, when they accompany her at a concert.'[20]

In 1976, Ella was awarded an honorary Doctorate of Humane Letters at Dartmouth College, which cited her as 'one of the most effective ambassadors our country has ever had'.

That year Norman Granz, whose Pablo records had not approached the commercial success of his earlier Verve recordings, showed the world that he was indulging only himself by launching a new concert series called the Pablo Jazz Festival. First, in May 1975, he got together the two stars whom he had continued to represent no matter where he was – Ella Fitzgerald and Oscar Peterson – and recorded an album, 'Ella and Oscar'.

Consumer Reports reviewed the album, and if that magazine can be a Bible for dishwasher-buyers, then by all means it must know about the best jazz records as well. The reviewer, Martin Bookspan wrote:

> The reunion of the three [Granz, Ella, and Peterson] results in a disc that is an instant jazz classic. Has Ella ever sounded more seductive, has she ever imbued lyrics with quite the sensitivity and perception that leaps out of these grooves, and has the voice as voice ever been under more firm control, responding to her every turn and inflection? Similarly, has Oscar Peterson ever been more free and daring, yet forming a perfect partnership? In four of the nine numbers bassist Ray Brown adds further luster to a most distinguished release.[21]

Ella and Oscar appeared at Carnegie Hall in November 1976 in the Pablo Jazz Festival, along with guitarist Joe Pass, becoming well known for his brilliant solos, and with Count Basie's Orchestra (without Count Basie, who had recently suffered a heart attack). One critic noted that she seemed looser and more genuinely jovially communicative than she had appeared in the past. She was pleased to be working with Peterson again.

Now that Norman Granz was back in the domestic recording business, he seemed to be trying to make up for the more than a decade he'd lost. His output on Pablo was prodigious, as if he didn't have many more years to document the work of the great jazz musicians. Ella did a great deal of recording in the middle seventies.

She did two albums with the guitarist Joe Pass, in February 1975 and in February 1976. The first was a live recording at Ronnie Scott's club in London, with the Tommy Flanagan Trio. The second was just Ella and Joe and was titled 'Fitzgerald and Pass . . . Again'. The cuts included ''Tis Autumn', 'Solitude', 'Nature Boy', 'Tennessee Waltz', and 'Rain', among others. Ella won the 1976 Grammy Award for Best Jazz Vocal Performance for this album – her seventh Grammy, and her first since 1962, ending a hiatus from the Grammy Awards that had lasted much too long.

Granz was busily chronicling the music of other old-time jazz greats. He recorded no fewer than sixteen albums at the Montreux '77 jazz festival, including 'Ella Fitzgerald with the Tommy Flanagan Trio', 'Count Basie Big Band', 'Oscar Peterson Jam' and 'Pablo All-Stars Jam'. Twenty years earlier, in 1957, he had put out about a dozen albums on the Newport Jazz Festival, but this was an amazing output, even for him.

Meanwhile, Granz was seeing to it that the important albums that Ella had recorded for Verve would be available to a new audience. In 1977 he reissued such classic albums as 'Ella Fitzgerald and Louis Armstrong: *Porgy and Bess*', 'Ella Fitzgerald: The Cole Porter Songbook', 'Norman Granz Jam Sessions: The Charlie Parker Sides' and 'Charlie Parker: The Verve Years (1950–51)'. For Ella, who was still recording, the reissues of her earlier work were a marvellous complement to her current Pablo records.

She now included more of those classic sides in her stage shows, among them Granz's lavish Pablo Jazz Festival, held in Los Angeles in February 1978.

Earlier that same year, Ella was honoured at the American Music Awards, which was televised. When Lou Rawls presented her with the annual 'American Music Award of Merit' she beamed, but simply

Bowing to necessity, Ella finally started wearing glasses onstage, although she hated to. Here she performs at An Evening at Pops.
Author's Collection

said thank you. She would much rather have been asked to sing than to speak.

Sing she continued to do. Her touring schedule was back up to thirty-six weeks a year, and she rarely cancelled. Says Keter Betts,

> Maybe twelve years ago, we were up in Kalamazoo, Michigan. We were in the night before to rehearse and Ella had an abscess on one of her back teeth. At the rehearsal the next day, her jaw had swollen up quite a bit. The people who were giving the concert – the conductor and all – wanted to cancel it because they didn't think she was up to it. But she said, 'I'm going on anyhow.' She went on that night, and it was really swollen up, but she sang like nothing had happened. And the next morning her jaw was out like a small cantaloupe. She flew to LA and went right to the dentist's office. The people in Kalamazoo said they got people up there who were ready to cancel if they had a hangnail.[22]

Ella is proud to be a trouper in the old theatrical sense, and when she cannot perform she has good reason. In early March 1978, she had to bow out of a sold-out weekend performance in London because she was suffering from chills and fever. She also had to postpone a concert scheduled at Avery Fisher Hall in New York for March 19. But she was soon back on the concert trail, performing at Avery Fisher Hall in early April.

'Miss Fitzgerald was greeted with a roaring ovation and was cheered continuously throughout her program,' wrote John S. Wilson. 'She responded with one of the finest performances she has given in New York. She was in superb voice – using a darkly silken low register on Cole Porter's "Dream Dancing", hitting some glass-shattering stabs as she scatted through "How High the Moon," even putting an unaccustomed shout into "St Louis Blues" (Miss Fitzgerald has never been known as a belter). Even her patter between songs, an area in which she has never seemed at ease, had an assurance and ease that matched the confidence with which she approached her singing.'[23]

Pam Day, a flight attendant for Continental Airlines recalls,

> It was in the late 1970s (probably '78–'79) that I had Ella Fitzgerald on a flight from Chicago to Los Angeles. Coincidentally, Billy Eckstine happened to be on the same flight, seated in the rear of

first class, while Ella sat in the front row, opposite side. Neither knew the other was aboard until about an hour out when Billy saw Ella, came over to her, sat down – she was traveling alone – and they had a very long, happy talk.

What was so interesting about Ella Fitzgerald, however, was that while she sat alone after Billy had left, she very, very softly began singing – 'scatting,' I suppose you would call it – to herself. This went on, off and on, for over an hour, up to the time when the plane landed in Los Angeles.

My jumpseat was up front, so I had my own private concert. Her eyes were closed, and she didn't notice my watching, my listening. This was for no one's benefit anyway, and it wasn't a rehearsal-type thing either. She sang because she flat out loved to sing, and I was absolutely amazed she loved it so much.[24]

In June, Ella appeared at the Newport Jazz Festival, New York. Wrote Harold Fuller of New York *News World*,

I approached her [concert] with caution, because I had been told wrongly that she was having problems with her voice and I might be in tears at concert's end. I wasn't. I was elated as Ms Fitzgerald swung her way through 13 songs with the help of Tommy Flanagan and trio, who'd opened the festivities with their own set . . . I can truthfully say that her voice is in fine shape. She would be singing along and suddenly hit a high note with stunning accuracy. In addition, she used her voice as a musical instrument and played the band's parts. She did it several times Saturday night, but the most notable occasions were 'One Note Samba' and 'How High the Moon.' Her timing was absolutely perfect and several times I caught [drummer Jimmy] Smith with looks of amazement on his face.[25]

It was a heady time for a sixty-year-old woman with eye problems. In some ways, the seventies were like the fifties all over again. Norman Granz was recording up a storm, there were Pablo Jazz Festivals that brought together the old Granz gang, and for Ella, it was once again, like a new beginning.

11 The *Grande Dame* of Vocal Jazz

To celebrate her new beginning, Ella bought a thirteen-room house in Beverly Hills, rather than redecorate, yet again, her old house. Besides, she needed more room for her family, not to mention the trophies, medals, plaques and citations that lined the walls and filled the shelves. There were no complaints from white neighbours this time.

The awards and honours continued, among them an honorary Doctorate of Humane Letters from Talledega College in Alabama, the key to the City of Birmingham from Mayor Richard Arrington, and a proclamation from Alabama Governor Fob James, all evidence of the New South sensibility, at least where black celebrities were concerned.

In the autumn of 1979, Ella received one of the nation's highest honours when she, along with Aaron Copland, Henry Fonda, Martha Graham and Tennessee Williams, was cited for lifetime achievement in the performing arts at the Kennedy Center for the Performing Arts in Washington, DC. The group was the second to be so honoured, the first Kennedy Center awards having been bestowed upon Marian Anderson, Fred Astaire, George Balanchine, Richard Rodgers and Arthur Rubinstein the previous year.

The evening of December 2, 1979, began with a five o'clock White House reception, complete with champagne, buffet dinner and music by the United States Marine Band. President Carter was not at that reception, nor at the Kennedy Center programme that followed. On November 4, 1979, the United States embassy in Teheran, Iran, had been invaded by followers of the Ayatollah Khomeini who had taken a group of Americans hostage. First Lady Mrs Roselyn Carter explained to the assembled guests, 'As you know, President Carter has had to cancel his public appearances in this time of crisis and he is particularly disappointed that he could not be here tonight to commemorate these outstanding artists – these five Americans are among the most talented that have ever lived.'[1]

The programme at the Kennedy Center was a lavish two hours filled with tributes by stars to the stars, readings, biographical and performance film, live performances, and standing ovations. Peggy Lee said of Ella, 'Ella Fitzgerald has become the standard by which the rest of us are measured.' For Ella, who said she had not slept at all the night before, it was a high point in her career, and she could not keep back the tears. They trickled down her cheeks, but she still managed to move in place to the beat of Count Basie's orchestra.

The final note to a marvellous decade came when Ella was voted into the *Down Beat* Hall of Fame, the third woman so honoured (the others were Billie Holiday and Bessie Smith).

In the 1980s, Ella continued to amass awards. In the fall of 1980, she received the Rose Award, from Lord & Taylor department stores, given annually to a person who has made an outstanding contribution to the arts, environment, education, and so on (other recipients have included Hal Prince and Lady Bird Johnson).

In February 1982, Ella Fitzgerald and James Cagney were named man and woman of the year by Harvard's Hasty Pudding Club, which bills itself as the nation's oldest theatrical organisation and which had been putting on all-male reviews for one hundred and thirty-four years. The ceremonies included a parade through Harvard Square, a performance of selected scenes from the club's production, *Sealed With a Quiche*, and the presentation to Ella and Jimmy of the Hasty Pudding pot. In 1983 she became the first woman to receive the Whitney M. Young, Jr, Award of the Los Angeles Urban League, given annually to those who have built bridges among the races or generations.

The litany of honours goes on. In June 1987, she was the recipient of an honorary Doctor of Music degree from Yale University. It was about her seventh such honorary degree, but this one was special.

Referring to her first gig with Chick Webb at a Yale fraternity party fifty years earlier, she said, 'I'm just thrilled. This is where you might say it all started.'[2]

Also in June 1987, she was among eleven recipients of the National Medal of Arts awarded by President Ronald Reagan. Other recipients included Romare Bearden, the artist, Isamu Noguchi, the sculptor and Dr Armand Hammer, the industrialist and art patron.

By 1980, the words 'legendary' and 'Ella' were more and more often written and spoken in tandem. Ella, who turned sixty-two that year, disliked being called legendary, saying, 'It makes me feel like a relic.' Ironically, she also objected to being called 'Miss Fitzgerald' – 'It's uncomfortably formal' – forty-odd years after she had once objected to *not* being called Miss Fitzgerald.

She understood that she risked becoming an icon whose music was no longer taken as seriously as was her age and tenure in the music world. In the 1970s and 1980s, she was forced to acquire a thicker skin so as not to be devastated by critics who began to note evidence of diminished capacity with some frequency.

The years had begun to tell on her vocal chords. In the late 1970s, reviewers had begun to comment on a deeper, darker tone. By the 1980s, this tone change had begun to affect her singing of ballads in particular. To compensate, at first she leaned more heavily on her earlier old standbys, especially swing tunes, and jazzed almost everything.

Reviewing 'Ella Fitzgerald and André Previn Do Gershwin', released in 1984 on Pablo Today, Derrick Stewart-Baxter wrote, 'I don't know when I have been so close to tears as when I first heard it. Here is an old, old lady, with little or nothing more to give, except a big heart and supreme artistry. Alas, time has caught up and she, poor dear, has little left to give us. Every bar she sings sounds like an effort – it is heart rending – but I would not be without this disc for "all the tea in China" (as the saying goes).'[3]

And in a review of an Ella Fitzgerald/Joe Pass concert at Carnegie Hall in June 1985, Stephen Holden wrote, '. . . her voice has lost much of its fiber and tonal certainty . . . When Miss Fitzgerald settles on a note, the tone is often thin and wobbly, and sometimes flat. Yet with the considerable resources she still commands, Miss Fitzgerald remains a marvel of inventiveness, especially in her rhythmic scatting.[4]

Not only was she a marvel of inventiveness, she was also a wonder of flexibility. After staying away from ballads for a time, which pleased neither her nor her fans, she adjusted her presentation. For the first time in her career, she began to infuse them with some real story-telling, getting inside the lyrics, connecting them with her own experiences, and producing some compelling reflections on the human condition. After fifty years, Ella Fitzgerald was at last opening herself up to her audiences and exhibiting some sincere feeling.

At the same time, she began to seem more at ease onstage. Over the years, critics had remarked about her visible discomfort, the way her patter between songs seemed stilted and rote-like, the way she seemed to feel exposed and eager to get on with the next song as if it were a welcome shield from direct contact with the audience. As critic John McDonough once put it, 'If the musician in Fitzgerald should ever fail, the actor in her could not pick up the slack.'[5] Only on occasion, especially when she performed with Oscar Peterson, had a discernible melting taken place. Now, she seemed more willing to communicate with audiences. Some of her patter was still perfunctory, but she exhibited a warmth and confidence that was refreshing.

Ella spent the late 1970s through the middle 1980s recording frequently and seeing earlier albums reissued. She also won more Grammy Awards, including two in 1980 for 'Fine and Mellow' and 'A Perfect Match – Ella and Basie'. In February 1979, she went into the Pablo Today recording studios with Count Basie and his Orchestra to record 'Ella Fitzgerald/Count Basie: A Classy Pair'. Ray Brown was in the Basie Band; Ella and her former husband had been recording together for thirty years by this time. Released in 1982, it was 'unreservedly recommended' by *Jazznews International*.

The new decade began for Ella with a reissue of her Verve 'Duke Ellington Songbook'. Other notable reissues included 'Ella in Hollywood', originally recorded in 1957, 'Ella Fitzgerald/Billie Holiday: At Newport', which had also been recorded in 1957, and 'Whisper Not', which Ella had recorded with the Marty Paitch Orchestra in 1965. New albums included 'Ella à Nice', a belated issue of a taped concert in 1971 in Nice, France, 'Digital III at Montreux', for which she won her eleventh Grammy award in 1981, and 'The Best Is Yet To Come', recorded on the Pablo Today label, and for which she won her twelfth Grammy Award in 1984 (Ella has won more Grammys than any other female jazz singer). Several of these albums were also issued in compact disc (CD) format.

Decca, which had now been taken over by MCA, was doing a brisk business in Ella reissues, although evidence of the comparatively impoverished material she sang for Decca is found in the total lack of CDs in release from her long Decca era. In 1981, at Granz's urging, Ella sued MCA Records, which had bought her contracts with Decca dating to 1951, accusing MCA of misrepresenting her sales and earnings. The suit asked one million dollars, plus a complete audit of her account at MCA. Details of the eventual settlement are not known.

A whole new generation of Ella fans was buying these albums. Jonathan Schwartz of *Esquire* wrote in November, 1985.

> I am here to honor Ella, to tell you that the sound of her voice has been recorded more voluminously than the music made by any other single human being who ever lived, except for Bing Crosby . . . Ella is closing in on Crosby. Quietly, on the Pablo label: Ella singing Jobim, Ella with Nelson Riddle, Ella in the South of France, Ella recording in the mid-eighties, having first stepped into the studio four years before Germany invaded Poland . . . Just those albums, the enormous ELLA bins at Music and Memories on Ventura Boulevard in Sherman Oaks, at Tower Records on lower Broadway in Manhattan, at the Coop in Harvard Square, at HMV record shop in Oxford Circus, London. Ella bins. Ella displays, as if she were some kind of resurrected Beatle.[6]

In 1988, when Quincy Jones began work on 'Back on the Block', his long-awaited new album that would celebrate forty years of African/American music, he naturally included Ella among the jazz veterans he wanted to record. On the cut, 'Jazz Corner of the World', Ella, James Moody, Miles Davis, Sarah Vaughan and Dizzy Gillespie sang or played jazz solos, each introduced by brief, rhymed tributes by rap stars Kool Moe Dee and Big Daddy Kane. Ella had a great time and enjoyed the opportunity to 'be current'. But she had to be talked into it. Said Jones, 'The thing about Ella is that *she doesn't think she can sing*. She's the sweetest woman on the planet, but she still doesn't get it.'[7]

By the 1970s, television was ubiquitous, and Ella appeared very often in the later 1970s and early 1980s, such exposure serving to further popularise her and her music. Specials with Frank Sinatra and Duke Ellington in the middle 1970s have come to be regarded as classics. By the late 1970s, she was practically a regular on any musical variety special, including 'Captain and Tennille', not to mention PBS series like 'Pop: The Great Singers'.

In November 1979, in Chicago, Ella taped her own TV special for PBS, on which she appeared with Roy Eldridge on guest trumpet, Zoot Sims on guest tenor, Joe Pass on guest guitar, and the Count Basie Band. Oscar Peterson was also supposed to have been there. He'd planned to fly from his home in Mississauga, Canada, until a train derailment five blocks from his house caught him in the middle of what was then called the largest mass evacuation in North American history.

Even without Peterson, the taping of the special went remarkably well. Norman Granz was on hand to see that all went smoothly. Taping began at 12:45 p.m., and by 2:00, when everyone broke for lunch, the first half of the show was in the can. A rather formalised homage-paying by Basie to Ella and vice-versa, it had been marred only by a couple of flubbed lyrics by Ella, necessitating retakes. For the more informal, relaxed numbers in the second half of the show, all went well until it came time for Ella's numbers with Joe Pass.

'The start was awkward and Granz stopped the take,' wrote John McDonough, who attended the taping.

A second try went perfectly. The final business of the afternoon was to tape the show's opening and closing tunes, both of which will feature only Ella and Joe. 'Am I Blue' was done in one take, but the final tune, 'Once In A While,' proved the most troublesome of the day. There were no less than seven takes. On two occasions there were technical problems. A frog crept into Ella's voice on the final note of another. And several times Ella drew a blank on the lyric, a problem many singers can have with ballads. The pace is so slow, the mind can sometimes wander from the words.

Through it all Granz exercised a knowing, never intrusive control. Stopwatch in hand, he scribbled notes to himself in a small log. Ella especially relied on him for counsel, criticism and assurance. In any case, it was all wrapped up in less than six hours, including lunch.[8]

The actual show aired on December 9, one week after Ella was honoured at the Kennedy Center.

Perhaps Ella's most important foray into television was in a commercial for Memorex cassette tapes. To demonstrate how accurately the tapes recorded sound, the commercial first featured her singing, with her pure amplified voice shattering a glass. Meanwhile, her singing had been recorded on a Memorex tape, and when it was played, Ella's recorded voice shattered another glass. 'Is it live or is it Memorex?' asked the unseen announcer. Not only did this commercial prove highly successful for Memorex, it made the name Ella Fitzgerald a household word in hundreds of thousands of new homes.

Of course, for the literal-minded young, the Memorex commercial set a standard for Ella's singing that was difficult for her to maintain. After a concert given especially for the children of Columbia, South Carolina, one boy was heard to remark, 'Well, I liked her singing all right, but she didn't break no glass.'

Live performances had always been the medium that had sustained Ella emotionally and professionally. Although in the 1970s she had cut down on her exhausting performance schedule, in the early 1980s, Ella increased the number of weeks of touring she did in a year, building back up to forty-two weeks at one point in 1984–5.

In the age of jet travel, Ella's musical 'family' could be far-flung but still perform together often. Ella lived in Los Angeles, Keter Betts in Silver Springs, Maryland, Arlene in New York City. 'Good old airplanes,' says Keter Betts. 'We would be in New Orleans for two weeks at the Fairmont, and then we'd close, and then we'd say, "Okay, see you in three weeks in San Francisco." At one time we were really scattered. The piano player was living in Arizona and the drummer was living in Copenhagen.'9

Sadly, the small travelling family had lost two of its members by the early 1980s. Ella's secretary/travelling companion, Arlene, died suddenly. 'That was hard on all of us,' says Betts. 'It was just the six of us – Ella, Arlene, Pete, and the trio. We had just finished playing in York, Pennsylvania, on a Saturday night, and then they had a big party for us at the hotel. I drove them back to Washington the next morning and from there they went to their respective homes. We said, "See you in two weeks" at wherever we were going to play next. That Tuesday night or Wednesday, Pete called to say that Arlene had died. So we got back together sooner than expected – for Arlene's funeral.'10

In 1979, Tommy Flanagan suffered a heart attack and had to withdraw from performing for a time. He now performs regularly. He and Ella have had little further contact, which is usual for Ella. For all their closeness professionally, she has rarely maintained friendships with her musicians once she has ceased to work with them. Paul Smith took over. 'He's still with her,' said the late Mel Lewis in 1989, 'and he's protective, too. He sort of takes care of her.'[11] The Paul Smith Trio included Smith on piano, Betts on bass, and Mickey Roker on drums.

Ella's heavy touring schedule included frequent trips to Europe. In November 1980 she appeared in London at the Royal Festival Hall with the Oscar Peterson Trio and the Jimmy Rowles Trio (Rowles having substituted for Paul Smith for this tour).

Back to London in April 1981, she and Peterson held forth at the Palladium. The reviewer for *Variety* felt that her 'faltering attempts at patter evinced tiredness after her transatlantic journey or, maybe, a career well into its fifth decade'.[12] Maybe indeed. Ella celebrated her sixty-third birthday that month. However, two shows a night for six days at Grosvenor House in London with Oscar Peterson in November 1982 (tickets were priced at $125 each and were very scarce) were still within her capability.

Her domestic touring schedule was equally demanding. That summer, the Ohio Valley Kool Jazz Festival, which had merged with George Wein's Newport Jazz Festival, came to New York. From a modest, two-day event in Newport, Rhode Island, in 1954, the jazz festival that had been nurtured by the New Orleans stride pianist was now the largest musical event of its kind, taking place in twenty-two cities from June to November. No jazz festival, whatever its name, was complete without Ella, and she was there, with the Jimmy Rowles Trio, plus guests Clark Terry and Zoot Sims.

In November, Ella performed at the University of South Carolina in Columbia for the Katanni Foundation, a black arts organisation for the city's public schools. (It was a youngster in this audience who complained that she hadn't broken any glasses.) Afterward, she was the overnight guest, along with Jesse Jackson, Jackson's mother, and Jackson's grandmother, at the mansion of Governor and Mrs Richard W. Riley. Jesse Jackson was in Columbia campaigning for a new Voting Rights Act.

Accompanied by the Paul Smith Trio, and often appearing with Joe Pass, Ella consistently wowed audiences at the Kennedy Center (two encores, both in response to standing ovations by the entire, sold-out house in June 1983), at a Kool Jazz Festival concert at Carnegie Hall later that same month, and even aboard a Continental Airlines flight to promote the brief resurrection of Continental's Pub compartments. (Amidst the hubbub of a ten-seat compartment packed with reporters and photographers, and conscious that artist LeRoy Neiman was sketching her for a later portrait to be produced at the behest of the airline, Ella tried to keep her composure, even though she was overheard to complain, 'My stockings are starting to fall down.')[13]

That summer, the Kool Jazz Festival included a salute to women in jazz. Naturally, Ella, the *grande dame* of vocal jazz', as one reviewer put it, led the way in a two-show event at Carnegie Hall. Once again, she was accompanied by the Count Basie orchestra, which had become a classic pairing over the years. Unfortunately, the chemistry wasn't right that evening. Several reviewers complained that with the Basie band Ella was shrill and mechanical-sounding and that she only relaxed once she was paired with her own Jimmy Smith Trio.

But that was an off night. More often, Ella was right on, no matter what her accompaniment. In the summer of 1985, she performed with Oscar Peterson at Wolf Trap. Reviewing the televised broadcast of the concert the following year, Jon Pareles wrote in *The New York Times*, 'Ella Fitzgerald . . . takes daredevil chances with every song. Demurely snapping her fingers, she darts in and around the beat, leaps from register to register and transforms the sound of her voice from Louis Armstrong's trumpet (in "Lucky So and So") to a melodic drum (in a scat-singing workout on "A Night in Tunisia").'[14]

Almost exactly in the middle of the decade, however, time and Ella's exhausting schedule caught up with her. In August 1985, she complained of 'shortness of breath' and spent a week at George Washington University hospital in Washington, DC, for respiratory problems. Sarah Vaughan filled in for her at the Ravinia Festival in Highland Park, Illinois, where Ella was scheduled to perform next. A hospital spokesman said, 'The breathing problem was apparently due to fluid in the lungs. She's in good condition and resting comfortably.' Doctors advised her to rest at home for five weeks before resuming her touring schedule. But within a month she was performing a concert at the Hollywood Bowl.

The audience gasped when they saw her, for she had lost a considerable amount of weight and looked shrivelled and drawn. Yet she seemed the essence of vitality. Her amazing onstage energy never deserted her. But her voice was another matter. Especially on ballads, it seemed wobbly and uncertain, and Ella seemed incapable of sustaining her vibrato. But it was a chilly evening and an outside concert, and she had not performed at the Hollywood Bowl for nearly a decade.

Thus, that concert was hardly the basis for judging her future career.

Ella's breathing problems did affect her singing. Her uncertain breath control caused her to collaborate more in concert with various instrumentalists and to emphasise her scat singing, thereby lessening the need for the long-held notes of ballads. Moreover, her extreme weight loss added to the perception that she was *not* healthy. But she belied that perception by maintaining an ambitious schedule, including the opening of George Wein's JVC (formerly Kool, formerly Newport, and named after the audio company that now sponsored it) Jazz Festival in June 1986.

Two months later, in mid-August 1986, following a performance in Lewiston, New York, Ella again suffered a respiratory problem and congestive heart failure and was hospitalised at Niagara Falls Medical Center. Her condition was described by her attending physician, as a 'temporary thing . . . something like pneumonia'. She had not suffered a heart attack, he added. Ella was released from the hospital after three days and flown to Cedars Sinai Medical Center in Los Angeles, where she was admitted on August 19. There, on September 3, she underwent quintuple bypass surgery.

Short of a heart transplant, that procedure is the most radical cardiac surgery that can be performed. While it is now done more and more frequently, it is not without risk. Nor is the post-surgery drug treatment risk-free, for the medication must be finely balanced to avoid complications, and potentially serious side effects. Ella did not perform again for six months.

By the late winter of 1986–7, Ella was champing at the bit, and eager to get back on the stage. Rehearsing at home one day, she hit a high note and set off the fire alarm. 'Is it Memorex or is it an alarm?' she joked to the firefighters who soon arrived on the scene.

Summoned to Los Angeles to begin rehearsing with Ella for her comeback, the members of her trio were pleased with her progress. 'When she came back from the heart thing, she was stronger, much stronger,' says Keter Betts. 'That's why she had the operation.'[15]

Her first post-operation concert was not until the spring of 1987. 'We played El Camino College (near Los Angeles) in March,' she said in June of 1987. 'That was the first date that the doctors allowed me to work. I had no idea it was completely sold out. When I came out, everybody said, "We love you Ella." That's like medicine for me.'

In June, she appeared at Franklin and Marshall College in Lancaster, Pennsylvania, still frail but nibbling on pretzels and drinking soda in her trailer/dressing room. A crowd of five thousand five hundred turned out to hear her at the football field, and once again Ella characterised her reception as 'part of my medicine'.[16]

In August 1987, she was hospitalised again for more than a month, this time for complications from diabetes that caused pain and swelling in her right foot. Released from the hospital, Ella was forced to undergo another prolonged stretch of semi-inactivity, during which she had therapy twice a week. She missed the road and was delighted when her doctors allowed her to return to performing in March, when she played three nights in Palm Springs.

A perennial part of the JVC Jazz Festival, she turned in a strong performance in June 1988. That same year, during a concert at the Hollywood Bowl, she took a tumble onstage as she was moving downstage during the show. All three members of the Paul Smith Trio rushed to her aid. 'It's okay. I'm okay. I'll just sing from down here,' she said, trying to make light of the incident. After a brief rest backstage, she returned to sing 'Since I Fell For You'. In June 1989 she again appeared at the JVC Jazz Festival in New York. Aware that she was now viewed as frail and ailing, she responded to the customary standing ovation that greeted her arrival onstage with, 'Don't spoil me – you can do that after and I'll feel good.'[17]

By July 1989, her stage demeanour was being described as 'vigorous'. Perhaps she had slowed, but there was no *stopping* Ella, at least not yet.

In the early autumn of 1989, she and the trio went abroad for the first time in three years. 'We went to Paris and did a big thing over there at the Moulin Rouge,' says Keter Betts. 'The wife of the president of France had a big show. Ella was the feature attraction, and other stars made cameo appearances – Jane Russell, Lauren Bacall, Greg Louganis, Jerry Lewis, Tony Curtis . . . Norman Granz met us over there. Now, we only do basically two or three one-nighters a month. We would prefer a week here or there so we could get some consistency, but this is the doctor's orders so we're complying with them.'[18]

Says Marian Logan, 'The only thing I noticed is that she forgets lyrics sometimes. But the wonderful thing about her is that she makes up lyrics right on the spot, right while she's standing there. And then she starts laughing, and people in the audience who know the lyrics, know when she's flubbed, but she still sounds great.'[19]

Says Phil Schapp, 'She just takes over an audience and wraps them

In 1987 Ella received the National Medal of Arts from President Ronald Reagan. It was just one of many accolades that accrued to her in the fifth decade of her career, but it was special in its acknowledgement of her as a national treasure.
National Archives, office of Presidential Libraries

up in her arms and makes them love her. When she walks out on the stage, [the cry] wells up from the audience, "We love you, Ella, we love you, Ella." They just take her in, and she just takes them in. It's a great experience to see that.'[20]

Audiences now included more young people than ever before. By the late 1980s, classic jazz was enjoying a major renaissance, and not just among listeners. For the first time in two decades, young musicians were seriously playing traditional jazz. Since the later 1960s, with the advent of electronics, the sounds of instruments had been distorted, and jazz had been heavily laced with funk and rock, technical precision ignored in favour of volume and simple dance rhythms. With the popularity of New Orleans trumpeter Wynton Marsalis, whose skill in classical music was as great as his skill in classic jazz and whose proselytising about the technical difficulty of classic jazz caused young musicians to sit up and take note, even younger jazz musicians were paying attention to technical precision, melody and instrumental tone. In 1980, few musicians under forty were playing classic jazz; by 1990, there were prodigies as young as thirteen playing and recording. Just as they appreciated the classic jazz musicians of the past, they also appreciated the classic jazz singers, and with the death of Sarah Vaughan, Ella stood almost alone as an exemplar of jazz singing in its heyday.

As the last decade of the twentieth century began, one of the major musical legends of the century struggled to maintain the consistency and level of her performances, not to mention an ambitious performing schedule (1990 was planned as her busiest year in some time), all the while battling persistent health problems.

On February 12, 1990, the music world paid tribute to Ella at Avery Fisher Hall in a benefit concert for the American Heart Association's Ella Fitzgerald Research Fellowship Fund. Called 'Hearts for Ella', the concert brought together a host of giants, including Benny Carter, Lena Horne, Joe Williams, Jessye Norman, Bobby McFerrin, Linda Ronstadt, Cab Calloway, George Shearing, André Previn, Dizzy Gillespie, and Honi Coles. Each sang, or danced, or played a valentine to Ella.

Ella herself did not perform, but enjoyed the show from a seat of honour in the audience. When at last Joe Williams escorted her to the stage, she was unsteady, but her voice was strong as she sang and scatted 'Honeysuckle Rose'. Later, she cancelled her appearance at a party for her.

In May, Ella's first album in almost five years was released. She had begun recording 'All That Jazz' the previous spring, and she had felt rusty. For that matter, Norman Granz, on whose Pablo Today label the album was issued, had not been in a recording studio in nearly four years, but he was more confident by nature than Ella. Unsure of herself, through Granz she turned down requests from music writers to attend the recording sessions, but the album was wonderful. Backed by Benny Carter, Clark Terry and Harry Edison, she sang ten standards, including 'Dream a Little Dream' and 'Jersey Bounce', in a clear, still-youthful voice with consummate musicianship.

A few weeks after the album was issued, Ella gave a concert in Paris and was named a Commander of Arts and Letters, that country's top award for excellence in the arts.

Back in the United States, she performed in Minneapolis on June 16 and at the JVC Jazz Festival in New York on June 29. Peter Watrous wrote in *The New York Times* of her concert at Avery Fisher Hall, 'Miss Fitzgerald swooped in and out of octaves, changed tones, fooled around with rhythms, added quotations to songs, and turned play into a serious affirmation of an art.'

Ella and her small entourage then headed back to Europe to give concerts at several jazz festivals. But in The Hague, Netherlands, where she was scheduled to perform in the North Sea Jazz Festival and to be honoured at a special gala, she became ill in her hotel and was hospitalised for dehydration and exhaustion. She was forced to return to the United States and to cancel appearances at jazz festivals in Montreux and Antibes.

Ella Fitzgerald is not alone among aging musicians who seem to shed decades when onstage but who pay dearly for the expenditure of energy and emotion when they are out of the spotlight. With thirty concerts scheduled for the year 1990, efforts to shield her from extraneous, energy-sapping activity on the part of those around her were thus well-intended, but the effect was increasing isolation. In seeking to protect her, those people whose job it is to arrange her appearance and oversee her professional life risk denying her the opportunity to see old friends and acquaintances whose company she would enjoy.

Says Marian Logan,

She used to hold my son, Chip, in her lap when he was a little boy. So when Chip graduated from college, I sent her some pictures and she said she never got them. I told her, 'You better tell that Mary Jane to let you see some of your mail,' because I had written her on my good Tiffany blue stationery, with my name on the envelope. She said, 'Well, I get so much mail,' and I said, 'Well, you ought to go through the mail because some mail you want to see.' I sent her another batch after she was here at the JVC festival last summer.

I talk to her about once a month, and I called her after she was here at the festival. She was so upset that I didn't go to see her. I said, 'Ella, I was there, and they wouldn't let me in.' She said, 'I saw your name on the list, and I sent Phoebe down to get you.' I said, 'But they wouldn't let me in, and I finally got tired of trying.'

I told her I loved the dress she wore in the second act. She's always so happy to hear things like that. I said, 'Ella, you looked gorgeous in that second act dress.' She said, 'Girl, that thing is thirty years old.' I said, 'Well you ought to wear it more often, because it looks beautiful on you.'[21]

Even friends in Los Angeles report that Ella is hard to get to, so insulated has she become by those who surround her. 'It's mainly by Granz and his people,' says one. 'She won't do anything without his say-so.' 'She's always been a very lonely person,' says Marian Logan.[22]

These days, Ella tends to stay close to home. About every other day, she has her driver take her shopping at Carl's Market on the corner of Santa Monica Boulevard and Doheney Street in Los Angeles. When she doesn't feel like cooking, she calls up her friend Maurice Prince of Maurice's Snack 'n' Chat on West Pico Boulevard, and Maurice will go to Ella's house and cook for her.

Her family members are very important to her. Ray, Jr, after living for a time in Alaska, is now located in Seattle, Washington, where he has a small band. Although reportedly he and his mother do not get along, he visits on holidays. So do her sister and her nieces and nephews. Ray, Jr's daughter, Alice, was born in 1985 in Alaska, and Ella is delighted to have a grandchild. 'She dotes on that child,' says Marian Logan. 'She has a great need to have some continuation of herself somewhere, and that grandchild is it, for her.'[23]

On occasion, most recently in 1985, Ella has expressed a desire to write her memoirs, explaining, 'I'd like to write as an inspiration to younger people who feel that, because they come from poor families, they don't have a chance.'[24] However, at this writing, she has made no effort to begin such a project. Given her extreme emotional repression, an autobiography would be very difficult for her.

It is hard to imagine how a woman so universally loved by strangers has remained so personally elusive. But then again, her very unreachability has contributed to her mystique and perhaps, in some measure, to her attraction. During most of her career, Ella has trod the fine line between distance and isolation successfully. If she had been more accessible offstage, she may not have become such a legend. But in the past few years, she has crossed that line and become practically a recluse offstage, threatening the affection that both friends and fans feel for her with a frustrating mysteriousness. Most acquaintances who will talk about her either insist on avoiding the subject of her personal life or say that they know little about it. Those who do not like her are dismissive, as if reluctant to attach any importance to what she does offstage.

While Ella may not have given of herself as a person as much as friends and fans would like, there is no question as to her generosity as a performer, and it is that which we should celebrate even as we continue to wonder why the offstage Ella has never chosen to share her life with her public.

Selected Bibliography

Basie, Count, as told to Albert Murray. *Good Morning Blues: The Auto-biography of Count Basie*. New York: Random House, 1985.

Bogle, Donald. *Toms, Coons, Mulattoes, Mammies, & Bucks: An Interpretive History of Blacks in American Films*. New York: Viking, 1973.

Bushell, Garvin, *Jazz from the Beginning*. Ann Arbor, MI: University of Michigan Press, 1988.

Chilton, John. *Billie's Blues*. Briarcliff Manor, NY: Stein & Day, 1975.

Chilton, John, and Max Jones. *Louis*. Briarcliff Manor, NY: Stein & Day, 1984.

Colin, Sid. *Ella: The Life and Times of Ella Fitzgerald*. London: Elm Tree Books/Hamish Hamilton Ltd., 1985.

Collier, James Lincoln. *Louis Armstrong: An American Genius*. New York: Oxford University Press, 1983.

Dance, Stanley. *The World of Count Basie*. New York: Scribner's, 1980.

——. *The World of Earl Hines*. New York: Scribner's, 1977.

Ellington, Duke. *Music is My Mistress*. Garden City, NY: Doubleday, 1973.

Ellington, Mercer, with Stanley Dance. *Duke Ellington in Person: An Intimate Memoir by Mercer Ellington*. Boston: Houghton Mifflin, 1978.

Feather, Leonard. *From Satchmo to Miles*. Briarcliff Manor, NY: Stein & Day, 1972.

Fox, Ted. *Showtime at the Apollo*. New York: Holt, Rinehart & Winston, 1983.

Giddings, Gary. *Jazz Tradition & Innovation: The 80's*. New York: Oxford University Press, 1985.

Gillespie, Dizzy, with Al Fraser. *To Be or Not To Bop: Memoirs*. Garden City, NY: Doubleday, 1979.

Gourse, Leslie. *Louis' Children: American Jazz Singers*. New York: Morrow/ Quill, 1984.

Grime, Kitty. *Jazz Voices*. New York: Quartet, 1983.

Hammond, John, with Irving Townsend. *John Hammond on Record: An Autobiography*. New York: Ridge Press/Summit Books, 1977.

Haskins, Jim. *The Cotton Club*. New York: New American Library, 1984.

——, with Lionel Hampton. *Hamp: An Autobiography*. New York: Amistad/ Warner, 1989.

——, with Kathleen Benson. *Nat King Cole: An Intimate Biography*. Briarcliff Manor, NY: Stein & Day, 1984.

Kliment, Bud. *Ella Fitzgerald: Singer*. New York: Chelsea House Publishers, 1988.

Schuller, Gunther. *The Swing Era: The Development of Jazz 1930–1945*. New York: Oxford University Press, 1989.

Shapiro, Nat, and Nat Hentoff. *Hear Me Talkin' To Ya: The Story of Jazz As Told By the Men Who Made It*. New York: Dover Press, 1955.

Smith, Joe. *Off the Record: An Oral History of Popular Music*. New York: Warner Books, 1988.

Tirro, Frank. *Jazz: A History*. New York: W. W. Norton, 1977.

Ulanov, Barry. *A History of Jazz in America*. New York: Viking, 1952.

Ella Fitzgerald's Grammy Awards

1958 – Best Solo Vocal Performance, Female: *Ella Fitzgerald Sings the Irving Berlin Song Book*
1958 – Best Jazz Performance, Individual: *Ella Fitzgerald Sings the Duke Ellington Song Book*
1959 – Best Vocal Performance, Female: *But Not For Me*
1959 – Best Jazz Performance, Soloist: *Ella Swings Lightly*
1960 – Best Vocal Performance, Single, Female: *Mack The Knife*
1962 – Best Solo Vocal Performance, Female: *Ella Swings Brightly with Nelson Riddle*
1976 – Best Jazz Vocal Performance: *Fitzgerald and Pass . . . Again*
1980 – Best Jazz Vocal: *Fine and Mellow*
1980 – Best Jazz Female Vocal Performance: *A Perfect Match/Ella and Basie*
1981 – Best Jazz Female Vocal Performance: *Digital III at Montreux*
1982 – Best Jazz Solo Vocal Performance, Female: *A Classy Pair*
1984 – Best Jazz Vocal Performance, Female: *The Best Is Yet To Come*
1990 – Best Jazz Vocal, Female: *All That Jazz*

Discography

Chick Webb and His Orchestra: Mario Bauza, Taft Jordan, Renald Jones, trumpets; Sandy Williams, trombone; Edgar Sampson, Pete Clark, altos; Elmer Williams, tenor; Joe Steele, piano; John Trueheart, guitar; John Kirby, bass; Chick Webb, drums; Wayman Carver, arranger; Charlie Linton, Ella Fitzgerald, vocals.

New York, June 12, 1935

39614-A **I'll chase the blues away** (ef, vcl), Br 02602.
39615-A **Down home rag** (wc, arr), De 785, DL9222, MCA 510014, Coral COPS3453.
39616-A **Are you here to stay?** (cl, vcl), De 494
39617-A **Love and kisses** (ef, vcl), –.
Bill Thomas (b) replaces Kirby.

New York, October 12, 1935

60054-A **Rhythm and romance** (ef, vcl), De 588.
60055-A **Moonlight and magnolias** (cl, vcl), –.
60056-A **I'll chase the blues away** (ef, vcl), 640.
60057-A **I may be wrong but I think you're wonderful** (tj, vcl), De 640.
60058-A **Facts and figures**, De 830, DL9222, MCA 510014, Coral COPS3453.

Radio Transcriptions, New York, February 1936

BB11208 **Big John special**, Pol 423248, Jazz Arch JA33, IAJRC 1.
You hit the stop (ef, vcl), Jazz Arch JA33.
Stompin' at the Savoy (es, arr), Pol 423248, Jazz Arch JA33, IAJRC 5.
Don't be that way (es, arr), Jazz Arch JA33, Pol 423248.
Shine (ef, vcl), –.
Go Harlem (es, arr), Pol 236524, De DL9222, AoH A/H32, Jazz Arch JA33.
Darktown strutters' ball (ef, vcl), Jazz Arch JA33.
Keepin' out of mischief now, Pol 423248, IAJRC 5, Jazz Arch JA33.
Nitwit serenade, Pol 423248, Jazz Arch JA33.
King Porter stomp, –, –, IAJRC 5.
If dreams come true (cl, vcl), Jazz Arch JA33.
Rhythm and romance (ef, vcl), –, IAJRC 5.

Teddy Wilson and His Orchestra: Frank Newton (tp), Jerry Blake (cl, as), John Trueheart (g), Lennie Stanfield (b), Cozy Cole (d), Ella Fitzgerald (vcl), Teddy Wilson (p).

New York, March 17, 1936

18829-1 **Christopher Columbus**, Br 7640, CBS 62876, 67289, 66274.
18830-1 **My melancholy baby** (ef, vcl), 7729, –.
18831-? **I know that you know** (unissued).
18832-1 **All my life** (ef, vcl), Br 7640, Col KG30788, CBS 67203, 62876, 66274, 67289.

Chick Webb and his Orchestra: same personnel as June 12, 1935

New York, April 7, 1936

60999-A,B **Love, you're just a laugh** (ef, vcl), (unissued).
61000-A **Crying my heart out for you** (ef, vcl), De 785.
61001-A **Under the spell of the blues** (ef, vcl), 831.
61002-A **When I get low I get high** (ef, vcl), 1123, Bandstand, 7125.

Nat Story (tb) Ted McRae (ts) replace Jones and Williams

New York, June 2, 1936

61123-A **Go Harlem** (es, arr), De 995, Dl9222, MCA 510014, Coral COPS3453.
61124-A **Sing me a swing song (and let me dance)** (ef, vcl), De 830), MCA 510119, Bandstand 7125.
61125-A **A little bit later on** (ef, vcl), De 831, Dl9222, MCA 510014, Coral COPS3453.
61126-A **Love, you're just a laugh** (ef, vcl), De 1114, MCA 510119, Swingfan (G) 1006.
61127-A **Devoting my time to you** (ef, vcl), De 995.

Mario Bauza, Bobby Stark, Taft Jordan (tp), Sandy Williams, Nat Story (tb), Pete Clark (cl, as, bar), Louis Jordan (as, vcl), Ted McRae (ts), Wayman Carver (ts, fl), Tommy Fulford (p), John Trueheart (g), Beverly Peer (b), Chick Webb (d), Ella Fitzgerlad (vcl).

New York, October 29, 1936

61361-A **(If you can't sing it) You'll have to swing it** (ef, vcl), De 1032, Historia 620, MCA 510068, Bandstand 7125.
61362-A **Swinging on the reservation** (ef, vcl), De 1065, Swingfan (G)1006, MCA 510068.
61363-A **I got the spring fever blues** (ef, vcl), De 1087, Swingfan (G)1006, MCA 510119.
61364-A **Vote for Mr. Rhythm** (ef, vcl), De 1032, Swingfan (G)1006, MCA 510119.
NOTE: Matrix 61364 on De M39023 issued under Ella Fitzgerald's name.

Benny Goodman and his Orchestra: Zeke Zarchy, Ziggy Elmann (tp), replace Bose and Erwin. Dick Clark (ts) out, Benny Goodman (as-1), Ella Fitzgerald (vcl), William Miller (arr).

New York, November 5, 1936

02458-1 **Somebody loves me** (fh, arr), Vic 25497, RCA (F)741059.
02459-1 **'Tain't no use** (bg, vcl), 25469.
02460-1 **Bugle call rag** (jm, arr), –, RCA (F) 741102.
02460-2 **Bugle call rag** (jm, arr), RCA (F) 741084.
02461-1 **Jam session** (jm, arr), 25497.
02463-1 **Goodnight, my love** (ef, vcl), 25461, RCA (F)731041.
02464-1 **Take another guess** (ef, vcl), –, –.
02465-1 **Did you mean it?** (ef, vcl, jm, arr), 25469, –.
NOTE: Complete session also on Bluebird AXM2-5532.

Chick Webb and His Orchestra: Mario Bauza, Bobby Stark, Taft Jordan (tp), Sandy Williams, Nat Story (tb), Pete Clark (cl, as, bar), Louis Jordan (as, vcl), Ted McRae (ts), Wayman Carver (ts, fl), Tommy Fulford (p), John Trueheart (g), Beverly Peer (b), Chick Webb (d), Ella Fitzgerald (vcl).

New York, November 18, 1936

Organ grinder's swing, MCA 2-4107.

Ella Fitzgerald and her Savoy Eight: Taft Jordan (tp), Sandy Williams (tb), Pete Clark (cl), Teddy McRae (ts, bar), Tommy Fulford (p), John Trueheart (g), Beverly Peer (b), Chick Webb (d), Ella Fitzgerald (vcl).

New York, November 18, 1936

61419-A **My last affair**, De 1061, Coral PC07333.
61420-A **Organ grinder's swing**, 1062, –.

New York, November 19, 1936

61421-A **Shine**, De 1062, Coral PC07333.
61422-B **Darktown strutters' ball**, 1061, –.
Vcl acc by the Mills Brothers (vcl) quartet.

New York, January 14, 1937

61529-A **Big boy blue**, De 1148, Coral 6.22065.

Chick Webb and His Orchestra: Mario Bauza, Bobby Stark, Taft Jordan (tp), Sandy Williams, Nat Story (tb), Pete Clark (cl, as, bar), Louis Jordan (as, vcl), Ted McRae (ts), Wayman Carver (ts, fl), Tommy Fulford (p), John Trueheart (g), Beverly Peer (b), Chick Webb (d), Ella Fitzgerald (vcl).

New York, January 14, 1937

61527-A **Take another guess** (ef, vcl), De 1123.
61528-A **Love marches on** (vcl, trio), 1115.

New York, January 15, 1937

61529-A **There's frost on the moon** (vcl, trio), De 1114.
61530-A **Gee, but you're swell** (lj, vcl), De 1115, MCA 510068.

New York, February 3, 1937

61576-A **Dedicated to you**, De 1148, Coral 6.22065.

Ella Fitzgerald and her Savoy Eight: same pers as November 18, 1936 but Louis Jordan (as), Bobby Johnson (g), replace Clark and Trueheart.

New York, May 24, 1937

62213-A **All over nothing at all**, De 1339.
62214-A **If you ever should leave**, 1302.
62215-A **Everyone's wrong but me**, –.
62216-A **Deep in the heart of the South**, 1339, Coral PC07333.

New York, December 21, 1937

62896-A **Bei mir bist du schoen**, De 1596, Coral PC07333.
62897-A **It's my turn now**, –.

Chick Webb and His Orchestra: Mario Bauza, Bobby Stark, Taft Jordan (tp), Sandy Williams, Nat Story (tb), Pete Clark (cl, as, bar), Louis Jordan (ad, vcl), Ted McRae (ts), Wayman Carver (ts, fl), Tommy Fulford (p), John Trueheart (g), Beverly Peer (b), Chick Webb (d), Ella Fitzgerald (vcl).

New York, February 8, 1937

That's a plenty, Jazz Pan LP2, Bandstand 7127
Big boy blue (ef, vcl), –.
Charlie Dixon (arr).

New York, March 24, 1937

62064-A **Rusty Hinge** (lj, vcl), De 1273, MCA 510068.
62065-A **Wake up and live** (vcl, trio), 1213.
62066-A **It's swell of you** (lj, vcl), –.
62067-A **You showed me the way** (ef, vcl), 1220.
62068-A **Clap hands! Here comes Charley**, –, DL9223, MCA 510020, Coral COPS1921, AoH A/H32.
62069-A **Cryin' mood** (ef, vcl), De 12173, MCA 510087, Bandstand 7125.
62072-A **Love is the thing, so they say** (ef, vcl), De 1356.
62073-A **That naughty waltz** (cd, arr), De 1356, DL9223, MCA 510020, Coral COPS1921.
NOTE: Matrices 62070/71 are by Louis Armstrong and his Orchestra, see there.

Chick Webb and his Little Chicks: Chauncey Haughton (cl), Wayman Carver (fl), Tommy Fulford (p), Beverly Peer (b), Chick Webb (d).

New York, September 21, 1937

62618-A   **In a little Spanish town**, De 1513, MCA 510068, 1759, MCA 2-4107, 510020.
62619-A   **I got rhythm**, De DL9223, Coral COPS1921.
62620-A   **I ain't got nobody**, De 1513, MCA 510068.

Chick Webb and his Orchestra: Same pers as for January 14, 1937 but Chauncey Haughton (cl, as), Bobby Johnson (g), replace Clark and Trueheart.

New York, October 27, 1937

62725-A   **Just a simple melody** (ef, vcl), De 1521, MCA 510087.
62726-A   **I got a guy** (ef, vcl), De 1618, Hist 620, MCA 510119.
62727-A   **Strictly jive**, De 1586, MCA 2-4107, 510068, AoH A/H32.
62728-A   **Holiday in Harlem** (ef, vcl), 1521, MCA 510087.

Chick Webb and his Little Chicks: same pers as September 21, 1937

New York, November 1, 1937

62737-B   **Sweet Sue, just you**, De 1759, MCA 510068, MCA 2-4107.

Chick Webb and his Orchestra: same as previous pers (big band), same date.
62738-A   **Rock it for me** (ef, vcl), De 1586, MCA 2-4107, MCA 510068, AoH A/H36.
62739-A   **Squeeze me** De 1716, MCA 2-4107, MCA 510020, Coral COPS1921, AoH A/H32.
62740-A   **Harlem Congo** (cd, arr), De 1681, MCA 2-4107, MCA 510020, Coral COPS1921, De DL9223.

New York, November 2, 1937

62743   **Hallelujah!** (unissued), De.
62744   **I want to be happy** (ef, vcl), –.

Chick Webb and his Orchestra: Same pers as October 27, 1937 but Garvin Bushell (cl, as) replaces Chauncey Haughton and Turk Van Lake (arr).

Broadcast, Savoy Ballroom, New York, December 10, 1937

Bronzeville stomp, Jazz Arch JA33.
She's tall, she's tan, she's terrific, –, (ef, vcl).
Honeysuckle rose (ef, vcl).

New York, December 17, 1937

62886-A **I want to be happy** (ef, vcl, tvl, arr), De 15039, 29239, Br 0138, A5131, MCA 510068.

62886-B **I want to be happy** (ef, vcl, tvl, arr), De Z778.

62887-A **The dipsy doodle** (ef, vcl), De 1587, MCA 2-4107, 510020, Coral COPS1921, De DL9223.

62888-A **If dreams come true** (ef, vcl), De 1716, MCA 2-4107, 510119, De DL9223, Swingfan (G)1006.

62889-A **Hallelujah!** (ef, vcl), De 15039, MCA 2-4107, 510020, Coral COPS1921, De DL9223.

62890-A **Midnite in a madhouse** (Midnite in Harlem*) De 1587, BM1104, M30113*, Br 02569*, A81449*, A505133*, De DL9223, AoH A/H32, Coral COPS1921.

62890-B **Midnite in a madhouse**, De Y5208.

Ella Fitzgerald and her Savoy Eight: Taft Jordan (tp), Sandy Williams (tb), Louis Jordan (as), Teddy McRae (ts, bar), Tommy Fulford (p), Bobby Johnson (g), Beverly Peer (b), Chick Webb (d), Ella Fitzgerald (vcl).

New York, January 25, 1938

63225-A **It's wonderful** De 1669, Coral PC07333.

63226-A **I was doing all right**, –.

Chick Webb and His Orchestra: same personnel as on October 27, but George Matthews (tb) added.

New York, May 2, 1938

63693-A **A-tisket, a-tasket** (ef + ens vcl), De 1840, MCA2-4107, De DL9223, AoH A/H16.

63694-A **Heart of mine** (ef, vcl), De 2721.

63695-A **I'm just a jitterbug** (ef, vcl), De 1899, MCA 510119, Swingfan (G)1006.

63696-C **Azure**, De 1899, AoH A/H32, MCA 510068.

NOTE: De 60730 and De 333298 on Matrix 63693 issued by Ella Fitzgerald.

New York, May 3, 1938

63707-A **Spinnin' the Webb** De 2021, DL9223, MCA 510020, Coral COPS1921.

63708-A **Liza (All the clouds 'll roll away)** De 1840, DL9223, MCA 510020, MCA 2-4107, AoH A/H32, Coral COPS1921.

Ella Fitzgerald and her Savoy Eight: same personnel as on January 25

New York, May 3, 1938

63703-A   **This time it's real** De 1806, Coral PC07333.
63704-A   **What do you know about love?** 1967, –.
63705-A   **You can't be mine (and someone else's too)** 1806, –.
63706-A   **We can't go on this way** 1846, –.
63709-B   **Saving myself for you** –, –.
63710-B   **If you only knew** 1967, –.
NOTE: Matrices in between recorded by Chick Webb and his Orchestra.

Chick Webb and His Orchestra: Hilton Jefferson (as) replaces Jordan.

New York, June 9, 1938

63934-A   **Pack up your sins and go to the devil** (ef, vcl), De 1894,
               MCA 510087, Swingfan (G)1006.
63935-A   **MacPherson is rehearsin' (to swing)** (ef, vcl), De 2080, MCA
               2-4107, 510068.
63936-A   **Everybody step** (ef, vcl), De 1894, MCA 510119, Swingfan
               (G)1006, Bandstand 7125.
63937-A   **Ella** (ef, tj, vcl), De 2148, AoH A/H36, MCA 510068.

New York, August 17, 1938

64459-A   **Wacky dust** (ef, vcl), De 2021, AoH A/H36, Stash 100, MCA
               510087.
64460-A   **Gotta pebble in my shoe** (ef, vcl), De 2231, MCA 510068.
64461-A   **I can't stop loving you** (ef, vcl), MCA 510119, De 2310,
               Swingfan (G)1006.
64464-A   **Who ya hunchin'?**, De 2231, DL9223, MCA 510020, Coral
               COPS1921.
64465-A   **I let a tear fall in the river** (ef, vcl), De 2080, Swingfan
               (G)1006, MCA 510119.

Ella Fitzgerald and her Savoy Eight: Hilton Jefferson (as) replaces Jordan.

New York, August 18, 1938

64426-A   **Strictly from Dixie** De 2202, Coral PC07333.
64463-A   **Woe is me** –, –.

Chick Webb and his Orchestra: Dick Vance, Bobby Stark, Taft Jordan (tp), Sandy Williams, Nat Story, George Matthews (tb), Hilton Jefferson, Garvin Bushell (cl, as), Ted McRae (ts), Wayman Carver (ts, fl), Tommy Fulford (p), Bobby Johnson (g), Beverly Peer (b), Chick Webb (d), Ella Fitzgerald (vcl).

New York, October 6, 1938

64573-A	**F. D. R. Jones** (ef, vcl), De 2105, MCA 2-4107, 510119, Swingfan (G)1006.
64574-A	**I love each move you make** (ef, vcl), De 2105, MCA 510119, Swingfan (G)1006.
64575-A	**It's foxy** (ef, vcl), De 2309, Swingfan (G)1006, MCA 510119.
64576-A	**I found my yellow basket** (ef, + ens vcl), De 2148, Historia 620 MCA 510119.

New York, January 9, 1939

Tea for two, Pol 423248.
How am I to know? –.
One o'clock jump, –.
The blue room, –.
Crazy rhythm, –.
Sugar foot stomp, –.
Grand Terrace rhythm, –.
By heck, 236524.
Blue skies, 423248.
Dinah, –.
Who *yuh* **hunchin'**, 236524.
Liza (all the clouds 'll roll away), 423248.

NOTE: The above 12 titles originally recorded by RCA Victor for NBC on Thesaurus transcriptions with 4 titles on each record in order as shown.

Chauncey Haughton (cl), Wayman Carver (fl), Tommy Fulford (p), Beverly Peer (b), Chick Webb (d).

Saturday Night Swing Club Program, New York, January 1939

Stompin' at the Savoy Jazz Archives JA33.

NBC Broadcast, Blue Room, Lincoln Hotel, New York, February 10, 1939

Let's get together (theme), Cicala (It)BJL8010.
Blue room, –, Pol 236524.
Deep in a dream (ef, vcl), –.
One o'clock jump, –, –.
That was my heart (ef, vcl), –.

New York, February 17, 1939

65039-A   **Undecided** (ef, vcl), De 2323, MCA 2-4107, De DL 9223, AoH A/H16, Coral COPS1921, MCA 510020.

65040-A   **'Tain't what you do (it's the way that cha do it)** (ef, vcl), De 2310, MCA 510119, 2-4107 2323, DL9223, MCA 510020.

65041-A   **In the groove at the grove** Coral COPS1921, AoH A/H32.

65042-A   **One side of me** (ef, vcl), De 2556, MCA 510087, AoH A/H32.

65043-A   **My heart belongs to daddy** (ef, vcl), De 2309, MCA 510087.

NOTE: Some issues on De 60730 and Brunswick 333298 by Ella Fitzgerald.

John Trueheart (g) replaces Johnson.

New York, March 2, 1939

65094-A   **Sugar pie** (ef, vcl), De 2665, AoH A/H36, Swingfan (G)1006, MCA 510087.

65095-A   **It's slumbertime along the Swanee** (ef, vcl), De 2389.

65096-A   **I'm up a tree** (ef, vcl), De 2468, AoH A/H36, MCA 510087.

65097-A   **Chew-chew-chew (your bubble gum)** (ef, vcl), De 2389, Historia 620, NCA 510119.

Ella Fitzgerald and her Savoy Eight: Trueheart (g) replaces Johnson.

New York, March 2, 1939

65092-A   **Once is enough for me**, De 2451, Coral PC07333.

65093-A   **I had to live and learn**, 2581.

New York, April 21, 1939

65441-A   **Don't worry 'bout me**, De 2451.

65442-A   **If anything happened to you**, 2481, Coral PC07333.

65443-A   **If that's what you're thinking**, 2581.

65444-A   **If you ever change your mind**, 2481, –.

Chick Webb and His Orchestra: same personnel as March 2.

New York, April 21, 1939

65445-A   **Have mercy** (ef, vcl), De 2468, Historia 620.

65446-A   **Little white lies** (ef, vcl), 2556, –, MCA 510087.

65447-A   **Coochi-coochi-coo** (ef, vcl), De 2803, AoH A/H36, MCA 510087.

65448-A   **That was my heart** (ef, vcl), 2665.

NOTE: Decca 2803 issued as 'Ella Fitzgerald with Chick Webb and his Orchestra'.

Southland Cafe, Boston, May 4, 1939

Let's get together (theme), Cicala (It)BJL8010, Col C1 CC11.
Poor little rich girl, (1), –, –.
New moon and old serenade (ef, vcl), –, –.
Breakin' em down, –, –.
If I didn't care (ef, vcl), –, –.
Stars and stripes forever, –, –.
I never knew heaven could speak (ef, vcl), –.
My wild Irish rose, (1), –, –.
Chew chew chew (ef, vcl), (1), –, –.

NOTE: (1) Also on First Time Records FTR1508.

Ella Fitzgerald and Her Famous Orchestra: Dick Vance, Bobby Stark, Taft Jordan (tp), George Matthews, Nat Story, Sandy Williams (tb), Garvin Bushell (cl, sop), Hilton Jefferson (as), Wayman Carver (as, ts, fl), Teddy McRae (ts, bar), Tommy Fulford (p), John Trueheart (g), Beverly Peer (b), Bill Beason (d), Ella Fitzgerald (vcl).

New York, June 29, 1939

65903-A	**Betcha nickel**, De 2904, Coral PC07334.
65904-A	**Stairway to the stars**, 2598, –.
65905-A	**I want the waiter (with the water)**, 2628, –.
65906-A	**That's all, brother**, –.
65907-A	**Out of nowhere**, 2598.

New York, August 18, 1939

66134-A	**My last goodbye**, De 2721.
66135-A	**Billy (I always dream of Bill)**, 2769.
66136-A	**Please tell me the truth**, –.
66137-A	**I'm not complainin'**, 3005.
66138-A	**Betcha nickel**, (unissued).

Chicago, October 12, 1939

91836-A	**You're gonna lose your gal**, De 2816.
91837-A	**After I say I'm sorry**, 2826.
91838-A	**Baby, what else can I do?** De 2826, Coral CP07334, AoH A/H36.
91839-A	**My wubba dolly**, De 2816.
91840-A	**Lindy hopper's delight**, (1), De 3186, Bandstand 7125, Br 87098.
91841-A	**Moon ray**, De 2904, Coral PC07334.

NOTE: (1) Ella Fitzgerald does not sing on this track.

'Savoy Ballroom', New York, December 1939

> **A-tisket, a-tasket**, (Opening theme), Musidisc 30JA5139.
> **Diga diga doo**, –.
> **'Tain't what you do**, –.
> **Breakin' down**, –.
> **Oh, Johnny**, –.
> **Traffic jam**, –.
> **Limehouse blues**, –.
> **I want the waiter with the water**, –.
> **Blue Lou**, –.
> **Confessin'**, –.
> **Swing out**, (closing theme), –.

Ella Fitzgerald (vcl) with Chick Webb's Orcestra: pers as before.

'Savoy Ballroom', New York, January 22, 1940

> **Theme (A-tisket, a-tasket)**, Coll Cl CC17.
> **Traffic jam**, –.
> **A lover is blue**.
> **Dodging the Dean**, –.
> **T'ain't what you do**, –.
> **I'm confessin'**, –.
> **Blue Lou**, –.
> **What's the matter with me**.
> **Waiter with the water**, –.
> **Sign off theme**, –.

'Savoy Ballroom', New York, January 25, 1940

> **Theme (A-tisket, a-tasket)**, Coll Cl CC17.
> **Limehouse blues**, –.
> **This changing world**.
> **Oh Johnny, oh Johnny**, –.
> **Digg digga doo**, –.
> **Thank your stars**.
> **Take it from the top**, –.
> **Vagabond dreams**.
> **Breakin' it up**, (1), –.
> **Theme (sign off)**, –.

NOTE: (1) On Collectors Classics as 'Breakin' em down'.

New York, January 26, 1940

67119-A	**Is there somebody else?** De 2988.
67120-A	**Sugar blues**, 3078, Coral PC07334.
67121-A	**The starlit hour**, 2988.
67122-A	**What's the matter with me?**, 3005.

Dick Vance, Irving Randolph, Taft Jordan (tp), George Matthews, John Haughton, Sandy Williams (tb), Chauncey Haughton, Eddie Barefield (cl, as), Teddy McRae (ts, bar), Sam Simons (ts), Roger Ramirez (p), John Trueheart (g), Beverly Peer (b), Bill Beason (d), Ella Fitzgerald (vcl).

New York, February 15, 1940

67194-A	**Busy as a bee**, De X-1937.	
67195-A	**Baby, won't you please come home?**, De 3186.	
67196-A	**If it weren't for you**, 3026.	
67197-A	**Sing song swing**, Coral PC07334, De 3026, AoH A/H36.	
67198-A	**Imagination**, 3078.	

Ella Fitzgerald (vcl) acc by Chick Webb Orchestra: prob pers as before.

'Roseland Ballroom', New York, February 26, 1940

Royal garden blues, Sunbeam SB205.
Sing song swing.
Sugar blues (ef, vcl), –.
Sweet Sue.
It's a blue world (ef, vcl), –.
Is there somebody else? (ef, vcl), –.
One moment please (ef, vcl), –.
I wanna be a rug-cutter, –.

'Roseland Ballroom', New York, March 4, 1940

Theme, Sunbeam SB205.
I got rhythm, –.
One cigarette for two.
Chewin' gum (ef, vcl), –.
Lover come back to me, –.
Who ya hunchin'?, –.
Sing song swing (ef, vcl), –.
Goin' and gettin' it, –.
Make believe, –.
Starlit hour (ef, vcl), –.
Sign off.

Tom Fulford (p) replaces Ramirez.

New York, March 20, 1940

67358-A	**Take it from the top** (1) De 3236	
67359-A	**Tea Dance** 3441	
67360-A	**Jubilee swing** (1) 3236, Bandstand BS7125	

NOTE: (1) Ella does not sing on these tracks

Webb on the air: Ella Fitzgerald and her Famous Orchestra: Dick Vance, Irving Randolph (tp), Taft Jordan (tp, vcl), George Matthews, John Haughton, Sandy Williams (tb), Eddie Barefield, Chauncey Haughton (cl, as), Teddy McRae (ts, bar), Sam Simons (ts), Tommy Fulford (p), John Trueheart (g), Beverly Peer (b), Bill Beason (d), Ella Fitzgerald (vcl).

New York, c. late March 1940

> **A-Tisket, a-tasket**, Jazz Trip 5.
> **Diga diga doo**, –.
> **'Tain't watcha do**, –.
> **Breakin' down**, (inst), –.
> **Oh Johnny, oh!** (tj, vcl), –.
> **Traffic jam**, (inst), –.
> **Limehouse blues**, (inst), –.
> **I want the waiter (with the water)**, –.
> **Blue Lou**, (inst), –.
> **I'm confessin' (That I love you)**, –.
> **Swing out** (inst), –.

James Archey, Floyd Brady, John McConnell (tb), Pete Clark (cl, as), replace Matthews, Haughton, Williams and Barefield.

New York, May 9, 1940

67699-A	**Deedle-de-dum**, De 3224.
67700-A	**Shake down the stars**, 3199.
67701-A	**Gulf coast blues**, 3224, Coral PC07334.
67706-A	**I fell in love with a dream**, 3199.

George Matthews, Earl Hardy (tb), Ulysses Livingston (g), replace Archey, Brady and Trueheart.

New York, September 25, 1940

68146-A	**Five o'clock whistle**, De 3420, Coral PC07334.
68147-A	**So long**, –.
68148-A, B	**Louisville, K6Y**, 3441.

George Dorsey (as) replaces Haughton

New York, November 8, 1940

68329-A	**Taking a chance on love**, De 3490.
68330-A	**Cabin in the sky**, –, Coral PC07334.
68331-A	**I'm the lonesomest gal in town**, 3662, AoH AH36.

New York, January 8, 1941

68558-A	**Three little words**, De 3608, Coral PC07334.
68559-A	**Hello Ma! I done it again**, 3612.
68560-A	**Wishful thinking**, –.
68561-A	**The one I love (belongs to somebody else)**, De 3608.
68562-A	**The muffin man**, 3666.

Dick Vance, Irving Randolph, Taft Jordan (tp), George Matthews, Earl Murphy, John McConnell (tb), Pete Clark, Chauncey Haughton (cl, as), Teddy McRae, Lonnie Simmons (ts), Tommy Fulford (p), Ulysses Livingston (g), Beverly Peer (b), Bill Beason (d), Ella Fitzgerald (vcl).

New York, March 31, 1941

68894-A	**Keep cool, fool**, De 3754, Coral PC07334.
68895-A	**No nothing**, –.
68896-A	**My man**, 4291, –.

Elmer Williams (ts) added and Jesse Price (d) replaces Beason.

Los Angeles, July 31, 1941

DLA2607-A	**I can't believe that you're in love with me**, De 18421.
DLA2608-A	**I must have that man**, De 18530, Coral PC07334.
DLA2609-A	**When my sugar walks down the street**, 18587.
DLA2610-A	**I got it bad (and that ain't good)**, 3968.
DLA2611-A	**Melinda the mousie**, –.
DLA2612-A	**Can't help lovin' dat man**, De 18421.

Vcl acc by Teddy McRae (ts), Tommy Fulford (p), Ulysses Livingston (g), Beverly Peer (b), Kenny Clarke (d).

New York, October 6, 1941

69784-A	**Jim**, De 4007, Coral 6.22178.
69785-A	**This love of mine**, –, –.

Eddie Barefield (as) Bill Beason (d) replace McRae and Clarke.

New York, October 28, 1941

69875-A	**Somebody nobody loves**, De 4082, Coral 6.22178.
69876-A	**You don't know what love is**, –.

New York, November 5, 1941

69905-A	**Who are you?**, De 4291, Coral 6.22178.
69906-A	**I'm thrilled**, 4073.
69907-A	**Make love to me**, –, –.

Vcl acc by the Four Keys: Bill Furness (p), Slim Furness (g), Peck Furness (b), Ernie Hatfield (d, vcl).

New York, March 11, 1942

70470-A   **I'm gettin' mighty lonesome**, De 4315.
70471-A   **When I come back crying (will you be laughing at me?)**, –.

Tommy Fulford (p) added.

New York, April 10, 1942

70652-A   **All I need is you**, De 18347.
70653-A   **Mama come home**, –, Coral 6.22065.

New York, July 31, 1942

71286-A   **My heart and I decided**, De 18530.
71287-A   **I put a four-leaf clover in your pocket**, De 18472, Coral 6.22065.
71288-A   **He's my guy**, De 18472, Coral 6.22178.

Vcl acc by John McGee (tp), Bill Doggett (p), Bernie McKay (g), Bob Haggart (b), Johnny Blowers (d), The Ink Spots: prob pers. Bill Kenny, Charles Fuqua, Ivory Watson and Happy Jones (vcl).

New York, November 3, 1943

71482-A   **Cow cow boogie**, De 18587.

Ella Fitzgerald (vcl) with unknown orchestra.

New York, March 21, 1944

71889   **Once too often**, De 18605.
71890   **Time alone will tell**, –.

Vcl acc by Orchestra and the Ink Spots (vcl quartet).

New York, August 30, 1944

72370-A   **Into each life some rain must fall**, De 23356, AoH AH16, Coral 6.22065.
72371-A   **I'm making believe**, De 23356.

Vcl acc by Johnny Long's Orchestra and The Song Spinners.

New York, November 6, 1944

72483-A   **And her tears flowed like wine**, De 18633, Coral 6.22065.
72484-A   **Confessin'**, –.

Vcl acc by the Ink Spots and orchestra.

New York, February 26, 1945

| 72746-A | **I'm beginning to see the light**, Coral 6.22065, De 23399. |
| 72747-A | **That's the way it is**, –. |

Ella Fitzgerald (vcl), acc by Renee de Knight (p), Hy White (g), Haig Stephens (b), George Wettling (d), the Delta Rhythm Boys (vcl).

New York, March 27, 1945

72798	**Paper moon (It's only a)**, De 23425, AoH AH16, Coral 6.22065.
72799	**Cry out of my heart** (unissued).
72800	**Cry out of my heart**, –.

Vcl acc by Randy Brooks and his Orchestra: prob pers. Randy Brooks, Ernie Englund, George Bardon (tp), Harry Brooks (tb), Eddie Caine, Paul Bardon (as), Stuart Anderson, John Lesko (ts), Eddie Shomer (bar), Shorty Allen (p), Paul Lajoie (b), Sonny Mann (d).

New York, August 29, 1945

| 73020 | **A kiss goodnight**, De 18713. |
| 73021 | **Benny's coming home on Saturday**, –. |

Vcl acc by Vic Schoen and his Orchestra: Ralph Mussilo, Charles Genduso, Louis Ruggiero (tp), William Pritchard (tb), Bennie Kaufman, Sid Cooper (as), Sid Rubin, Harry Feldman (ts), Moe Wechsler (p), Hy White (g), Felix Giobbe (b), Irv Kluger (d).

New York, October 4, 1945

| 73066-A | **Flying home**, De 23956, AoH AH16. |

Vcl acc by Louis Jordan's Tympany Five: Aaron Izenhall (tp), Louis Jordan (as, vcl), Josh Jackson (ts), Bill Davies (p), Carl Hogan (g), Jesse Simpkins (b), Eddie Byrd (d), Harry Dial (maracas), Vic Lourie (claves).

New York, October 8, 1945

73073-A	**Stone cold dead in de market**, De 23546.
73074-A	**Petootie pie**, –.
73081	**Petootie pie**, Coral 6.22178.

Ella Fitzgerald and her V-Disc Jumpers: Charlie Shavers (tp), Lou McGarity (tb), Peanuts Hucko (cl), Al Sears (ts), Buddy Weed (p), Remo Palmieri (g), Trigger Alpert (b), Buddy Rich (d).

New York, October 12, 1945

1596	**That's Rich**, V-Disc 603, Jazz Soc AA511.
1599	**I'll always be in love with you**, 569.
1661	**I'll see you in my dreams**, 730, –.

Vcl acc by Billy Kyle (p), Jimmy Shirley (g), Junior Raglin (b), Sylvester Payne (d).

Louis Armstrong and Ella Fitzgerald acc. by Bob Haggart's Orchestra: Louis Armstrong (tp, vcl), Billy Butterfield (tp), Bill Stregmeyer (cl, as), George Koenig (as), Jack Greenberg, Art Drellinger (ts), Molton Schatz (bar), Joe Bushkin (p), Danny Perri (g), Trigger Alpert (b), Cozy Cole (d), Ella Fitzgerald (vcl), Bob Haggart (cond).

New York, January 18, 1946

73285-A	**You won't be satisfied**, (la & ef vcl) De 23496, ED2027, DL8477. Br (E) 03644, OE9061, LAT8223, (G) 10118EPB, 87038LPBM, Coral COPS7397.
73286-A	**The frim fram sauce**, (la & ef vcl) De 23496, ED2027, DL8477, Br (E) 03644, OE9061, LAT8223, Br (G) 1011EPB, 87 038LPBM, De BM31040, Coral COPS7397

Ella Fitzgerald and her V-Disc Jumpers: same personnel as October 12, 1945.

New York, February 21, 1946

73388	**I'm just a lucky so and so**, De 18814, AoH AH45.
73389	**I didn't mean a word I said**, –, –.

Vcl acc by the Delta Rhythm Boys (vcl quartet) Renee de Knight (p), Jimmy Shirley (g), Lamont Moten (b), Eddie Bourne (d).

New York, August 29, 1946

73669	**For sentimental reasons**, De 23670, MCA (Jap) SV7006, AoH AH16.
73670	**It's a pity to say goodnight**, –, Coral 6.22065.

Buddy Rich and his V-Disc Speed Demons: Charlie Shavers (tp), Lou McGarity (tb), Peanuts Hucko (cl), Al Sears (ts), Buddy Weed (p), Remo Palmieri (g), Trigger Alpert (b), Buddy Rich (d), Ella Fitzgerald (vcl).

New York, October, 1946

> **That's Rich**, (ef vcl), V-Disc 569, Caracol 423.
> **I'll always be in love with you**, –, –.

Ella Fitzgerald vcl acc by Eddie Heywood and his Orchestra: Leonard Graham (tp), Al King (tb), Jimmy Powell (as), Eddie Heywood (p), Billy Taylor (b), William Purnell (d).

New York, January 24, 1947

73786   **Guilty**, De 23844.
73787   **Sentimental journey**, –, MCA (Jap)SV7006.

Vcl duet with Buddy Rich acc by Joe Mooney (accor), Nick Tagg (p), Sidney Catlett (d).

'WNEW Broadcast', New York, March 1, 1947

JD432   **Budella (Blue skies)**, V-Disc 775, Elec (Jap) KV122.

Vcl acc by Bob Haggart and his Orchestra: Andy Ferretti, Chris Griffin, Bob Peck (tp), Will Bradley, Jack Satterfield, Freddie Ohms (tb), Ernie Caceres (bar), Stan Freeman (p), Dan Perri (g), Bob Haggart (b), Morey Feld (d), Andy Love Quintet (vcl group-l).

New York, March 19, 1947

73818   **A Sunday kind of love** (1), De 23866, DL4129.
73819   **That's my desire** (1), De 23866, MCA (Jap) SV7006, De
              DL8695.
73820-A   **Lady be good!**, De 23956, DL8149, AoH AH16, AH45.

Ella Fitzgerald (vcl) prob acc by Bob Haggart Orchestra: prob pers. Andy Ferretti (tp), Will Bradley, Fred Ohms, Billy Rauch, Seymour Shaffer (tb), Art Drellinger (cl), Toots Mondello (as), Hymie Schertzer (ts), Stan Freeman (p), Dan Perri (g), Bob Haggart (b), Norris Shawker (d).

New York, July 11, 1947

74000   **You're breakin' in a new heart** (unissued).

Vcl acc by Bob Haggart and his Orchestra: definitely Haggart + above pers.

New York, July 22, 1947

74013   **Don't you think I oughta know?** De 24157.
74014   **You're breakin' in a new heart**, –.

Vcl acc by the Day Dreamers (vcl) acc by small combo.
Dizzie Gillespie and his Orchestra: Dizzy Gillespie, Dave Burns, Elmon Wright, Ray Orr, Matthew McKay (tp), Taswell Baird, Bill Shepherd (tb), Howard Johnson, John Brown (as), James Moody or George Nicholas, Joe Gayles (ts), Cecil Payne (bar), Milt Jackson (vib), John Lewis (p), Al McKibbon (b), Joe Harris (d), Kenny Hagood, Ella Fitzgerald (vcl).

Concert 'Carnegie Hall', New York, September 29, 1947

N1791E	**Festival in Cuba**, Arco AL8.
N1792-2E	**Panic in Puerto Rico**, –.
N1793-2E	**Bop salad**, –.
N1794-E	**A serenade in fifths**, –.
N1795-B2	**To be sure**, –.
	Toccata for trumpet and orchestra (unissued).
	Cubana be – Cubana bop, –.
	Salt peanuts, –.
	One bass hit, –.
	Oo-pop-a-da, –.
	Stairway to the stars, (ef, vcl), –.
	How high the moon, (ef, vcl), –.

Ella Fitzgerald vcl prob acc by Bob Haggart Orchestra: personnel same as in July 1947.

New York, December 18, 1947

74300	**I want to learn about love**, De 24581.
74301	**That old feeling**, 28049.

Vcl acc by Leonard Graham (tp), Ray Brown (b) + others.

New York, December 20, 1947

74322	**My baby likes to re-bop**, De 24332, Coral 6.22178.
74323	**No sense**, 24538, –.
74324-A	**How high the moon**, De 24387, AoH AH16, –.

Vcl acc by Illinois Jacquet (ts), Sir Charles Thompson (org), Hank Jones (p), Hy White (g), John Simmons (b), J. C. Heard (d).

New York, December 23, 1947

74386	**I've got a feeling I'm falling**, De 24232, Coral 6.22065.
74387	**You turned the tables on me**, 24387, –.
74392	**I cried and cried and cried**, 6.22178.
74393	**Robbins nest**, 24538, –.

Ella Fitzgerald (vcl) acc by The Song Spinners (vcl group) with large Orch.

New York, April 29, 1948

74537	**Tea leaves**, De 24446.

Ella Fitzgerald (vcl) with The Song Spinners (vcl group) but inst. acc. out.

New York, April 30, 1948

74538   **My happiness**, De 24446.

Vcl acc by Illinois Jacquet (ts) + unknown p, b and d.

New York, August 20, 1948

74590   **It's too soon**, De 24497, AoH AH16.
74591   **I can't go on without you**, –.

Vcl with unknown acc.

New York, November 10, 1948

74621   **To make a mistake is human**, De 24529.
74622   **In my dreams**, –.

Unknown tb, ts, poss Hank Jones (p), Ray Brown (b), unknown (d), Ella
Fitzgerald (vcl).

Broadcast, 'Royal Roost', New York, November 27 & December 4, 1948

        Lady be good, Alto AL706.
        I never knew, –.
        Love that boy (ef, vcl), –.
        Too soon to know (ef, vcl), –.
        Mr. Paganini (ef, vcl), –.
        Royal Roost bop boogie 1 (ef, vcl), –.
        Tiny's blues, –.
        Bop goes the weasel, –.
        Heat wave (ef vcl), –.
        Old mother Hubbard (ef, vcl), –.
        Royal Roost bop boogie 2 (ef, vcl), –.
        Flying home (ef, vcl), –.

NOTE: On the titles where *Ella Fitzgerald* is singing she is only
        accompanied by rhythm.

Lester Young and his Orchestra: Jessie Drakes (tp), Kai Winding (tb), Allen
Eager, Lester Young (ts), Hank Jones (p), Ted Briscoe (b), Roy Haynes (d),
Ella Fitzgerald (vcl).

'Royal Roost', New York, December 4, 1948

        Theme, Ambrosia 1.
        Bebop boogie (Boppin' boogie), Charlie Parker PLP409,
        ESP3017, Session SR103.
        I cover the waterfront, Session SR103.
        How high the moon, Vogue (E) 514, Charlie Parker 409.
        Sunday, –, –.
        Confessin', Session SR103.

Ella Fitzgerald (vcl) with unknown accompaniment.

New York, January 14, 1949

74686	**I couldn't stay away**, De 244562.
74687	**Old mother Hubbard**, 24581.
74688	**Someone like you**, 24562.

Ella Fitzgerald (vcl) with unknown acc.

'Royal Roost', New York, April 15, 1949

Old mother Hubbard, Session 5.
Mr Paganini, –.
There's a small hotel, –.
How high the moon?, –.

'Bop City', New York, April 23 & 30, 1949

Robbins' nest, Session 5.
As you desire me, –.
Thou swell, –.
Flyin' home, –.
Someone like you, –.
Again, –.
In a mellotone, –.
Lemon drop, –.

New York, April 28, 1949

74862	**Happy talk**, De DL8696.
74863	**I'm gonna wash that man right outa my hair**, De DL8696, MCA, (Jap) SV7006.
74864	**Black coffee**, De DL8696.
74865	**Lover's gold**, –.

Vcl acc by Louis Jordan and his Tympany Five: Aaron Izenhall (tp), Louis Jordan (as, vcl), Eddie Johnson (ts), Bill Davis (p), Carl Hogan (g), Dallas Bartley (b), Christopher Columbus (d).

New York, April 28 1949

| 74866 | **Baby it's cold outside**, De DL8477, MCA (Jap) SV7006. |
| 74867 | **Don't cry, cry baby**, –, Coral 6.22178. |

Vcl acc by Sonny Burke and his Orchestra: no details.

Los Angeles, July 20, 1949

| L5097 | **Crying**, De 34708. |
| L5098 | **A new shade of blue**, –. |

Vcl acc by Sy Oliver and his Orchestra: pers incl. Bernie Previn (tp), Henderson Chambers (tb), Billy Kyle (p), Sy Oliver (arr), and others.

New York, September 20, 1949

75279	**In the evening**, De 24780, Coral 6.22179.
75280	**Talk fast, my heart, talk fast**, –, –.
75281	**I'm waitin' for the junkman**, 24868, –.
75282	**Basin Street blues**, –, AoH AH16.

Vcl acc by Gordon Jenkins' Orchestra: vcl group included, no details.

New York, September 21, 1949

75287	**I hadn't anyone till you**, De 24900, AoH AH16.
75288	**Dream a little longer**, –.
75289	**Foolish tears**, 24773.
75290	**A man wrote a song**, –.

Vcl acc by the Mills Brothers (vcl group) with unknown acc.

Los Angeles, November 7, 1949

L5191	**Fairy tales**, De 24813.
L5192	**I gotta have my baby back**, –.

Vcl acc by Sy Oliver Orchestra: no details.

New York, February 2, 1950

75801	**Baby, won't you say you love me?**, De 24917.
75802	**Doncha go 'way mad**, –.

Vcl acc by Sy Oliver's Orchestra: Bernie Previn, Tony Faso, Paul Webster (tp), Henderson Chambers (tb), Milt Yaner, Sid Cooper (as), Jerry Jerome, Al Klink (ts), Hank Jones (p), Everett Barksdale (g), Ray Brown (b), Jimmy Crawford (d).

New York, March 6, 1950

75936	**Solid as a rock**, De 24958, Coral 6.22179.
75937	**I've got the world on a string**, 27120, AoH AH22.
75938	**Sugarfoot rag**, 24958, Coral 6.22179.
75939	**Peas and rice**, 27120.

Ella Fitzgerald (vcl) with unknown acc. combo.

'Birdland', New York, May 3, 1950

I hadn't anyone 'till you, Session 5.

Vcl acc by the Four Hits and a Miss (vcl) with unknown combo.

Los Angeles, May 9, 1950

L5594   **M-i-s-s-i-s-s-i-p-p-i**, De 27061, Coral 6.22065.
L5595   **I don't want the world**, –, –.

Vcl acc by Louis Jordan and his Tympany Five.

New York, August 15, 1950

76731   **Ain't nobody's business**, De 27200, Coral 6.22178.
76732   **I'll never be free**, –.

Louis Armstrong & Ella Fitzgerald acc by Sy Oliver's Orchestra: Paul Webster (tp), Hank D'Amico (cl), Frank Ludwig (ts), Hank Jones (p), Everett Barksdale (g), Ray Brown (b), Johnny Blowers (d), Sy Oliver (arr, cond), Louis Armstrong (tp, vcl), Ella Fitzgerald (vcl).

New York, August 25, 1950

76750   **Dream a little dream of me**, (la & ef, vcl), De 27209, ED2027, DL8477, Br (E)04614, OE9061, OE9274, LAT8223, (G) A82430, 86006LPB, (G/F) 10118EPB, 87038 LPBM, Coral COPS7397.
76751   **Can anyone explain**, (la & ef, vcl), De 27209, Br (E)04614, OE9274, (G) A82430, 86006LPB, (G/F) 10118EPB, 87038LPBM, Coral COPS7397.

Vcl acc by Ellis Larkins (p).

New York, September 11, 1950

76823   **Looking for a boy**, De 27369, De DL8378
76824   **My one and only love**, 27368, –.
76825   **How long has this been going on?**, 27370, –.
76826   **I've got a crush on you**, –, –.
NOTE: The above 4 also on MCA (F) 510149 and AoH AH45.

JATP All Stars: prob. Harry Edison (tp), Charlie Parker (as), Coleman Hawkins, Flip Phillips (ts), Hank Jones (p), Ray Brown (b), Buddy Rich (d), Ella Fitzgerald (vcl).

New York, September 1950

     Body and soul, JATP Film Soundtrack.

ELLA FITZGERALD

Vcl acc by Ellis Larkins (p).

New York, September 12, 1950

76834   **But not for me**, De 27369, DL8378
76835   **Soon**, 27371, –.
76836   **Someone to watch over me**, 27368, –.
76837   **Maybe**, 27371, –.
NOTE: The above four also on MCA (F) 510149 and AoH AH45.

Vcl acc by Charlie Shavers (tp), Hank Jones (p), John Collins (g), Ray Brown (b), Charlie Smith (d).

New York, September 26, 1950

76899   **Santa Claus got stuck in my chimney**, De 27255.
76900   **Molasses, molasses**, –.

Vcl acc by the Ink Spots with unknown small group.

New York, December 20, 1950

80291   **Little small town girl**, De 27419.
80292   **I still feel the same about you**, –, Coral 6.22065.
Sy Oliver and the Skylarks (vcl).

New York, January 12, 1951

80337-T4A   **Lonesome gal**, De 27453.
80338-T3A   **The bean bag song**, –, Coral 6.22065.

Vcl acc by Sy Oliver's Orchestra: Bernie Previn, Paul Webster, Tony Faso (tp), Mort Bullman (tb), Artie Baker, George Dorsey, Al Klink, Bill Holcomb (saxes), Hank Jones (p), Everett Barksdale (g), Sandy Bloch (b), Jimmy Crawford (d).

New York, March 27, 1951

80745-A   **Chesapeake and Ohio**, De 27602, Coral 6.22179.
80746-A   **Little man in a flying saucer**, 27578, –.
80747-A   **Because of rain**, 27602.
80748-A   **The hot canary**, 27578, –.

Vcl acc by Hank Jones (p), Everett Barksdale (g), Sandy Bloch (b), Jimmy Crawford (d).

New York, May 24, 1951

81075   **Even as you and I**, De 27634.
81076   **If you really love me**, –.
         Love you madly, 27693.

Ella Fitzgerald (vcl), acc by Bill Doggett (org), Hank Jones (p), Everett Barksdale (g), Arnold Fishkin (b), Johnny Blowers (d), Ray Charles Singers (vcl group).

New York, June 26, 1951

81214	**Mixed emotions**, De 27680, AoH AH22.
81215-A	**Smooth sailing**, 27693, –.
81216-A	**Come on a-my house**, 27680.

Vcl acc. by Sy Oliver and his Orchestra: Taft Jordan, Bernie Previn, Carl Poole (tp), Henderson Chambers, Frank Saracco (tb), Milt Yaner, Hymie Schertzer, Al Klink, Fred Williams, Stewart Blake (saxes), Hank Jones (p), Everett Barksdale (g), Sandy Bloch (b), Johnny Blowers (d).

New York, July 18, 1951

81286	**It's my own darn fault**, De DL8695.
81287	**I don't want to make a change**, 27948, Coral 6.22179.
81288	**There never was a baby**, 27724, DL8892.
81289	**Give a little get a little**, –, DL8695.

Louis Armstrong & Ella Fitzgerald with Dave Barbour's Orchestra: Larry Neill (tp), Frank Howard (tb), Jack Dumont, Chuck Gentry, Heinie Beau (saxes), Hank Jones (p), Ray Brown (b), Alvin Stoller (d), Dave Barbour (cond, poss g), Louis Armstrong (tp, vcl), Ella Fitzgerald (vcl).

Los Angeles, November 23, 1951

L6526	**Necessary evil**, De 27901, (F) MU60711, Br (E) OE9274, (G) A82623, (G/F) 87038LPBM.
L6527	**Oops!**, De 27901, (F) MU60711, Br (E) OE9274, (G) A82623, (G/F) 87038LPBM.
L6528	**Would you like to take a walk**, De28552, ED2027, DL8477, Br (E) 05112, OE9061, LAT8223, (G) A82803, (G/F) 87038LPBM, De MU60887.
L6529	**Who walks in when I walk out**, De 28552, (F) MU60887, Br (E) 05112 (G) A82803, (G/F) 87038LPBM.

Louis Armstrong and Bing Crosby: Louis Armstrong (tp, vcl) Bing Crosby, Ella Fitzgerald (vcl) acc by J. S. Trotter's Orchestra.

Hollywood, November 27, 1951

> **I get ideas**, (la, vcl).
> **Memphis blues**, (la, bc, ef, vcl).
> **A kiss to build a dream on**, (la, bc, vcl).

Vcl acc by Sonny Burke's Orchestra: Pete Candoli, Carlton McBeath, Mickey Mangano, Oliver Mitchell (tp), Paul Tauner, Jim Priddy, John Haliburton, Milt Bernhardt (tb), Clint Neagley, Hugo Loewenstein, Don Raffell, Hammond Russum, Chuck Gentry (saxes), Hank Jones (p), Laurindo Almeido (g), Joe Mondragon (b), Tommy Rowles (d).

Los Angeles, December 26, 1951

L6533-A **Baby doll**, De 27900.
L6534 **What does it take?**, 28034.
L6535 **Lady bug**, 27900.
L6536 **Lazy day**, 28034.

Vcl acc by Ray Brown's Orchestra: Bill Doggett (org), Hank Jones (p), Ray Brown (b), Rudy Taylor (d), Dick Jacobs (bells).

New York, January 4, 1952

82075 **Airmail special**, De 28126, Coral 6.22065.
82076 **Rough ridin'**, 27948.

Vcl acc by Sy Oliver's Orchestra: Taft Jordan, Bernie Previn, James Nottingham (tp), Mort Bullman, Al Grey (tb), Milt Yaner, Sid Cooper, Dick Jacobs, Sammy Taylor (saxes), Dave McRae (bar), Hank Jones (p), Everett Barksdale (g), Sandy Bloch (b), Jimmy Crawford (d).

New York, February 25, 1952

82319 **A guy is a guy**, De 28049.
82320 **Nowhere guy**, 28707, Coral 6.22179.
82321 **Gee but I'm glad to know**, 28131.
82322-A **Goody goody**, 28126.

Same pers but Bobby Byrne (tb), Milt Yaner, Sid Cooper (as), Dick Jacobs, Sam Taylor (ts).

New York, June 26, 1952

83009 **Ding-dong boogie**, (1) De 28321, Coral 6.22179.
83010-A **You'll have to swing it pt 1**, 28774, AoH 22.
83011-A **You'll have to swing it pt 2**, –, –.
83012 **Angel eyes**, 28707, MCA (Jap) SV7006.
83013 **Early autumn**, 29810, Coral 6.22179.
83014 **Preview**, (1), 28321, Coral 6.22178.
NOTE: (1) Vcl acc by Taylor (ts), Jones (p), Barksdale (g), Bloch (b), and Crawford (d) only.

Vcl acc by Leroy Kirkland's Orchestra: Phil Kraus (vib), Hank Jones (p), Hy White (g), George Duvivier (b), Stan Kane (d) + others.

New York, August 11–13, 1952

83243-1	**Trying**, De 28375.
83244	**The greatest there is**, 28930.
83247	**My Bonnie**, 28375.
83248	**Ella's contribution to the blues**, 29810.

New York, September 19, 1952

83429   **Walking by the river**, De 28433, AoH AH22.

Vcl acc by Lawson Haggart Jazz Band.

New York, October 15, 1952

83496   **Basin Street blues**

Vcl acc by Jerry Gray's Orchestra: Conrad Gozzo, John Best, Tom Patton, Whitey Thomas (tp), Milt Bernhardt, Jim Priddy, John Halliburton, George Arus (tb), Riley Weston, Dale Brown, John Rotella (as, cl, bar), Bob Cooper, Ronny Perry (ts), Hank Jones or Bob Hammack (p), Bobby Gibbons (g), Bob Stone (b), Alvin Stoller (d).

Los Angeles, November 30, 1952

L6955   **I can't lie to myself**, De 28589.
L6956   **Don't wake me up**, –.

Vcl acc by Sy Oliver's Orchestra: Taft Jordan, Jimmy Nottingham, Charlie Shavers (tp), Henderson Chambers, Frank Saracco (tb), Art Baker, George Dorsey (as), Sam Taylor, Mel Tait (ts), Manny Albam (bar), Hank Jones (p), Everett Barksdale (g), George Duvivier (b), Jimmy Crawford (d).

New York, February 13, 1953

83951-A   **Careless**, De 28671.
83952-A   **Blue Lou**, –.
83953-A   **I wonder what kind of man**, 28930, Coral 6.22179.

Vcl acc by Taft Jordan (tp), Bill Doggett (org), Sandy Bloch (b), Jimmy Crawford (d), The Ray Charles Singers (vcl group).

New York, June 11, 1953

84694   **When the hands of the clock pray at midnight**, De 28762.
84695-A   **Crying in the chapel**, –.

Concert 'Nichigeki Theatre', Tokyo, November 18, 1953

Ella Fitzgerald and her Quartet: Ella Fitzgerald (vcl), Raymond Tunia (p), Herb Ellis (g), Ray Brown (b), J. C. Heard (d), same location and date.

> **On the sunny side of the street**, Pablo 2620140.
> **Body and soul**, –.
> **Why don't you do right**, –.
> **Lady be good**, –.
> **I got it bad and that ain't good**, –.
> **How high the moon**, –.

Ella Fitzgerald (vcl) acc by the Jazz at the Philharmonic All Stars. Roy Eldridge, Charlie Shavers (tp), Bill Harris (tb), Willie Smith, Benny Carter (as), Flip Phillips, Ben Webster (ts), Oscar Peterson (p), Herb Ellis (g), Ray Brown (b), J. C. Heard (d), same location and date.

> **My funny Valentine**, Pablo 2620140.
> **Smooth sailin'**, –.
> **Frim fram sauce**, –.
> **Perdido**, –.

NOTE: The Ella Fitzgerald session also on Verve 2615015 and MV9078.

Vcl acc by Sy Oliver's Orchestra: Jimmy Nottingham, Taft Jordan, Charlie Shavers (tp), Frank Saracco, Jack Satterfield (tb), George Dorsey, Bill Holcomb (as), Sam Taylor (ts), Dave McRae (bar), Dave Martin (p), Everett Barksdale (g), Sandy Bloch (b), Jimmy Crawford (d), Lawrence Rivera (bgo).

New York, December 23, 1953

85590	**Empty ballroom**, De 29259, AoH AH22.	
85591	**If you don't, I know who will**, –, Coral 6.22179.	
85592-1	**Melancholy me**, De 29008.	
85593-1	**Somebody bad stole de wedding bell**, –.	

Vcl acc by John Scott Trotter's Orchestra: Red Nichols, Robert Guy, Ziggy Elman (tp), Joe Howard, Ted Vesely, Wendell Mayhew (tb), Phil Sunken, Matty Matlock, Dave Harris, Warren Baker, Larry Wright (saxes), Buddy Cole (p), Perry Botkin (g), Phil Stevens (b), Nick Fatool (d), plus string section.

Los Angeles, December 31, 1953

L7519-1	**Moanin' low**, De 29475, Coral 6839.	
L7520-1	**Takin' a chance on love**, –.	

Vcl acc by Gordon Jenkins' Orchestra.

New York, March 24, 1954

86079-1	**I wished on the moon**, De 29137, AoH AH22.
86080-1	**Baby**, 29108.
86081-1	**I need**, –.
86082-1	**Who's afraid?** 29137.

Vcl acc by Ellis Larkins (p).

New York, March 29, 1954

86087	**I'm glad there is you**, De DL8068.
86088	**What else could I do?**, –, Coral 6839, MCA 510149.
86089	**What is there to say?**, –.
86090	**Makin' whoopee**, MCA (F) 510149, De LD8068, Coral 6839.
86091	**Until the real thing comes along**, –.
86092	**People will say we're in love**, –.

New York, March 30, 1954

86093	**Please be kind**, De DL8068, Coral 6839, MCA (F) 510149.
86094	**Imagination**, –.
86095	**My heart belongs to daddy**, MCA (Jap) SV7006.
86096	**You leave me breathless**, MCA (F) 510149, Coral 6839.
86097	**Nice work if you can get it**, –, –, AoH AH45.
86098	**Stardust**, –, –, Coral 6839.

Vcl acc by Sy Oliver's Orchestra: no details.

New York, June 4, 1954

| 86356 | **Lullaby of Birdland**, De 29198, Coral 6.22179. |
| 86357 | **Later**, –. |

Vcl acc by André Previn's Orchestra.

Los Angeles, April 1, 1955

	You'll never know, De DL8155, Coral 6839.
	Thanks for the memory, –, –.
	It might as well be spring, –.
	I can't get started, –.

Vcl acc by Benny Carter's Orchestra.

Los Angeles, April 27, 1955

L8364	**Old devil moon**, De 29580, DL8155, Coral 6839.
L8365	**Lover come back to me**, –, –, AoH AH22.
	Between the devil and the deep blue sea, De DL8155, Coral 6839.
	That old black magic, –, AoH AH22.

Vcl acc by Don Abney (p), Joe Mondragon (b), Larry Bunker (d).

Hollywood, May 3, 1955

L8379   **Hard hearted Hannah**, Coral 6.22178, De 29689. De DL8166, AoH AH26, MCA (Jap) SV7006.

L8380   **Pete Kelly's blues**, De 29689, DL8166, AoH AH26, MCA (Jap) SV7006.

L8381   **Ella hums the blues**, De DL8166, MCA2-4064, AoH AH26.

Vcl acc by Toots Camarata and his Orchestra: Will Bradley, Frank Saracco, Cutty Cutshall (tb), Dick Moore, Lester Salomon (fhr), Hymie Schertzer (as), Don Abney (cel), Dick Hyman (p), Barry Galbraith (g), Sandy Bloch (b), Phil Kraus (d), plus vcl chorus.

New York, August 1, 1955

88435   **Soldier boy**, De 29648.

88436   **A satisfied mind**, –.

Vcl acc by Toots Camarata and his Orchestra: Jimmy Nottingham, Charlie Shavers, Dale McMickle (tp), Will Bradley, Frank Saracco, Cutty Cutshall, Ward Silloway (tb), Al Howard, Hymie Schertzer (as), Al Klink, Hal Feldman (ts), Don Abney (p), Al Casamenti (g), Eddie Safranski (b), Jimmy Crawford (d), Janet Putman (harp), plus string section.

New York, August 5, 1955

88456   **My one and only love**, De 29746, AoH 22, MCA SV7006.

88457   **The impatient years**, 29665.

88458   **But not like mine**, –.

88459   **The tender trap**, 29746.

Ella Fitzgerald & Frank Sinatra (vcl).

Hollywood, 1955

       Necessity (ef, fs, vcl), Chairman Records 6009.

NOTE: The above from a never released cartoon soundtrack.

Vcl acc by Buddy Bregman Orchestra.

Los Angeles, January, 1956

20054   **Stay here**, Verve 10012.

20055   **The sun forgot to shine**, 10021.

20056   **Too young for the blues**, 10002, MGV2036.

20057   **It's only a man**, –, –.

Vcl acc by Harry Edison (tp), plus others.

Los Angeles, February, 1956

20067	**It's all right with me**, Verve 10077, MGV4050, 4001-2.
20068	**Beale Street blues**, 10128.
Similar	
20075	**So in love**, Verve MGV4050, 4001-2.
20078	**Begin the beguine**, Verve MGV4049, MGV4066, 4001-2.

Vcl acc by Paul Smith (p), Barney Kessel (g), Joe Mondragon (b), Alvin Stoller (d).

Los Angeles, February 8, 1956

	I get a kick out of you, Verve MGV4049, MGV4066, 4001-2.
	Get out of town –, –.
	Miss Otis regrets, –, –.
	Easy to love, MGV4050, –.
	I concentrate on you, –, –.
20083	**Love for sale**, –, MGV4066, –.
20086	**Let's do it**, MGV4049, –.
20087	**All of you**, –, –, –.

Ella Fitzgerald (vcl) acc by Buddy Bregman's Orchestra: no details but strings included.

Los Angeles, February/March, 1956

20121	**Night and day**, Verve MGV4050, MGV4066, 4001-2.
20122	**A beautiful friendship**, MGV4063.
	All through the night, Verve MGV4049, MGV4066, 4001-2.
	Anything goes, –, –, –.
	Too darn hot, –, –.
	Do I love you?, –, –.
	From this moment on, –, –.
	Everytime we say goodbye, –, –, –.
	Just one of those things, –, –, –.
	I am in love, –, –.
	In the still of the night, –, –.
	Always true to you in my fashion, –, –.
	Ridin' high, Verve MGV4050, 4001-2.
	Don't fence me in, –, –.
	It's delovely, –, –, MGV4066.
	You're the top, –, –, –.
	Ace in the hole, –, –.
	I've got you under my skin, –, –, –.
	I love Paris, –, –.
	You do something to me, –, –.
	What is this thing called love, –, –, –.
	Why can't you behave?, –, –.

Vcl with Count Basie and his Orchestra.

New York, June 26, 1956

2900-4   **April in Paris**, (1, ef, jw, vcl), Clef 89172, MGC743,Verve
                MGV8030, (G/F)511038, Col (E)SEB10070, Kar AFF1122,
                KEP329.
2901   **Too close for comfort**, (ef, jw, vcl), Verve MGV8288.
2902-1   **Salty lips**, (ef, jw,. vcl) (unissued).
2903   **Every day (I have the blues)**, (ef, jw, vcl), Clef MGC743,
                Verve MGV8030, Col (E)SEB10070, Kar KEP329.

2904-5   **Party blues**, (ef, jw, vcl), Clef 89172, MGC743, Verve
                MGV8030, (E)VLP9127, Col (E)SEB10070, Kar AFF1122,
                KEP329.
2905-9   **Slats**, Verve MGV8291, ARS G422, Blue Star (F) GLP3648.
2906-3   **Don't worry 'bout me**, (jw, vcl), Verve MGV8288.
2907-4   **Low life**, Verve MGV8291, ARS G422, Blue Star (F)
                GLP3648, Kar KEP373.
                NOTE: (1) Ralph Burns (p, arr) added.

Vcl acc by Paul Smith (p) Barney Kessel (g) Joe Mondragon (b) Alvin Stoller
(d).

'Hollywood Bowl', Los Angeles, August 15, 1956

Love for sale, Verve MGV8231-2.
Just one of those things, –.
Little girl blue, –.
Too close for comfort, –.
I can't give you anything but love, –.
Airmail special, –.

Jazz at the Hollywood Bowl: Louis Armstrong (tp, vcl), Trummy Young
(tb), Edmond Hall (cl), Billy Kyle (p), Dale Jones (b), Barrett Deems (d), Ella
Fitzgerald (vcl).

Concert, Hollywood Bowl, Los Angeles, August 15, 1956

You won't be satisfied, (ef & la, vcl), Verve EPV5034,
MGV8231, (G)26145, VV20085.
Undecided, (ef, vcl), Verve EPV5033, MGV8231, (G)V90000,
26145.
When the saints go marchin' in, (1), Verve EPV5033,
MGV8231, (F)711051, (G)V90000, VV20085, Metro MS657.
NOTE: (1) Harry Edison, Roy Eldridge (tp), Illinois Jacquet, Flip Phillips
(ts), Herb Ellis (g), Ray Brown (b), added. Although Verve 2615006
is supposed to contain all the Armstrong sides recorded for Verve,
it has an incomplete version of the above 'When the saints'! All
other Verve's are indeed on this 10 LP album.

Ella Fitzgerald & Louis Armstrong: Louis Armstrong (tp, vcl), Oscar Peterson (p), Herb Ellis (g), Ray Brown (b), Buddy Rich (d), Ella Fitzgerald (vcl).

Los Angeles, August 18, 1956

20207-2	**They can't take that away from me**, Verve EPV5014, MGV4003, (Swed) EPV5007.
20208-8	**Isn't it a lovely day?**, Verve EPV5012, MGV4003, (Swed) EPV5008.
20209-5	**Tenderly**, Verve EPV5012, MGV4003, (Swed) EPV5007, Metro MS657.
20210	**Stars fell on Alabama**, Verve EPV5015, MGV4003, (Swed) EPV5006.
20211-5	**Cheek to cheek**, Verve EPV5012, MGV4003, (Swed) EPV5006.
20212-1	**Under a blanket of blue**, Verve EPV5015, MGV4003,(Swed) EPV5008, HMV7 EG8280.
20213-7	**Moonlight in Vermont**, Verve EPV5015, MGV4003, (Swed) EPV5008, HMV7 EG8280.
20214-6	**A foggy day**, Verve EPV5015, MGV4003, (Swed) EPV5006.
20215-6	**April in Paris**, Verve EPV5013, MGV4003, (Swed) EPV 5008, Metro MS567.
20216-1	**The nearness of you**, Verve EPV5007, MGV4003, (Swed) EPV5007.
20222-2	**Can't we be friends**, Verve 2015, 10023, MGV4003, (Du) EPV5046, (Swed) EPV5008. HMV7 EG8280.

Vcl acc by Buddy Bregman's Orchestra.

Los Angeles, August 21, 1956

20221	**The silent treatment**, Verve MGV2036.

ELLA FITZGERALD

Prob. same pers as above Buddy Bregman's Orchestra.

Los Angeles, August 1956
     A ship without a sail, Verve MGV4022, 4002-2
     Have you met Miss Jones?, –, –.
     You took advantage of me, –, –.
     The lady is a tramp, –, –.
     Johnny One Note, –, –.
     I wish I were in love again, –, –.
     Spring is here to stay, –, –.
     This can't be love, –, –.
     Where or when, –, –.
     Little girl blue, –, –.
     It never entered my mind, –, –.
     Bewitched, MGV4023, –.
     Mountain greenery, –, –.
     Wait till you see her, –, –.
     Ten cents a dance, –, –.
     My heart stood still, –, –.
     I've got five dollars, –, –.
     Lover, –, –.
     Isn't it romantic, –, –.
     Blue moon, –, –.
     Here in my arms, –, –.
     To keep my love alive, –, –.
     Thou swell, –, –.
     Dancing on the ceiling, –, –.
     Blue room, –, –.
     Everything I've got, –, –.
     I could write a book, –, –.
     My funny Valentine, –, –.
     Manhattan, –, –.
     With a song in my heart, –, –.
     Give it back to the Indians, –, –.
     I didn't know what time it was, –, –.
     My romance, –, –.
     There's a small hotel, –, –.
NOTE: The entire session also on Verve (F)2610044.

Ella Fitzgerald (vcl) acc by Stuff Smith (vln), Ben Webster (ts), Paul Smith (p), Barney Kessell) (g), Joe Mondragon (b), Alvin Stoller (d).

Los Angeles, September 4 or 16, 1956

20252-4   **I let a song go out of my heart**, Verve MGV4009-2.
20253-1   **Rocks in my bed**, MGV4008-21.
20254-3   **Cotton tail**, –.
20255-1   **Just squeeze me**, –.
20256-4   **Do nothin' till you hear from me**, –.
20257-6   **Solitude**, (only g acc), –.
20258-2   **Sophisticated lady**, –.
20259-1   **Just a-sittin; and a-rockin'**, –.
20260-4   **It don't mean a thing**, –.
20261-1   **Prelude to a kiss**, MGV4008-2.
20262-3   **Don't get around much anymore**, –.
20263   **Satin doll**, MGV4009-2.
               Azure, (g acc only), –.
               In a sentimental mood, (g acc only), MGV4009-2.

Vcl acc by Russ Garcia's Orchestra: no details.

Los Angeles, January 20, 1957

20575   **Hear my heart**, Verve 10031.
20576   **Hotta chocolata**, –.

Vcl with Duke Ellington and his Orchestra: Cat Anderson, Dizzy Gillespie (tp), Johnny Hodges (as), Jimmy Hamilton (cl, ts), John Sanders (tb), Duke Ellington, Billy Strayhorn (p), Jimmy Woods (b), Sam Woodyard (d).

New York, June 24, 1957

21033   **Day dream**, (ef, vcl), (1), Verve MGV4008-2, Bar 80102.
21034-6   **Take the 'A' train**, (ef, vcl, 2), –, –.
Ella Fitzgerald (vcl) added.

New York, June 25, 1957

21036   **Everything but you**, (ef, vcl), Verve MGV4009-2, Bar 80105.
21037   **I got it bad**, (ef, vcl), –, –.
21038   **Drop me off at Harlem**, (ef, vcl), MGV4008-2, 80102.
21039   **Lost in meditation**, (ef, vcl), –, –.
21040   **I ain't got nothin' but the blues**, (ef, vcl), –, –.

ELLA FITZGERALD

Ella Fitzgerald with Duke Ellington Orchestra.

New York, June 26, 1957

21049	**Clementine**, (ef, vcl), Verve MGV4008-2, Bar 80102.
21050	**Lush life**, (ef, vcl), (unissued).
21051	**I'm beginning to see the light**,(ef, vcl),(1), –, –.
21052	**I didn't know about you**, (ef, vcl), (1), –, –.
21053	**Rockin' in rhythm**, (ef, vcl), (1), –, –.
	I'm just a lucky so and so, (ef, vcl), MGV4009-2, 80105.

Ella Fitzgerald with Duke Ellington Orchestra: Billy Strayhorn (p-1).

New York, June 27, 1957

21064	**Caravan**, (ef, vcl), Verve MGV4008-2, Bar 80102.
21065	**Bli-blip**, (ef, vcl), MGV4009-2,80105.
21066	**Chelsea bridge**, (ef, vcl), –, –.
21067	**Perdido**, (ef, vcl), MGV4008-2, 80102.
	All too soon, (ef, vcl), MGV4009-2, 80105.
	The 'B' and 'D' blues, (ef, vcl), –.

Vcl acc by Don Abney (p), Wendell Marshall (b), Jo Jones (d).

Newport Jazz Festival, July 4, 1957

	This can't be love, Verve MGV8234.
	I got it bad, –.
	Body and soul, –.
	April in Paris, –.
	I've got a crush on you, –.
	Airmail special, –.
	I can't give you anything but love, –.

Louis Armstrong and Ella Fitzgerald: Louis Armstrong (tp, vcl), Oscar Peterson (p), Herb Ellis (g), Ray Brown (b), Louis Bellson (d), Ella Fitzgerald (vcl).

Los Angeles, July 22 & 23, 1957

21132	**Love is here to stay**, (la, ef, vcl), Verve MGV4006-2, MGV4018, (Du)EPV5054, (Swed) VEP5038. HMV 7EG8436.
21133	**Learning the blues**, (la, ef, vcl), Verve MGV4006-2, MGV4018, (Du) EPV5053, (Swed) VEP5037.
21134	**Autumn in New York**, (la, ef, vcl), Verve MGV4006-1, MGV4017, (Du) EPV5049, Metro (S), 601.
21135	**Let's call the whole thing off**, (la, ef, vcl), Verve MGV4006-2, MGV4018, (Du) EPV5053, (Swed) VEP5037.
21136	**They all laughed**, (1) (la, ef, vcl), Verve MGV4006-1, MGV4017, (Du) EPV5050, (Swed) VEP5038, Metro M(S)601.
21137	**Gee baby ain't I good to you**, Verve MGV4006-1, MGV4017, (Du) EPV5051, (Swed) VEP5038, Metro M(S)601.
21138	**Stompin' at the Savoy**, (la, ef, vcl), Verve MGV4006-1, MGV4017, (Du) EPV5050, (Swed) VEP5036, Metro M(S)601.

NOTE: (1) Louis Armstrong does not play tp.

Vcl acc by Oscar Peterson (p), Herb Ellis (g), Ray Brown (b), Louie Bellson (d).

Los Angeles, July 23, 1957

21141   **Ill wind**, Verve MGV4018.
              These foolish things, –.
              Comes love, MGV4017.

Frank De Vol's Orchestra: no details.

Los Angeles, July 24, 1957

21163   **Moonlight in Vermont**, Verve MGV4034.
21164   **Stairway to the stars**, –.
21166   **A-tisket, a-tasket**, MGV4063.
21169   **Goody goody**, –.
21170   **St Louis blues**, –.
              Moonlight becomes you, –.
              You turned the tables on me, –.
              Gipsy in my soul, –.

Louis Armstrong and Ella Fitzgerald: same as before with Ella Fitzgerald (vcl) added.

Los Angeles, August 13, 1957

21267-6   **I won't dance**, (1 & ef, la vcl), Verve MGV4006-1,
              MGV4017, (Du) EPV5054, (Swed) VEP5036, Metro M(S)601.
21268-5   **A fine romance**, (la, ef, vcl), Verve MGV4006-2, MGV4018,
              (Du) EPV5054, (Swed) VEP5038, HMV 7EG8486.
21269-9   **Don't be that way**, (1, ef & la, vcl), Verve MGC4006-1,
              MGV4017, (Du) EPV5049, Metro M(S)510, M(S)601, Adria
              655043.
21270-7   **I'm puttin' all my eggs in one basket**, (la, ef, vcl), Verve
              MGV4006-2, MGV4018, (Du) EPV5052, (Swed) EPV5037.
21271-12   **I've got my love to keep me warm**, (ef, la, vcl), Verve
              MGV4006-2, MGV4018, (Du) EPV5051, (Swed) EPV5036.
NOTE: (1) Louis Armstrong does not play tp. Three more titles without
        Louis were recorded on the above session dates 'Comes love', 'Ill
        wind', and 'These foolish things'.

Louis Armstrong and Ella Fitzgerald acc by strings, p, g, b and d.

Los Angeles, August 8, 1957

21290-2 **Summertime**, (la, ef, vcl), Verve MGV4011, HMV 7EG8489, (Du) EPV5098, (Swed) VEP5055, MGVS-6040.

21291-6 **Bess you is my woman**, (la, ef, vcl) Verve MGV4011, HMV 7EG8490, (Du) EPV5099, (Swed) VEP5056, MGVS-6040.

21292-10 **I got plenty o' nuttin'** (la, ef, vcl), Verve MGV4011, (Du) EPV5099, (Swed) VEP5056, HMV 7EG8489.

21293-2 **It ain't necessarily so** (la, ef, vcl), Verve MGV4011, (Du) EPV5098, (Swed) VEP5055, MGVS-6040, HMV 7EG8490.

21294-6 **There's a boat that's leaving soon for New York**, (la, ef, vcl), Verve MGV4011, (Du) EPV5115, MGVS-6040.

21295-9 **A woman is a sometime thing**, (la, vcl), Verve MGV4011, (Du) EPV5115, MGVS-6040.

21296-9 **Oh Lord I'm on my way**, (la & choir, vcl), Verve MGV4011, (Du) EPV5098, (Swed) VEP5055, MGVS6040.

21298 **Bess oh where is my Bess** (la, vcl), Verve MGV4011.

Vcl acc by Russ Garcia's Orchestra: no details.

Los Angeles, August 18, 1957

21360 **I want to stay here**, Verve MGV4011-2.
21361 **My man's gone now**, –.
21362 **What you want with Bess**, –.
21363 **Buzzard song**, –.
21364 **Oh doctor Jesus**, –.
21365 **Here comes de honeyman**, (medley), –.
21366 **Strawberry woman**, (medley), –.

Duke Ellington and his Orchestra: Quentin Jackson (tb), replaces Henderson and Billy Strayhorn (p, talking), added (1), Duke Ellington (p, talking) on (2).

New York, August, 1957

Portrait of Ella Fitzgerald: Verve MGV4009-2, Bar 80105, HMV CLP1227/1228, VSP SVSP57024.
1. **Royal ancestry** (2).
2. **All heart** (2).
3. **Beyond category** (2).
4. **Total jazz** (1, 2).

Vcl acc by Oscar Peterson (p), Herb Ellis (g), Ray Brown (b), Jo Jones (d).

'Chicago Opera House', October 19, 1957

> **Don't cha go way mad**, Verve MGV8264.
> **It's all right with me**, –.
> **Bewitched**, –.
> **These foolish things**, –.
> **Ill wind**, –.
> **Goody goody**, Verve MGV8264.
> **Moonlight in Vermont**, –.

Vcl acc by Roy Eldridge (tp), Jay Jay Johnson (tb), Sonny Stitt (as), Lester Young (ts), Illinois Jacquet, Coleman Hawkins, Stan Getz, Flip Phillips (ts), Oscar Peterson (p), Herb Ellis (g), Ray Brown (b), Connie Kay (d).

'Philharmonic Hall', Los Angeles, October 25, 1957

> **Stompin' at the Savoy**, Verve MGV8264.
> **Lady be good**, –.

Ella (vcl) acc by Ben Webster (ts), Oscar Peterson (p), Herb Ellis (g), Ray Brown (b), Alvin Stoller (d).

Los Angeles, October 26, 1957

> **Mood indigo** (bw out), Verve MGV4009-1.
> **In a mellow tone**, –.
> **Love you madly**, –.
> **Lush life** (op only), –.
> **Squatty roo**, –.

Vcl acc by Paul Weston's Orchestra: Stan Getz (ts) + others.

Los Angeles, October, 1957

21732	**What will I tell my heart**, Verve MGV4004.
	There's a lull in my life, –.
	More than you know, –.
	I never had a chance, –.
	Close your eyes, –.
	We'll be together again, –.
	Then I'll be tired of you, –.
	Like someone in love, –.
21738	**Midnight sun**, –.
	You're blasé, –.
	I thought about you, –.
	Night wind, –.
	What's new, –.
	How long has this been going on?, –.
	Hurry home, –.

Vcl acc by Paul Weston's Orchestra: prob similar to above.

Los Angeles, March 16 & 18, 1958

22119	**Isn't this a lovely day**, Verve MGV4031, MGV4019-2.
22120	**All by myself**, MGV4030, –.
22121	**Let's go slummin' on Park Avenue**, MGV4031, –.
22122	**I'm puttin' all my eggs in one basket**, –, –.
22123	**Always**, –, –.
22124	**I used to be colorblind**, MGV4030, –.
22125	**You can have him**, –, –.
22126	**How's chances**, MGV4031, –.
22127	**No strings (I'm fancy free)**, –, –.
22128	**You keep coming back like a song**, –, –.
22129	**Summertime**, –, –.
22130	**How deep is the ocean**, MGV4030. –.
22131	**You're laughing at me**, –, –.
22132	**Russian lullaby**, –, –.
22133	**Change partners**, MGV4031, –.
22134	**Now it can be told**, –, –.
22135	**How about me**, MGV4030, –.
22136	**Get thee behind me Satan**, –, –.
22137	**Reaching for the moon**, MGV4031, –.
22138	**I've got my love to keep me warm**, –, –.
22139	**Heat wave**, –, –.
22140	**Cheek to cheek**, MGV4030, –.
22141	**The song is ended**, MGV4031, –.
22142	**Blue skies** (1), Playboy PB1958-2, Verve 4036.
22143	**Lazy**, Verve MGV4030, MGV4019-2.
22144	**Let's face the music and dance**, –, –.
22145	**It's a lovely day**, MGV4031, –.
22146	**Puttin' on the Ritz**, MGV4030, –.
22147	**Remember**, Verve MGV4030, MGV4019-2.
22148	**Alexander's ragtime band**, –, –.
22149	**Let yourself go**, –, –.
22150	**Top hat white tie and tails**, –, –.
22151	**Teach me to cry**, 10130.
22152	**Swingin' shepherd blues**, –.

NOTE: (1) The accompaniment of matrix 22142 includes Harry Edison, although this is Paul Weston's Orchestra. The personnel has been changed during the different recordings of the songs.

Vcl acc by Lou Levy (p), Max Bennett (b), Gus Johnson (d), Dick Hyman (org-l).

New York, c. 1958

22290   **Travelin' light**, Verve 10143.
22291   **Your red wagon** (1), –, MGV8320.

Vcl acc by Nelson Riddle's Orchestra: no details.

Los Angeles, November 1958

22525   **He loves and she loves**, Verve MGV4027, 4029-5.
              Bidin' my time, MGV4026, –.
              Aren't you glad we did?, –, –.
              You've got what gets me, MGV4027, –.
              I can't be bothered now, MGV4028, –.

Vcl acc by Marty Paich's Dektette: Don Fagerquist, Al Porcino (tp), Bob Enevoldsen (vtb, ts), Vince DeRosa (fhr), John Kitzmiller (tu), Bud Shank (as), Bill Holman (ts), Med Flory (bar), Lou Levy (p), Joe Mondragon (b), Mel Lewis (d), Marty Paich (arr, cond).

Los Angeles, November 22 & 23, 1958

22563   **You hit the spot**, Verve MGV4021.
22564   **Blues in the night**, –.
22565   **What's your story morning glory**, –.
22566   **Just you just me**, –.
22567   **My kinda love**, –.
22568   **If I were a bell**, –.
22569-3   **Teardrops from my eyes**, –.
22570   **You're an old smoothie**, –.
22571   **As long as I live**, –.
22572   **Knock me a kiss**, –.
22573   **Gotta be this or that**, –.
22574   **720 in the books**, –.
22575   **Moonlight on the Ganges**, –.
22576-4   **Oh what a night for love**, –.
22577-2   **Little jazz**, –.
22578   **Little white lies**, –.
22579   **You brought a new kind of love**, –.
22580-1   **Dreams are made for children**, 10158.

Vcl acc by Frank De Vol Orchestra: Harry Edison (tp), plus 4 other tp, 4 tb, 5 reeds, p, g, b and d.

Los Angeles, November 24, 1958

22581-1	**East of the sun**, Verve MGV4032.
22582-4	**Lullaby of Broadway**, –.
22583-2	**Let's fall in love again**, –.
22584-4	**I remember you**, –.
22585-3	**Sweet and lovely**, –.
22586-1	**Can't we be friends**, –.
22587-7	**Out of this world**, –.
22588-1	**Makin' whoopee**, –.

Vcl acc by Nelson Riddle's Orchestra: Don Fagerquist (tp), Bob Cooper (tb), Alvin Stoller (d) plus others and string section.

Los Angeles, 1959

22617-5	**Soon**, Verve MGV4026.
22618-8	**I got rhythm**, –.
22619-3	**Our love is here to stay**, –.
22620-9	**They can't take that away from me**, –.
22621-2	**How long has this been going on?**, Verve MGV4024, MGV4029-5.
22622-3	**A foggy day**, MGV4026, –.
22623-5	**The man I love**, –, –.
22624	
22625	
22626-5	**I've got beginners luck**, MGV4024, –.
22627	
22628-3	**Slap that bass**, MGV4027, –.
22629-3	**Clap hands here comes Charlie**, MGV4026, –.
22630	
22631-6	**That certain feeling**, MGV4025, –.
22632-5	**Embraceable you**, MGV4028, –.
22633-3	**I've got a crush on you**, MGV4026, –.
22634-2	**But not for me**, MGV4024, –.
22635-9	**Lady be good**, –, –.

Ella Fitzgerald (vcl) with unknown acc.

Los Angeles

22749-5	**This can't be love**, Verve MGV4026, MGV4029-5.
22750-5	**Of thee I swing**, MGV4026, –.
22751-4	**I was doing all right**, MGV4027, –.
22752-6	**Funny face**, MGV4028, –.
22753-6	**Fascinating rhythm**, –, –.

Ella Fitzgerald (vcl) with unknown acc.

22763-6	**I'm thru with love**, Verve MGV4034, MGV4029-5.
22768-4	**My one and only love**, MGV4024, –.
22769-2	**Someone to watch over me**, MGV 4025, –.
22770-2	**Nice work if you can get it**, MGV4024, –.
22771-3	**Love walked in**, MGV4027, –.
22772-10	**But not for me**, MGV4024, –.
22773-5	**Let's call the whole thing off**, –, –.
22774-6	**Lookin' for a boy**, MGV4025, –.
22775-10	**Lorelei** (Nelson Riddle Orch), MGV4028, –.
22776-3	**Let's kiss and make up**, –, –.
22777-6	**They all laughed**, MGV4025, –.

Ella Fitzgerald (vcl) acc by Russ Garcia's Orchestra.

Los Angeles, late 1959

22892-6	**Like young**, Verve MGV4036.
22893	
22894-4	**Beat me daddy eight to the bar**, MGV4036.
22895-4	**The Christmas song**, 10182.
22896-4	**The secret of Christmas**, –.
	Cool breeze, MGV4036.

Vcl acc by Frank De Vol's Orchestra: no details.

Los Angeles, July 11, 1959

26413-5	**My old flame**, Verve MGV4032.
26414-2	**Gone with the wind**, –.
26415-8	**That old feeling**, –.
26416	
26417-2	**Moonlight serenade**, –.
26418-3	**You make me feel so young**, MGV4036.

Vcl acc by Nelson Riddle's Orchestra: Don Fagerquist (tp), Bob Cooper (ts), Alvin Stoller (d) plus strings and other musicians.

Los Angeles, July 1959

26433-7	**Shall we dance**, Verve, MGV4027,MGV4029-5.
26434-3	**That certain feeling**, MGV4026, –.
26435-7	**What love has done to me**, MGV4028, –.
26436-7	**Boy wanted**, MGV4026, –.
26437-3	**Half of it dearie blues**, MGV4027, –.
26438-6	**'S Wonderful**, Verve MGV4025, MGV4029-5.
26439-3	**Who cares**, MGV4025, –.
26440-8	**Treat me rough**, MGV4027, –.
26441-3	**Strike up the band**, MGV4026, –.
26442-12	**Sam and Delilah**, MGV4024, –.
26443-3	**By Strauss**, MGV4025, –.
26444-11	**My cousin from Milwaukee**, –, –.
26445-9	**Things are looking up**, MGV4024, –.
26446-5	**Stiff upper lip**, MGV4026, –.
26447-12	**Oh so nice**, MGV4028, –.
26448-5	**Just another rhumba**, MGV4024, –.
26449-6	**Somebody from somewhere**, MGV4025, –.
26450-4	**Love is sweeping this country**, MGV4027, –.
26451-6	**For you for me forevermore**, MGV4026,–.
26452-6	**Are not you friends**, –, –.
26453-4	**Isn't it a pity**, MGV4027, –.
26454-6	**My real American folk song**, MGV4025, –.

Vcl acc by Frank de Vol Orchestra.

Hollywood, 1960

You go to my head, Verve MGV4034.
Willow weep for me, –.
Spring will be a little late this year, –.
Everything happens to me, –.
Lost in a fog, –.
I've grown accustomed to his face, –.
I'll never be the same, –.
So rare, –.
Tenderly, –.
Somebody loves me, MGV4036.
Cheerful little earful, –.

Ella Fitzgerald (vcl), acc by Paul Smith (p), Jim Hall (g), Wilfred Middlebrooks (b), Gus Johnson (d).

'Deutschland-Hallen', Berlin, February 13, 1960

26607	**Gone with the wind**, Verve MGV4041.
26608	**Misty**, –.
26609	**The lady is a tramp**, –.
26610	**The man I love**, –.
26611	**Summertime**, –.
26612	**Too darn hot**, –.
26613	**Lorelei**, –, MGV4063.
26614	**Mack the knife**, –.
26615	**How high the moon**, –.

Vcl acc by Frank de Vol's Orchestra.

Los Angeles, 1960

26717	**Santa Claus**, Verve MGV4042.
26718	**Jingle bells**, –.
26719	**Frosty the snowman**, –.
26722	**Rudolf the red nosed reindeer**, –.
26723	**Good morning blues**, –.
26724	**Winter wonderland**, –.
26725	**Let it snow**, –.
26726	**What are you doing on New Year's eve**, –.
26727	**White Christmas**, –.
26728	**Have yourself a merry Christmas**, –.
26741	**The Christmas song**, Verve MGV4042.
26742	**Sleigh ride**, –.

Ella Fitzgerald (vcl) acc by Paul Smith (p) plus rhythm.

Los Angeles, 1960

Black coffee, Verve MGV4043.
Angel eyes, –.
I cried for you, –.
I can't give you anything but love, –.
Then you've never been blue, –.
I hadn't anyone till you, Verve MGV4043.
My melancholy baby, –.
Misty, –.
September song, –.
One for my baby, –.
Who's sorry now, –.
I'm getting sentimental over you, –.
Reach for tomorrow, –.

Ella Fitzgerald (vcl), acc by Billy May's Orchestra: 4 tp, 3-4 tb, 4-5 saxes, p, g, b, d.

Los Angeles, 1960–61

                  Blues in the night, Verve MGV4057, MGV4046-2.
                  Let's fall in love, –, –.
                  Stormy weather, –, –.
                  Between the devil and the deep blue sea, –, –.
                  My shining hour, –, –.
                  Hooray for love, –, –.
                  This time the dream's on me, –, –.
                  That old black magic, –, –.
                  Ill wind, –, –.
                  I've got the world on a string, –, –.
                  Let's take a walk, –, –.
                  Acc-ent-tchu-ate the positive, –, –.
                  Come rain or come shine, MGV4058, –.
                  When the sun comes out, –, –.
                  As long as I live, –, –.
                  Happiness is a thing called Joe, –, –.
                  It's only a paper moon, –, –.
                  The man that got away, –, –.
                  One for my baby, –, –.
                  It was written in the stars, –, –.
                  Get happy, –, –.
                  I gotta right to sing the blues, –, –.
                  Out of this world, –, –.
                  Over the rainbow, –, –.

Vcl acc by Lou Levy (p), Jim Hall (g), Wilfred Middlebrooks (b), Gus Johnson (d).

Crescendo Club, Hollywood, summer 1961

27036	**You'll have to swing it Mr. Paganini**, Verve MGV4052.
27038	**I've got the world on a string**, –.
27039	**You're driving me crazy**, –.
27040	**Just in time**, –.
27042	**Blue moon**, –.
27044	**This could be the start of something big**, –.
27045	**Baby won't you please come home**, –.
27048	**It might as well be spring**, –.
27049	**Take the 'A' train**, –.
27050	**Stairway to the stars**, –.
27051	**Satin doll**, –.
27075	**Airmail special**, –.

Vcl acc by Nelson Riddle's Orchestra: pers including Ronnie Lang (as).

Los Angeles, 1961

               Don't be that way, Verve MGV4054.
               When your lover has gone, –.
               Love me or leave me, –.
               I hear music, –.
               What am I here for?, –.
               I'm gonna go fishing, –.
               I won't dance, –.
               I only have eyes for you, –.
               The gentleman is a dope, –.
               Mean to me, –.
               Alone together, –.
               Pick yourself up, –.
61VK609   **Call me darling**, Verve 10238.

Ella Fitzgerald (vcl), acc by Lou Levy (p), Herb Ellis (g), Joe Mondragon (b), Stan Levey (d).

Los Angeles, June 22, 23 & 24, 1961

               Cry me a river, Verve MGV4053.
               Clap hands here comes Charlie, –.
               A night in Tunisia, –.
               You're my thrill, –.
               My reverie, –.
               Stella by starlight, –.
               Jersey bounce, –.
               Good morning heartache, –.
               I was born to be blue, –.
               Spring can really hang you up the most, –.
               The music goes round and round, –.
               Signing off, –.
               'Round midnight, –.
               This year's kisses, –.

Vcl acc by Nelson Riddle's Orchestra: 4-5 tp, Ronnie Lang (as) 4-5 saxes, p. g, b, d and vib. plus string section except on titles marked (1).

Los Angeles, 1962

        Sweet and slow, Verve MGV4055.
        Georgia on my mind, (1) –.
        I can't get started, (1) –.
        Street of dreams, –.
        Imagination, –.
        The very thought of you, –.
        It's a blue world, –.
        Darn that dream, (1) –.
        He's funny that way, –.
        I wished on the moon, –.
        It's a pity to say goodnight,
        My one and only love,
        Body and soul,

Ella Fitzgerald (vcl) acc by Knud Jorgensen (p), Jimmy Woode (b), William Schiöpffe (d).

Copenhagen, August 25, 1961

        You'll have to swing it, Verve V90012.
        Ich fühle mich crazy, –.

Vcl acc by Ernie Royal, Taft Jordan (tp), Phil Woods (as), Bill Doggett (org), Gus Johnson (d) plus others.

New York, May 1962

62VK272   **I'll always be in love with you**, Verve MGV4056.
        Rough ridin', –.
        You can depend on me, –.
        Broadway, –.
        Runnin' wild, –.
        Show me the way to get out of this world, –.
        Hallelujah, I love him so, –.
        I can't face the music,
        No moon at all, –.
        Laughing on the outside, –.
        After you've gone, –.

No details, prob. as above or similar.

62VK317   **What is this thing called love**, Verve 10238.

Ella Fitzgerald (vcl) acc by Marty Paich and his Orchestra.

Los Angeles, September 1962

62VK631   **Desafinado**, Verve 10274, MGV4063.
62VK632   **Stardust bossa nova**, -.

Vcl acc by Paul Smith (p), Wilfred Middlebrooks (b), Stan Levey (d).

Crescendo Club, Los Angeles, December 1962

62VK714   **Ol' man Mose**, Verve 10288.
62VK785   **Bill Bailey won't you please come home**, MGV4063.

Vcl acc Count Basie and his Orchestra: Don Rader, Joe Newman, Sonny Cohn, Al Aarons, Fip Ricard (tp), Harry Coker, Benny Powell, Grover Mitchell, Urbie Green (tb), Marshall Royal (as, cal), Eric Dixon, Frank Wess, Frank Foster (as, tx, fl), Charlie Fowlkes (bar), Count Basie (p), Freddie Green (g), Buddy Catlett (b), Sonny Payne (d).

New York, July 16, 1963

63VK501   **Pleasingly plump**, (inst), Verve V10329, MGV(6)8549.
63VK504   **Into each life some rain must fall**, V10305, MGV(6)4061, (E)SS517, VLP(S)9050, VLP9091.

New York, July 16 & 17, 1963

63VK511   **Shiny stockings**, Verve V10305, MGV(6)4061, (E)SS517, VLP(S)9050, VLP9091.
                Dream a little dream of me, (1), Verve MGV(6)4061, (E)VLP(S)9050.
                Them there eyes, (1), −, −.
                Deed I do, −, −.
                Ain't misbehavin', −, −.
                On the sunny side of the street, −, −.
                Satin doll, −, −.
                Honeysuckle rose, −, −.
                Tea for two, −, −.
                I'm beginning to see the light, −, −.
                My last affair, −, −.

NOTE: (1) Joe Newman, Urbie Green, Frank Foster, Count Basie, Freddie Green, Buddy Catlett and Sonny Payne only.

Vcl acc by Nelson Riddle's Orchestra: + strings.

Los Angeles, September, 1963

                Let's begin, Verve MGV4060, (E)SVLP9080.
                A fine romance, –, –.
                All the things you are, –, –.
                I'll be hard to handle, –, –.
                You couldn't be cuter, –, –.
                She didn't say yes, –, –.
                I'm old fashioned, –, –.
                Remind me, –, –.
                The way you look tonight, –, –.
                Yesterdays,–, –.
                Can't help lovin' that man, –,–.
                Why was I born?, –, –.

These are the blues: Ella Fitzgerald (vcl), acc by Roy Eldridge (tp), Wild Bill Davis (org), Herb Ellis (g), Ray Brown (b), Gus Johnson (d).

New York, October 27–28, 1963

63VK675   **See see rider**, Verve MGV4062 (G)2332083.
63VK676   **Trouble in mind**, –, –.
                Jailhouse blues, –, –.
                In the evening (when the sun goes down), –, –.
                You don't know my mind, –, –.
                How long, how long blues, –, –.
                Hear me talking to ya, –, –.
                Cherry Red, –, –.
                Downhearted blues, –, –.
                St. Louis blues, –, –.

Vcl acc by Frank de Vol's Orchestra: horns on (1) Zoot Sims (ts-2, fl-3, vib-4), cel, g, b, d, and bgo on (5) + string section.

New York, March 3–4, 1964

                Miss Otis regrets (4), Verve MGV4064.
                My man (mon homme) (1, 3), –.
                How high the moon (2, 4), –.
                Volare (Nel blu, dipinto di blue), (3, 4), –.
                The thrill is gone (1, 3, 5), –.
                Memories of you (2), –.
                Lullaby of the leaves (2, 4), –.
                Pete Kelly's blues (2, 4), –.
                Call me darling, Verve 58984.

English Orchestra under the leadership of Johnnie Spence (arr, dir) tp's, tb's, reeds, p, g, b, d.

London, April 7, 1964

64VK335	**Can't buy me love**, Verve MGV4064.
64VK336	**Hello Dolly**, –.
	The sweetest sounds, –.
	People, –.

No details.

1964

64VK502	**I've grown accustomed to her face**, Verve, 10337.
64VK518	**Ringo beat**, 10340, 58123.
64VK519	**I'm fallin' in love**, –, –.
	Hernando's hideaway
	If I were a bell
	Warm all over
	Almost like being in love
	Dites moi
64KV660	**I could have danced all night**
	Show me
	No other love
	Steam heat
	Whatever Lola wants
	Guys and dolls
	Somebody somewhere

Ella Fitzgerald (vcl), acc by Roy Eldridge (tp), Tommy Flanagan (p), Bill Yancey (b), Gus Johnson (d).

Jazz Festival, Juan-Les-Pins, France, July 1964

64VK555	**Day in day out**, Barclay GLP3716, Verve MGV4065.
64VK556	**Just a sittin' and a rockin'**, –, –.
64VK557	**The lady is a tramp**, –, –.
64VK558	**Summertime (re out)**, –, –.
64VK559	**St. Louis blues**, –, –.
64VK560	**Honeysuckle rose**, –, –.
	They can't take that away from me, –, –.
	You'd be so nice to come home to, –, –.
	Somewhere in the night (re out), –, –.
	I've got you under my skin, –, –.
	The cricket song, –, –.
	How high the moon, –, –.
	Goody goody, –, –.
	The boy from Ipanema, –.
	Cutie pants, –.

Ella Fitzgerald (vcl) acc by Nelson Riddle's Orchestra: Buddy DeFranco (cl), Willie Smith (as), Paul Smith (p), Frank Flynn (vib) plus others.

Los Angeles, October 20, 1964

Early autumn, Verve MGV4067.
Too marvellous for words, –.
Day in day out, –.
Laura, –.
This time the dreams on me, –.
Skylark, –.
Single O, –.
Something gotta give, –.
Travellin' light, –.
Midnight sun, –.
Dream, –.
I remember you, –.
When a woman loves a man, –.

No details.

65VK399   **She's just a quiet girl**, Verve 10359.
65VK400   **We three**, –.

Vcl acc by Tommy Flanagan (p), Keter Betts (b), Gus Johnson (d).

Musikhalle, Hamburg, March 26, 1965

Walk right in, Verve MGV4069.
That old black magic, –.
Body and soul, –.
Here's that rainy day again, –.
65VK448   **And the angels sing**, –.
65VK508   **A hard day's night**, –.
Ellington medley: Mood indigo
               Do nothin' till you hear from me
               It don't mean a thing
The boy from Ipanema, Verve MGV4069.
Don't rain on my parade, –.
Angel eyes, –.
Smooth sailing, –.
Old McDonald had a farm, –.

Vcl acc by Duke Ellington and his Orchestra on (1) rhythm on (2).

66VK342   **Duke's Place** (2), Verve 10408.
The shadow of your smile, –.

Duke Ellington/Ella Fitzgerald: Duke Ellington and his Orchestra: Cat Anderson, Cootie Williams, Mercer Ellington, Herbie Jones (tp), Lawrence Brown, Chuck Connors, Buster Cooper (tb), Jimmy Hamilton (cl, ts), Russell Procope (as, cl), Johnny Hodges (as), Paul Gonsalves (ts), Harry Carney (bar, cl), Duke Ellington (p), Jimmy Jones (p-1), replacing Duke, John Lamb (b), Louie Bellson (d), Ella Fitzgerald (vcl).

Los Angeles, October 1965

> **A flower is a lovesome thing** (1), Verve (V6)4070.
> **Something to live for,** (1), –.
> **Azure,** –.
> **I like the sunrise,** (1), –.
> **Passion flower,** (1), –.
> **Cotton tail** (1 + de also p), –.
> **Imagine my frustration** (*), –.
> **What am I here for?,** –.
> **Duke's place,** –.
> **The brown-skin gal** (1), –.

NOTE: (*)Original title of Imagine is in fact 'Feelin' kinda blue'.

Vcl acc by Jimmy Jones (p), Jim Hughart (b), Grady Tate (d).

Juan-Les-Pins, July 28–29, 1966

101595	**Jazz samba** (1), Verve MGV4072-2.
101596	**Goin' out of my head,** –.
101597	**How long has this been goin' on?,** –.
101598	**Misty,** –.
101599	**The more I see you,** –.
101600	**Lullaby of Birdland,** –.

NOTE: (1) With Ellington band but above rhythm.

Vcl acc by The Duke Ellington Orchestra: Cootie Williams, Cat Anderson, Herbie Jones, Mercer Ellington (tp), Lawrence Brown, Buster Cooper, Chuck Connors (tb), Jimmy Hamilton (cl, ts), Johnny Hodges, Russell Procope (as), Paul Gonsalves (ts), Harry Carney (bar), Duke Ellington (p), John Lamb (b), Sam Woodyard (d).

Juan-Les-Pins, July 28, 1966

| 101601 | **Mack the Knife**, Verve MGV4072-2. |

Ray Nance (tp, vln, vcl), Ben Webster (ts) added.

Juan-Les-Pins, July 29, 1966

| 101602 | **It don't mean a thing**, Verve MGV4072-2. |
| 101603 | **Just squeeze me,** –. |

Vcl acc by Marty Paich's Orchestra: Harry Edison (tp), Jimmy Rowles (b), Chuck Berghofer (b), Louis Bellson (d), plus others.

Los Angeles, August 1966

100669	**Sweet Georgia Brown**, Verve MGV4071, (E)SVLP9148.
100670	**Whisper not**, –, –.
100671	**I said no**, –, –.
100672	**Thanks for the memory**, –, –.
100673	**Spring can really hang you up the most**, –, –.
100674	**Old McDonald had a farm**, –, –.

Vcl acc by Marty Paich's Orchestra: Stu Williamson (tp), Bill Perkins (ts), Jimmy Rowles (p), Al Viola (g), Joe Mondragon (b), Shelly Manne (d).

Los Angeles, August 1966

100675	**Time after time**, Verve MGV4071, (E)SVLP9148.
100676	**You've changed**, –, –.
100677	**I've got your number**, –, –.
100678	**Lover man**, –, –.
100679	**Wives and lovers**, –, –.
100680	**Matchmaker**, –, –.

Ella Fitzgerald and her Orchestra: prob full Ellington band with Ella's rhythm section: Cootie Williams, Cat Anderson, Mercer Ellington, Herbie Jones (tp), Chuck Connors, Buster Cooper, Lawrence Brown (tb), Jimmy Hamilton (cl, ts), Russell Procope, Johnny Hodges (as), Paul Gonsalves (ts), Harry Carney (b-cl, bar), Jimmy Jones (p), Jim Hughart (b), Ed Thigpen (d).

'The Greek Theatre', Los Angeles, September 14 & 25, 1966

The moment of truth
These boots are made for walking
Stardust
I'm just a lucky so and so (1)

NOTE: (1) small combo (tp) prob. Cat Anderson acc by rhythm only.

1966

These boots are made for walkin', Stateside SS569, SE1044.
Stardust, –, –.
The moment of truth, Stateside SE1044.
I'm just a lucky so and so, –.

No details.

Live, c. 1967

> **Gone with the wind**, Verve V6-8748.
> **The man I love**, –.
> **Summertime**, –.
> **The lady is a tramp**, –.
> **Boy from Ipanema**, –.
> **That old black magic**, –.
> **Just a-sittin' and a-rockin'**, –.
> **They can't take that away from me**, –.
> **I've got you under my skin**, –.
> **Body and soul**, –.
> **St. Louis blues**, –.
> **Stompin' at the Savoy**, –.

Ella Fitzgerald (vcl) acc by Ralph Carmichael Chorus and Orchestra: no details.

Los Angeles, February 1967

56900	**God will take care**, Cap T2685.
56901	**What a friend we have in Jesus**, –.
56902	**God will be with you till we meet again**, –.
56903	**Abide with me**, –.
56904	**In the garden**, –.
56905	**Brighten the corner where you can**, –.
56906	**I shall not be moved**, –.
56907	**Just a closer walk with thee**, –.
56912	**Throw out the lifeline**, Cap T2685.
56913	**The old rugged cross**, –.
56914	**Rock of ages**, –.
56915	**I need thee every hour**, –.
56916	**Let the lower lights be burning**, –.
56917	**The church in the wildwood**, –.

Christmas: Ella Fitzgerald (vcl) prob acc with the same group as above.

Los Angeles, July 19, 1967

57998	**Silent night**, Cap T2805.
57999	**Hark the herald angels sing**, –.
58000	**Angels we have heard on high**, –.
58001	**We three kings**, –.

Los Angeles, July 20, 1967

58006	**O little town of Bethlehem**, Cap T2805.
58007	**Away in a manger**, –.
58008	**It came upon a midnight clear**, –.
58009	**Sleep, my little Lord Jesus**, –.
58010	**Joy to the world**, –.
58011	**O holy night**, –.
58012	**O come all ye faithful**, –.
58013	**God rest ye merry gentlemen**, –.

Los Angeles, July 21, 1967

58033	**The first Noel**, Cap T2805.

Misty blue: Ella Fitzgerald (vcl) acc by Sid Feller Orchestra: no details.

Los Angeles, December 20, 1967

58921	**I taught him everything he knows**, Cap T2888.
58922	**Don't touch me**, –.
58923	**Turn the world around**, –.
58924	**Walking in the sunshine**, –.

Los Angeles, December 21, 1967

58936	**It's only love**, Cap T2888.
58937	**Born to lose**, –.
58938	**The chokin' kind**, –.
58939	**Misty blue**, –.

Los Angeles, December 22, 1967

58944	**Evil on your mind**, Cap T2888.
58945	**Don't let the doorknob hit you**, –.
58946	**This gun don't care**, –.

30 by Ella: Ella Fitzgerald (vcl), acc by Benny Carter's Music: Harry Edison (tp), Benny Carter (as), George Auld (ts), Jimmy Jones (p, celeste), John Collins (g), Bob West (el-b), Panama Francis (d).

Los Angeles, July 1968

59798	**Medley:**	**No regrets**, Cap T2960, (F)STTX340776.
		I've got a feeling I'm falling
		Don't blame me, (inst).
		Deep Purple
		Rain
		You're a sweetheart
59799	**Medley:**	**On Green Dolphin Street**, –, –.
		How am I to know?
		Just friends
		I cried for you
		Seems like old times
		You stepped out of a dream

Louie Bellson (d) replaces Francis.

Los Angeles, July-August 1968

59819	**Medley:**	**If I give my heart to you**, Cap T260, (F)STTX340776.
		Once in a while
		Ebb tide
		The lamp is low
		Where are you
		Think of you
59820	**Medley:**	**My mother's eyes**
		Try a little tenderness
		I got it bad
		Everything I have is yours
		I never knew
		Goodnight my love

Los Angeles, August 1968

59892   **Medley: Candy**, Cap T2960, (F)STTX340776.
                      All I do is dream of you
                      Spring is here, (inst).
                      720 in the books
                      It happened in Monterey
                      What can I say after I say I'm sorry
59893   **Hawaiian war chant**, Cap 2267.
59894   **Medley: Four or five times**, T2960.
                      Maybe
                      Takin' a chance on love, (inst).
                      Elmer's tune at sundown
                      It's a wonderful world

Ella Fitzgerald (vcl), Benny Carter (arr, cond).

New York, 1968

26883   **It's up to me and you**, Cap 2212.

Sunshine of your love: Ella Fitzgerald (vcl), acc by Ernie Heckscher Big Band: pers. incl. Allen Smith (tp), Tommy Flanagan (p, cond), Frank De La Rosa (b), Ed Thigpen (d), Marty Paich, Frank De Vol, Tee Carson and Bill Holman (arr).

'Fairmont Hotel', San Francisco, February/March 1969

                      Hey Jude (pr, arr), MPS 15250ST, BASF 20712.
                      Sunshine of your love (mp, arr), MPS 15250ST, BASF 20712.
                      This girls's in love (fdv, arr), –, –.
                      Watch what happens (tc, arr), –, –.
                      Alright, okay, you win (mp, arr), –, –.
                      Give me the simple life (bh, arr), –, –.

Ella Fitzgerald (vcl), acc by own Trio: Tommy Flanagan (p), Frank De La Rosa (b), Ed Thigpen (d), same place and date.

                      Useless landscape, MPS 15250ST, BASF 20712.
                      Old devil moon, –, –.
                      Don' cha go' way mad, –, –.
                      A house is not a home, –, –.
                      Trouble is a man, –, –.
                      Love you madly, –, –.

NOTE: The above recording was made by Norman Granz during a live performance. The original title on MPS was 'Sunshine of your love' but when BASF bought up the SABA label they released it again under a BASF number and retitled the LP 'Watch what happens'.

Ella: Ella Fitzgerald (vcl), acc by studio band with Richard Perry, Mike Vickers and John Cameron (arr).

London, May 26, 28, 29 & 30, 1969

> **Get ready**, Reprise RS6354.
> **The hunter gets captured by the game**, –.
> **Yellow man**, –.
> **I'll never fall in love again**, –.
> **Got to get you into my life**, –.
> **I wonder why**, –.
> **Open your window**, –.
> **Savoy truffle**, –.
> **Ooh, baby, baby**, –.
> **Knock on wood**, –.

NOTE: The above also on Midi (G)MID4008.

Vcl acc by Orchestra under Dir. of Gerald Wilson (arr, cond), Bobby Bryant, Larry McGuire, Alex Rodriguez, Paul Hubinon, Harry Edison (tp), J. J. Johnson, Jimmy Cleveland, Mike Wimberley, Britt Woodman, Bill Tole, Alexander Thomas, Thurman Green (tb), Arthur Maebe (fhr), Henry de Vega (as), Anthony Ortega, Ernie Watts, William Green (fl, pic), Marshall Royal (as, cl, fl), Harold Land, Ray Bojorquez (ts), Richard Aplanalp (bar), Tommy Flanagan (p), Joe Sample (org, el-p), Vic Feldman/Bobby Hutcherson (vib), Herb Ellis/Dennis Budimir (g), Ray Brown (b), Louie Bellson (d), Modeste Duran, Franzisco de Souza (bgo, cga), Things ain't what they used to be:

Hollywood, 1970

> **Sunny**, Reprise RS6432m 44122.
> **Mas que nada**, –, –.
> **A man and a woman**, –, –.
> **Days of wine and roses**, –, –.
> **Black coffee**, –, –.
> **Tuxedo junction**, –, –.
> **I heard it through the grapevine**, –, –.
> **Don't dream of anybody but me**, –, –.
> **Things ain't what they used to be**, –, –.
> **Willow weep for me**, –, –.
> **Manteca**, –, –.
> **Just when we're falling in love**, –, –.

ELLA FITZGERALD

Ella Fitzgerald (vcl), Tommy Flanagan (p), Frank De Rosa (b), Ed Thigpen (d).

Nice Jazz Festival, July 21, 1971

Night and day, CBS (F)64812.
The many faces of Cole Porter, –.
    Get out of town
    Easy to love
    You do something to me
The ballad medley, CBS (F)64812.
    Body and soul
    The man I love
    Porgy
The bossa scene, –.
    The girl from Ipanema
    Fly me to the moon
    O nosso amor
    Cielito lindo
    Magdalena
    Aqua de beber
Summertime, –.
They can't take that away from me, –.
Aspects of Duke
    Mood indigo
    Do nothin' till you hear from me
    It don't mean a thing
Something, –.
St. Louis blues, –.
Close to you, –.
Put a little love in your heart, –.

Last time: Mercer Ellington, Cootie Williams, Money Johnson, Edward Preston (tp), Malcolm Taylor, Chuck Connors, Booty Wood, James Cheatham, John Coles (tb), Russell Procope, Harold Minerve (as), Harold Ashby (ts, cl), Paul Gonsalves, Norris Turney (ts), Harry Carney (bar), Duke Ellington (p), Wild Bill Davis (org), Joe Benjamin (b), Rufus Jones (d), Nell Brookshire, Ella Fitzgerald (vcl).

Warsaw, Poland, October 30, 1971

> **I'm beginning to see the light**, Poljazz (P)SX0673.
> **Duke's tune**, –.
> **Things ain't what they used to be**, –.
> **Unknown no 1 (+ Hello Dolly)** (mj, vcl), –.
> **La plus belle Africaine**.
> **I got the blues** (nb, vcl).
> **Medley: Sophisticated lady**
>   **Caravan**
> **Satin doll**.
> **Unknown no 2.**
> **Lotus Blossom**.

Vcl acc by Count Basie and his Orchestra: George Minger, Paul Cohen, Sonny Cohn, Waymon Reed (tp), Al Grey, Bill Hughes (tb), Bobby Plater, Curtis Peagler (as, cl), Jimmy Forrest (ts), Eric Dixon (ts, fl), J. C. Williams (bar), Count Basie (p), Freddie Green (g), Norman Keenan (b), Harold Jones (d), Quincy Jones, Marty Paich, Gerald Wilson (arr).

Civil Auditorium, Santa Monica, CA, June 2, 1972

> **You've got a friend** (mp, arr), Pablo PB1000.
> **What's goin' on?** (gw, arr), –.
> **Shiny stockings** (qj, arr), –.
> **Cole Porter medley**, –.
>   **Too darn hot** (mp, arr),
>   **It's all right with me** (mp, arr).
> **Sanford & Son theme** (mp, arr), –.
> **I can't stop lovin' you** (mp, arr), –.

JATP All Stars: Roy Eldridge, Harry Edison (tp), Al Grey (tb), Stan Getz, Eddie Davis (ts), Count Basie (p), Freddie Green (g), Ray Brown (b), Ed Thigpen (d), Ella Fitzgerald (vcl).

Same place and date

> **C jam blues**

Ella Fitzgerald and Cole Porter: Charles Turner, Al Aarons, Carroll Lewis, Shorty Sherock (tp), J. J. Johnson, Bill Watrous, Dick Noel (tb), Christopher Riddle (b-tb), Wilbur Schwartz, Harry Klee (fl), Bill Green, Mahlon Clark (cl), Gordon Schoneberg, Norman Benno (oboe), Bobby Tricarico, Don Christlieb (bar), Paul Smith (p), Ralph Grasso (g), John Heard (b), Louie Bellson (d), Nelson Riddle (arr).

Hollywood, June 9, 1972

        I've got you under my skin, Pablo 2310-814.
        I concentrate on you, –.
        My heart belongs to daddy, –.
        Love for sale, –.
        So near and yet so far, –.
        Down in the depths, –.
        Just one of those things, –.
        I get a kick out of you, –.
        All of you, –.
        Anything goes, –.
        At long last love, Pablo 2310-814.
        C'est magnifique, –.
        Without love, –.

Ella Fitzgerald (vcl), acc by the Count Basie Orchestra plus The Tommy Flanagan Trio: George Minger, Paul Cohen, George Cohn, Waymon Reed (tp), William Hughes, Melvin Wanzo, Frank Hooks, Al Grey (tb), John Williams, Eric Dixon, Jimmy Forrest, Robert Plater, Curtis Peagler (saxes), Count Basie (p), Freddie Green (g), Norman Keenan (b), Harold Jones (d), Tommy Flanagan (p), Frank De La Rosa (b), Ed Thigpen (d).

Palo Alto, August 2, 1972

        Shiny stockings, Pablo 2625701.
        You've got a friend, –.
        What's going wrong, –.

Vcl acc by Tommy Flanagan Trio: same trio as before, same date.

        Spring can really hang you up the most, Pablo 2625701.
        Madalena, –.

Count Basie Orchestra added: same as before, same date.

        The Cole Porter Medley, Pablo 2625701.
            Too darn hot
            It's all right with me
        Sanford & Son theme, –.
        I can't stop lovin' you, –.

Ella Fitzgerald acc by Tommy Flanagan Trio, Count Basie Orchestra plus The Philharmonic All Stars: Roy Eldridge, Harry Edison (tp), Al Grey (tb), Stan Getz, Eddie 'Lockjaw' Davis (ts), Oscar Peterson (p), Freddie Green (g), Ray Brown (b), Ed Thigpen (d), same date.

> **Finale: C jam blues**, Pablo 2625701.
> **At long last love**, Pablo 2310-814.
> **C'est magnifique**, –.
> **Without love**, –.

Take love easy: Ella Fitzgerald (vcl), Joe Pass (g).

1973

> **Take love easy**, Pablo 2310-702.
> **Once I loved**, –.
> **Don't be that way**, –.
> **You're blasé**, –.
> **Lush life**, –.
> **A foggy day**, –.
> **Gee baby ain't I good to you**, –.
> **You go to my head**, –.
> **I want to talk about you**, –.

Newport Jazz Festival/Live at Carnegie Hall: Ella Fitzgerald (vcl), Tommy Flanagan (p), Joe Pass (g), Keter Betts (b), Freddie Waits (d).

Newport Jazz Festival, July 5, 1973

> **I've gotta be me**, Col KG32557.
> **Good morning heartache**, –.
> **Miss Otis regrets**, –.
> **Medley: Don't worry 'bout me** (ef, jp only), –.
>   **These foolish things** (ef, jp only).
> **Any old blues**, –.

Ella Fitzgerald acc by the Chick Webb Orchestra: Taft Jordan, Dick Vance, Francis Williams, Frank Lo Pinto (tp), George Matthews, Al Cobb, Garnett Brown, Jack Jeffers (tb), Eddie Barefield, Chauncy Haughton, Pete Clarke, Arthur Clarke, Bob Ashton, Haywood Henry (reeds), Cliff Smalls (p), Lawrence Lucy (g), Beverly Peer (b), same date.

> **A-tisket, a-tasket**, Col KG32557.
> **Indian summer**, –.
> **Smooth sailing**, –.

Ella Fitzgerald (vcl), Ellis Larkins (p), same date.

> **You turned the tables on me**, –.
> **Nice work if you can get it**, –.
> **I've got a crush on you**, –.

Ella Fitzgerald (vcl), Roy Eldridge (tp), Al Grey (tb), Eddie 'Lockjaw' Davis
(ts), Tommy Flanagan (p), Joe Pass (g), Keeter Betts (b), Freddie Waits (d),
same date.

> **I can't get started**, Col KG32557.
> **The young man with a horn**, –.
> **'Round midnight**, –.
> **Star dust**, –.
> **C jam blues**, –.
> **Medley: Taking a chance on love**, –.
>   **I'm in the mood for love**, –.
>   **Lemon drop**
>   **Some of these days**
>   **People**

Fine and mellow: Ella Fitzgerald (vcl), acc by Clark Terry (tp, flhrn), Zoot
Sims, Eddie 'Lockjaw' Davis (ts), Harry Edison (tp), Tommy Flanagan (p),
Joe Pass (g), Ray Brown (b), Louie Bellson (d).

Los Angeles, January 8, 1974

> **Fine and mellow**, Pablo 2310-829.
> **I'm just a lucky so and so**, –.
> **(I don't stand) A ghost of a chance with you**, Pablo 2310-829.
> **Rockin' in rhythm**, –.
> **I'm in the mood for love**, –.
> **'Round midnight**, –.
> **I can't give you anything but love**, –.
> **The man I love**, –.
> **Polka dots and moonbeams**, –.

In London: Ella Fitzgerald (vcl), Tommy Flanagan (p), Joe Pass (g), Keter
Betts (b), Bobby Durham (d).

'Ronnie Scott's Club', London, April 11, 1974

> **Sweet Georgia Brown**, Pablo 2310-711.
> **They can't take that away from me**, –.
> **Everytime we say goodbye**, –.
> **The man I love**, –.
> **It don't mean a thing**, –.
> **You've got a friend**, –.
> **Lemon drop**, –.
> **The very thought of you**, –.
> **Happy blues**, –.

Ella and Oscar: Ella Fitzgerald (vcl), Oscar Peterson (p).

Los Angeles, May 19, 1975

> **Mean to me**, Pablo 2310-759.
> **How long has this been going on**, –.
> **When your lover has gone**, –.
> **More than you ever know**, –.
> **There's a lull in my life**, –.

Ray Brown (b), added, same date.

> **Midnight sun**, –.
> **I hear music**, –.
> **Street of dreams**, –.
> **April in Paris**, –.

Ella Fitzgerald (vcl), Tommy Flanagan (p), Keter Betts (b), Bobby Durham (d).

Live, Montreux Jazz Festival, July 17, 1975

> **The man I love**, Pablo 2625-707.
> **Caravan**, 2310-751.
> **Satin doll**, –.
> **Wave**, –.
> **Teach me tonight**, –.
> **It's all right with me**, –.
> **Let's do it**, –.
> **How high the moon**, –.
> **The girl from Ipanema**, –.
> **'T'ain't nobody's bizness**, –.

Again: Ella Fitzgerald (vcl), Joe Pass (g).

Los Angeles, February 8, 1976

> **I ain't got nothin' but the blues**, Pablo 2310-772.
> **'Tis autumn**, –.
> **I didn't know about you**, –.
> **You took advantage of me**, –.
> **I've got the world on a string**, –.
> **All too soon**, –.
> **The one I love belongs to somebody else**, –.
> **Solitude**, –.
> **Nature boy**, –.
> **Tennessee waltz**, –.
> **One note samba**, –.
> **My old flame**, –.
> **That old feeling**, –.
> **Rain**, –.

Montreux '77: Ella Fitzgerald (vcl), acc by Tommy Flanagan (p), Keter Betts (b), Bobby Durham (d).

Montreux, July 15, 1977

> **Too close for comfort**, Pablo 2306-206.
> **I ain't got nothin' but the blues**, –.
> **My man**, –.
> **Come rain or come shine**, –.
> **Day by day**, –.
> **Ordinary fool**, –.
> **One note samba**, –.
> **I let a song go out of my heart**, –.
> **Billie's bounce**, –.
> **You are the sunshine of my life**, –.

Ella Fitzgerald (vcl) acc by Nelson Riddle Orchestra: Charles Turner, Al Aarons, Carroll Lewis, Shorty Sherock (tp), J. J. Johnson, Bill Watrous, Dick Noel (tb), Chris Riddle (b-tb), Harry Klee, Wilbur Schwartz (fl), Bill Green, Mahlon Clark (cl), Gordon Schonberg, Norman Benno (oboe), Bob Tricarico, Don Christlieb (bar), Paul Smith (p), Ralph Grasso (g), John Heard (b), Louie Bellson (d), Nelson Riddle (arr, cond).

Los Angeles, February 13, 1978

> **Dream dancing**, Pablo, 2310-814.
> **After you**, –.

Lady time: Ella Fitzgerald (vcl), Jackie Davis (org), Louie Bellson (d).

Los Angeles, June 19 & 20, 1978

> **I'm walkin'**, Pablo 2310-825.
> **All or nothing at all**, –.
> **I never had a chance**, –.
> **I cried for you (now it's your turn to cry over me)**, –.
> **Since I fell for you**, –.
> **And the angels sing**, –.
> **I'm confessin' (that I love you)**, –.
> **Mack the Knife**, –.
> **That's my desire**, –.
> **I'm in the mood for love**, –.

A classy Pair: Ella Fitzgerald sings, Count Basie plays: Ella Fitzgerald (vcl), Pete Minger, Sonny Cohn, Ray Brown, Nolan Smith (tp), Mel Wanzo, Bill Hughes, Booty Wood, Dennis Wilson (tb), Bobby Plater, Danny Turner, Kenny Hing, Eric Dixon, Charlie Fowlkes (saxes), Count Basie (p), Freddie Green (g), John Clayton (b), Butch Miles (d).

Hollywood, February 15, 1979

> **Organ grinder's swing**, Pablo 2312-132.
> **Just a sittin' and a rockin'**, −.
> **My kind of trouble is you**, −.
> **Ain't misbehavin'**, −.
> **Teach me tonight**, −.
> **I'm getting sentimental over you**, −.
> **Don't worry 'bout me**, −.
> **Honeysuckle rose**, −.
> **Sweet Lorraine**, −.

A perfect match: Ella & Basie: Ella Fitzgerald (vcl), acc by Count Basie Orchestra: Pete Minger, Sonny Cohn, Paul Cohen, Ray Brown (tp), Mitchell "Bootie" Wood, Bill Hughes, Mel Wanzo, Dennis Wilson (tb), Bobby Plater, Danny Turner (as), Kenny Hing, Eric Dixon (ts), Charlie Fowlkes (bar), Paul Smith (p), Count Basie (p-l), Freddie Green (g), Keter Betts (b), Mickey Roker (d).

Montreux, July 12, 1979

> **Please don't talk about me when I'm gone**, Pablo 2312-110.
> **Sweet Georgia Brown**, −.
> **Some other spring**, −.
> **Make me rainbows**, −.
> **After you've gone**, −.
> **Round about midnight**, −.
> **Fine and mellow**, −.
> **You've changed**, −.
> **Honeysuckle rose**, −.
> **St. Louis blues**, −.
> **Basella** (1), −.

Digital III at Montreux: Ella Fitzgerald (vcl), Paul Smith (p), Keter Betts (b), Mickey Roker (d) same date.

> **(I don't stand a) Ghost of a chance (with you)**, Pablo D2308223.
> **Flying home**, −.

NOTE: Rest of the above LP see Count Basie and Joe Pass.

Ella Abraca Jobim/Sing the Antonio Carlos Jobim Songbook: Vcl acc by
Clark Terry (tp), Zoot Sims (ts), Toots Thielemans (hca), Terry Trotter,
Mike Lang, Clarence McDonald (keyboards), Joe Pass (el-g), Oscar Castro-
Neves, Paul Jackson, Mitch Holder, Roland Bautiste (g), Abraham Laboriel
(b), Alex Acuna (d), Paulhino Da Costa (perc), Erich Bulling (arr, cond), coll.
pers.

Hollywood, September 17–19, 1980 & March 18–20, 1981

   Somewhere in the hills, Pablo 2630-201.
   The girl from Ipanema, –.
   Dindi, –.
   Off key (Desafinado), –.
   Water to drink (Agua de beber), –.
   Triste, –.
   How insensitive, –.
   He's a Carioca, –.
   A felicidade, –.
   This love that I found, –.
   Dreamer, –.
   Quiet nights of quiet stars (Corcovado), –.
   Bonita, –.
   One note samba, –.
   Wave, –.
   Don't ever go away, –.
   Song of the jet, –.
   Useless landscape, –.

The best is yet to come: Ella Fitzgerald (vcl), acc by Al Aarons (tp), Bill
Watrous (tb), Bob Cooper (ts), Marshall Royal (as), Hubert Laws, Wilbur
Schwartz, Ronnie Lang, Bill Green (fl), David Allen Duke, Gale Robinson,
Joe Meyer, Richard Klein (fhr), Jimmy Rowles (p), Art Hillery (org), Joe Pass
(g), Tommy Tedesco (g-l), Jim Hughart (b), Shelly Manne (d), Jerome
Kessler, Dennis Karmazyn, Christine Ermacoff, Barbara Jane Hunter,
Nancy Stein, Robert L. Martin, Frederick Seykora, Judy Perett (cello),
Nelson Riddle (arr, cond).

Hollywood, February 4–5, 1982

   I wonder where our love has gone (1), Pablo 2312-138.
   Don't be that way, –.
   God bless the child, –.
   You're driving me crazy, –.
   Good-bye (1), –.
   Any old time, –.
   Autumn in New York (1), Pablo 2312-138.
   The best is yet to come, –.
   Deep purple (1), –.
   Somewhere in the night (1), –.

Speak Love: Joe Pass (g), Ella Fitzgerald (vcl).

Hollywood, March 21 & 22, 1982

          Speak low, Pablo D233 0888.
          Comes love, –.
          There's no you, –.
          I may be wrong (but I think you're wonderful), –.
          At last, –.
          The thrill is gone, –.
          Gone with the wind, –.
          Blue & sentimental, –.
          Girl talk, –.
          Georgia on my mind, –.

Nice work if you can get it: Ella Fitzgerald and André Previn do Gershwin: Ella Fitzgerald (vcl), André Previn (p), Niels-Henning Ørsted Pedersen (b).

New York, May 23, 1983

          A foggy day, Pablo Today D2312-140.
          Nice work if you can get it, –.
          But not for me, –.
          Let's call the whole thing off, –.
          How long has this been going on, –.
          Who cares?, –.
          They can't take that away from me, –.
          Medley: I've got a crush on you, –.
                  Someone to watch over me, –.
                  Embraceable you, –.

Ella à Nice: Ella Fitzgerald with Tommy Flanagan (p), Ed Thigpen (d), and Frank De La Rosa (b).

Nice, France, July 21, 1971, Pablo Live 2308-234 p. 1983

          Night and Day
          The Many Faces of Cole Porter
          The Ballad Medley
          The Bossa Scene
          Summertime
          They Can't Take That Away From Me
          Aspects of Duke
          Something
          St. Louis Blues
          Close To You
          Put A Little Love In Your Heart

ELLA FITZGERALD

Stockholm Concert: Ella Fitzgerald (vcl), with Duke Ellington and his Orchestra.

Stockholm, Sweden 1966. Pablo Live: 2308-242

    Imagine My Frustration
    Duke's Place
    Satin Doll
    Something to Live For
    Wives & Lovers
    So danco Samba
    Let's Do It
    Lover Man
    Cottontail

Notes

Chapter 1

1   'Half a Century of Song With the Great "Ella"', *New York Times* (June 15, 1986), p. C1.
2   Interview with Billy Taylor, *Sunday Morning* (CBS-TV, January 13, 1985).
3   'Ella Fitzgerald Plans to Write Her Autobiography,' *Jet* (October 21, 1985), p. 62.
4   Interview on *Essence* (NBC-TV, July 12, 1986).
5   Ibid.
6   Bud Kliment, *Ella Fitzgerald* (New York: Chelsea House, 1988), p. 22.
7   Joe Smith, *Off the Record* (New York: Warner, 1988), p. 14.
8   According to some sources, the first amateur contest she entered was at the Apollo Theater, which later became far better known than the Harlem Opera House.
9   Kliment, p. 18.
10 Ibid.
11 Some sources say the cash prize was $10.
12 According to some sources, it was the Lafayette Theater, but by this time the Lafayette no longer had amateur contests.
13 David Hinckley, 'Ella, The Object of Their Affection,' New York *Daily News* (February 12, 1990), p. 29.
14 'First Lady of Song' (December 1949), p. 41.
15 'She Who Is Ella,' *Time* (November 27, 1984), p. 86.
16 *Essence* interview.
17 'Half a Century of Song with the Great "Ella",' *New York Times* (June 15, 1986), p. 31.

Chapter 2

1   Kliment, p. 31.
2   Garvin Bushell, *Jazz From the Beginning* (Ann Arbor: University of Michigan Press, 1988), p. 101.
3   Duke Ellington, *Music is My Mistress* (New York: Doubleday, 1973), p. 100.
4   *A History of Jazz in America* (New York: Viking, 1952), p. 171.
5   Ellington, ibid.
6   Kliment, p. 36.
7   Sid Colin, *Ella: The Life and Times of Ella Fitzgerald* (London: Elm Tree, 1986), p. 20.
8   Kliment, p. 41.
9   Interview, May 9, 1988.

10   Colin, pp. 27–8.
11   Interview, August 14, 1989.
12   Bushell, p. 102.
13   Interview, August 11, 1989.
14   *Time* (November 27, 1984), p. 91.
15   Interview, May 9, 1988.
16   *Time*, ibid.
17   Nat Shapiro and Nat Hentoff, *Hear Me Talkin' to Ya: The Story of Jazz As Told By the Men Who Made It* (New York: Dover, 1955), pp. 195–6.
18   *Hamp: An Autobiography* (New York: Amistad/Warner, 1989), p. 30
19   Kliment, pp. 45–6.
20   Shapiro and Hentoff, p. 194.
21   Kliment, p. 49.

Chapter 3

 1   Stanley Dance, *The World of Earl Hines* (New York: Scribner's, 1977), p. 257.
 2   Kliment, p. 52.
 3   Schuller, p. 293, n. 27.
 4   Kliment, p. 57.
 5   Interview, August 11, 1989.
 6   Bushell, p. 101.
 7   Ibid., p. 103.
 8   Letter to author from Abe and Harriet Rothstein, April 11, 1989.
 9   Letter to author from E. E. Gariepy, July 6, 1989.
10   Letter to author from Dave Burchfield, April 10, 1989.
11   Interview, April, 14, 1989.
12   Kliment, p. 55.
13   Bushell, p. 101.
14   Kliment, p. 56.
15   Colin, p. 55.

Chapter 4

 1   Interview, August 14, 1989.
 2   Colin, p. 56.
 3   April 1940.
 4   Interview, August 11, 1989.
 5   Ibid.
 6   Colin, p. 58.
 7   Bushell, p. 104.
 8   Interview, August 11, 1989.
 9   Ibid.
10   Ibid.

11 Colin, pp. 60–1.
12 Interview, August 14, 1989.
13 Ibid.
14 Interview, August 11, 1989.
15 Ibid.
16 McDonough, p. 31.
17 Dizzy Gillespie with Al Fraser, *To Be Or Not To Bop* (Garden City, NY: Doubleday, 1979), p. 133.
18 Interview, August 11, 1989.
19 Ibid.
20 Interview, August 14, 1989.
21 Leslie Gourse, *Louis' Children: American Jazz Singers* (New York: William Morrow, 1984), p. 257.

Chapter 5

1 Interview, May 9, 1989.
2 Interview, August 15, 1989.
3 Interview, August 15, 1989.
4 *John Hammond on Record* (New York: Summit Books, 1977), p. 255.
5 Letter to author from Abe and Harriet Rothstein, April 11, 1989.
6 Interview, August 15, 1989.
7 Ibid.
8 Kliment, p. 63.
9 Hammond, p. 273.
10 Interview, May 5, 1990.
11 Ibid.
12 Ibid.
13 Ibid.
14 Ibid.
15 Gillespie, p. 273.
16 Interview, March 8, 1988.
17 Gillespie, Ibid.
18 Stanley Dance, *The World of Count Basie* (New York: Scribner's, 1980), pp. 333–4.
19 Colin, p. 92.

Chapter 6

1 Gillespie, p. 272.
2 Interview, May 8, 1989.
3 Interview, December 8, 1989.
4 John McDonough, 'Jazz: Revisiting Norman Granz,' *Wall Street Journal* (September 5, 1989), p. A12.
5 Colin, p. 102.

6 Kliment, pp. 72–3.
7 'The Jazz Business,' *Time* (March 2, 1953), p. 40.
8 Colin, p. 87.
9 Interview, December 8, 1989.
10 Colin, Ibid.
11 Ibid.
12 Letters to author July 24, 1989, and September 16, 1989.
13 'Ella Admires Bebop But Prefers to Sing Ballads,' *Ebony* (May 1949), p. 46.
14 Jim Haskins, with Kathleen Benson, *Nat King Cole: An Intimate Biography* (Briarcliff Manor, NY: Stein & Day, 1984), p. 118.
15 Interview, August 19, 1989.
16 Letter to author, June 5, 1989.
17 Interview, December 8, 1989.
18 Colin, p. 96.
19 *Vancouver Sun* (August 1, 1989), no page.
20 'Sunday Morning,' CBS-TV (October 1, 1989).
21 Kitty Grime, *Jazz Voices* (New York: Quartet, 1983).
22 Interview, December 8, 1989.

Chapter 7

1 Interview, May 23, 1988.
2 Haskins with Benson, p. 126.
3 *Time* (March 3, 1953), no page.
4 *New York Amsterdam News* (November 17, 1936), no page.
5 Colin, p. 100.
6 Leonard Feather, 'Ella Today (And Yesterday Too),' *Down Beat* (November 18, 1965), p. 22.
7 Interview, May 9, 1989.
8 'Any Style Will Do' (June 7, 1954), p. 82.
9 August 19, 1955.
10 Gillespie, pp. 407–8.
11 Ibid., p. 407.
12 'The Ella Fitzgerald/Norman Granz Songbooks: Locus Classicus of American Song,' *Hi-Fidelity* (March 1980), p. 47.
13 Ibid., p. 48.
14 Smith, p. 15.
15 Source unidentified, clippings file, Schomburg Center for Research in Black Culture.
16 James Goodrich, 'On the Record,' *Tan* (July 1957), pp. 13, 61.
17 Ibid., p. 61.

Chapter 8

1 Smith, p. 18.
2 Letter to author from Victoria Secunda, October 1, 1989.
3 'Ella Fitzgerald, Norway Friend Now Deny They're Married,' *Jet* (August 15, 1957), pp. 20–1.
4 August 24, 1957.
5 Victoria Secunda letter.
6 Gourse, p. 257.
7 John McDonough, 'Pablo Patriarch: The Norman Granz Story Part II,' *Down Beat* (November 1979), p. 35.
8 Ellington, pp. 236–7.
9 'Duke Ellington and Queen Ella' (April 12, 1958), p. 50.
10 Ellington, p. 238.
11 'Music: Gingham and Ginger Ale,' *Good Housekeeping* (February 1958), p. 40.
12 Rufus Blair, 'Audience Appreciation,' *The Afro-American* (February 8, 1958), p. 5; Rufus Blair, 'Ella Fitzgerald Sees "Rock 'n' Roll" Decline,' *The Afro-American* (March 20, 1958), p. 7.
13 'Ella Fitzgerald Talks "Rock 'n' Roll" Vs. Jazz,' *Chicago Defender* (April 5, 1958), no page.
14 Dance, *World of Count Basie*, p. 295.
15 'Ella Fitzgerald Joins Duke Ellington in a Jazz Concert at Carnegie Hall,' (April 7, 1958), no page.
16 Colin, pp. 115–16.
17 Interview, May 9, 1989.
18 'What Ella Does Best,' *Newsweek* (June 23, 1958), p. 67.
19 Hammond, p. 341.
20 'Hot Air,' (April 1972).

Chapter 9

1 Haskins with Benson, p. 156.
2 Ibid.
3 Interview, May 8, 1989.
4 'The Perennial Ella' (March 25, 1961), p. 194.
5 '11,000 Hear Ella Fitzgerald at Forest Hills Stadium' (August 7, 1961), no page.
6 Interview, August 19, 1989.
7 December 13, 1963.
8 McDonough, *Down Beat* (November 1979), p. 31.
9 Interview, July 2, 1989.
10 Ibid.
11 Interview, May 8, 1989.
12 Interview, July 2, 1989.
13 *Jazz: A History* (New York: Norton, 1977), pp. 322–3.

14   Interview, July 2, 1989.
15   Ibid.
16   Colin, p. 126.
17   Feather, p. 23.
18   Letter to author, October 1, 1989.
19   Colin, p. 127.

Chapter 10

 1   Interview, August 19, 1989.
 2   Interview, May 23, 1988.
 3   Interview, May 9, 1988.
 4   Interview, November 23, 1989.
 5   April 1972.
 6   Interview, November 13, 1989.
 7   April 1972.
 8   Ibid.
 9   Jay M. Steinberg and Pat Salvo, 'That Great Jazz Feeling,' *Sepia* (October 1979), p. 57.
10   McDonough, *Down Beat* (November 1979), p. 36.
11   'Ain't But a Few of Us Left,' *Progressive* (September 1982), p. 51.
12   John Chilton and Max Jones, *Louis* (Briarcliff Manor, NY: Stein & Day, 1984), p. 125.
13   Ibid.
14   'Ella, Basie Join Hands in California Stand' (February 1, 1973), p. 11.
15   'Ella Fitzgerald's Solo on "Lemon Drop"' (Oct./Nov. 1987), no page.
16   Steinberg and Salvo, Ibid.
17   April 1972.
18   Steinberg and Salvo, Ibid.
19   'Sinatra, Basie and Ella Fitzgerald Appear for Audience of Old Admirers,' *The New York Times* (September 10, 1975), no page.
20   'A New Jazz Reissue Series from Verve' (May 1977), p. 98.
21   'Jazz,' *Consumer Reports* (October 1976), p. 584.
22   Interview, November 13, 1989.
23   'Jazz: Ella Fitzgerald Wins Ovation' (April 4, 1978), p. C6.
24   Letter to author, April 8, 1989.
25   'Spin Off' (June 26, 1978), no page.

Chapter 11

 1   Arthur Unger, 'JFK Center Tribute: It Was Better on TV,' *Christian Science Monitor* (December 28, 1979), no page.
 2   John Rockwell, 'Half a Century of Song with the Great "Ella",' *New York Times* (June 15, 1986), p. 30.

3   'Ella Fitzgerald and André Previn Do Gershwin,' *Jazz Journal International* (September 1984), no page.
4   'Joe Pass is Surprise Guest of Fitzgerald at Carnegie' (June 24, 1985), no page.
5   'Ella Fitzgerald: Songbird Lives:' *The Wall Street Journal* (May 31, 1990), p. A12.
6   'Ella,' *Esquire* (November 1985), pp. 98–9, 102.
7   David Hinckley, 'Ella, The Object of Their Affection,' New York *Daily News* (February 12, 1990), p. 29.
8   'Caught! An Evening with Ella Fitzgerald,' *Down Beat* (February 1980), pp. 57–8.
9   Interview, November 13, 1989.
10 Ibid.
11 Interview, May 8, 1989.
12 'Ella Fitzgerald, Oscar Peterson (Palladium, London)' (April 22, 1981), p. 178.
13 Bob Greene, 'The Sky's the Limit,' *Esquire* (May 1983), p. 14.
14 'Fitzgerald and Peterson Perform at Wolf Trap,' (August 25, 1986), no page.
15 Interview, November 13, 1989.
16 Mary Ellen Wright, 'Ella Helps F&M Blow Out its 200 Candles,' *Lancaster Sunday News* (June 8, 1987), no page.
17 (June 27, 1989), no page.
18 Interview, November 13, 1989.
19 Interview, August 19, 1989.
20 Interview, May 23, 1988.
21 Interview, August 19, 1989.
22 Ibid.
23 Ibid.
24 'Ella Fitzgerald Plans to Write her Autobiography,' *Jet* (October 21, 1985), p. 62.

Index

Index

Figures in italics refer to captions.

Aarons, Al 162
Abbott and Costello 68
Ahbez, Eden 97
Ali, Bardu 28, 31–2, 33, *48*, 54, 59, 63
Ali Brothers 32
Alix, Mae 27
Allen, David 147
Allen, Red 122
Allen, Steve 116, 117
Anderson, Ernestine 147
Anderson, Ivie 37
Anderson, Marian 172
Andrews Sisters 13, 51
Anthony, Ray 116
Archey, James 64
Arlen, Harold 146
Arlene 146, 147, 160, 178
Armstrong, Louis 14, 42, 49, 82, 103, 108, 109, 115, 116, 126, 128, 133, 154, 158, 163, 164, 180
Armstrong, Lucille 158
Ashby, Irving 109
Ashton, Bob 164

Bailey, Mildred 45, 55
Bailey, Pearl 115, 116
Barefield, Eddie 63–4, 71, 72, 154, 156, 164
Barksdale, Everett 108
Barnet, Charlie 110
Basie, Count 37, 55, 74, 101, 124, 125–6, 137, 144, 156, 162, 164, 166, 167, 173, 177
Bates, Peg-Leg 63, 78
Bauza, Mario 45, 47, *48*
Beason, Bill 54, 59, 66, 72

Beatles 148, 149
Bechet, Sidney 64
Belafonte, Harry 116, 144
Bellison, Louie 162, 165
Bennett, Max 138
Bennett, Tony 144
Benno, Norman 162
Benny Goodman Quartet 44
Benny Goodman Story, The 121–2
Berg, Billy 69, 80, 94
Berliner, Dr Miller 163
Bernstein, Leonard 144
Berry, Chuck 135
Betts, Keter 158, 160, 170, 178, 179, 181, 182
Bill Haley and His Comets 135, 137
Billy May's Orchestra 146
Bladid Jazz 116
Blowers, Johnny 108
Blue Rhythm 116
Bob Haggart and His Orchestra 88
Booker, George 27
Bookspan, Martin 167
Boone, Pat 135
Boswell, Connee 13, 21, 23
Boswell, Helvetia 13
Boswell, Martha 13
Boswell Sisters 13, 22, 23, 25
Bradshaw, Tiny 27
Brady, Floyd 64
Bregman, Buddy 123, 126
Brice, Fannie 22
Bricktop 123
Brown, Alice 186
Brown, Garnett 164
Brown, Jasbo 'Jas' 15

Brown, Ralph   79, 126
Brown, Ray   85, 88, 90, 92, 93, 95, 96, 98, 99, *102*, 104, 105, 108–12, 116, 118, 124, 158, 160, 162, 165, 167, 175
Brown, Ray, Jr   101, 111, 116, 144, 145, 152, 163, 186
Brubeck, Dave   144
Bruce, Marian *see* Logan, Marian
Bryant, Willie   62
Buchanan, Charles   17, 33, 58, 62
Buddy Bregman's Orchestra   122
Burns, Dave   86
Bushell, Garvin   28, 32, 35, 47, 49, 54, 59, 63
Byrd, Eddie   82

Cab Calloway and the Missourians   17
Cagney, James   173
Calloway, Cab   47, 53, 54, 64, 65, 71, 74, 184
Carter, Benny   23, 24, 25, 30, 65, 155, 184, 185
Carter, Jimmy   172–3
Carter, Roselyn   173
Carver, Wayman   *48*, 59
Cavallo, Pete   160
Charles Singers   108
Charleston Bearcats   17
Charlie Johnson's Paradise Band   18
Chick Webb Orchestra   156
  becomes resident at Savoy   31
  Linton featured singer of   32
  height of popularity   47, 49
  first trip to West Coast   53
  tours the South   54

becomes Ella Fitzgerald and Her Famous Orchestra   58
resuscitated   164
Christian, Charlie   83
Christlieb, Don   162
Clark, Mahlon   162
Clarke, Arthur   164
Clarke, Kenny   72
Clark, Pete   43, 64, 164
Clinton, Larry   51
Clooney, Rosemary   107, 108, 116
Cobb, Al   164
Cohen, Sidney   22, 23
Cole, Nat King   69, 75, 97, 98, 105, 134–7, 139, 142, 144, 153
Coles, Honi   184
Colin, Sid   100, 137
Comfort, Joe   153
Corinne, Kitty   111
Count Basie Orchestra   163, 167, 175, 177, 180
Crawford, Jimmy   108
Crosby, Bing   45, 109, 134, 176
Crosby, Bob   74

Dankworth, Johnny   110
Dave Barbour's Orchestra   108
Dave Brubeck Quartet   124
Davis, Bill   82
Davis, Eddie (Lockjaw)   164, 165
Davis, Miles   139, 176
Davis, Sammy, Jr   144
Dawn, Dolly   13
Day, Pam   170–71
De Rosa, Frank   160
Dee, Kool Moe   176
Delta Rhythm Boys   81
Dial, Harry   82
Diddley, Bo   135
Dixon, Ike   18
Doggett, Bill   78–9, 81, 108

Dorsey, Jimmy 45
Douglass, Bill 152
Duke Ellington and His
 Orchestra 18, 34, 39,
 155
Duncan Mayor's Savoy
 Bearcats 17
Dupree, Rich 78
Durante, Jimmy 144

Eckstine, Billy 78, 85, 98,
 105, 115, 116, 170–71
Eddie Condon's Orchestra 124
Edison, Harry 105, 122, 162,
 165, 185
Eldridge, Roy 118, 137, 162,
 164, 177
Ella Fitzgerald and Her Famous
 Orchestra 58, 59, 60, 65,
 66, 67, 70, 71
Ella Fitzgerald and Her Savoy
 Eight 44, 45
Ellington, Edward Kennedy
 'Duke' 16, 24, 30, 31, 39,
 74, 79, 101, 115, 126, 132,
 133, 137, 142, 153, 156,
 158, 164, 165, 176
Ellington, Mercer 101
Ellis, Herb 109, 126, 127, 146,
 153
England, Leon 39

Faubus, Governor Orval 139
Feather, Leonard 152
Feldman, Al (later Van
 Alexander) 50
Fess Williams and His
 Royal Flush Orchestra
 17, 18, 28
Fields, Dorothy 22
Fields, Gracie 100
Fields, Sidney 72
Fishkin, Arnold 108
Fitzgerald, Ella;
 voice 10, 11, 23, 26, 36, 37,
 100, 107, 118, 164, 171,
 174, 176, 180
 style 10–11, 23, 33, 35–6,
 97, 100, 150
 birth 11
 at school 12, 13–14
 and racism 12, 42, 44,
 117–19, 120, 121, 146
 favourite black singers 13
 cursory musical
 education 14
 influences 14
 appearance 14, 18, 26, 33,
 34, 36, 52–3, 88, 100,
 106, 108, 134, 138,
 180
 enjoys jazz dancing 14–15
 visits Harlem clubs 16
 as sidewalk entertainer 18,
 20
 amateur contest at Harlem
 Opera House 21–2
 audition with Fletcher
 Henderson 23–5
 and mother's death 25, 26
 and orphanage legend 25–6
 drops out of school 26
 first professional
 engagement 27
 gig at Yale 33
 becomes Webb's girl
 singer 34
 first recording
 session 36–7
 records ballads with
 Webb 40
 celebrates eighteenth
 birthday 41
 records with Goodman 42–3
 first song-writing 44
 voted top female
 vocalist (1937) 45
 bond with Webb 46
 and Ink Spots 47, 78, 79,
 81, 108

Fitzgerald, Ella – *cont.*
  compared with Billie
    Holiday   49
  singing lacks emotional
    depth   49–50
  records 'A-Tisket,
    A-Tasket'   51–2
  first tour in the
    South   54, 56
  and Webb's
    death   56, 57, 58
  becomes bandleader   58–9,
      60
  and Webb memorial
    engagement   63
  eating problem   67
  in *Ride 'Em Cowboy*   68–9,
      76, 100
  and breakup of band   71, 72
  marries Benny Kornegay 72
  marriage annulled   73
  and Four Keys   75–6
  matures   79
  work with US armed
    forces   80
  dubbed 'The First Lady of
    Song'   88
  contract with JATP   96
  records 'Nature Boy'   97–8
  marries Ray Brown   98
  at London
    Palladium   99–101, 179
  adopts Ray, Jr   101
  imitates Armstrong in 'Basin
    Street Blues'   103
  throat problems   103, 112
  untouched by fame   103
  loyalty to fans   103–5
  Granz becomes unofficial
    adviser   106–7, 114
  first LP   107
  first recording session with
    Armstrong   108–9
  relationship with
    Peterson   110

  divorce   111, 112, 116
  stormy relationship with
    Granz   115–16
  celebrates eighteen years
    in the music
    business   116–17
  makes second
    film   118, 121
  first top-selling
    album   123–4
  appears at Waldorf-Astoria
    with Basie   125–6
  romantic rumours   129–31
  abdominal   abscess   132,
      133–4
  on rock 'n' roll   135–6
  appears in *St Louis
    Woman*   136
  moves to Beverly Hills   145
  and Tommy
    Flanagan   149–50
  exhaustion   151–4, 185
  and son's music   152–3
  debut with Boston
    Pops   157
  eye problems   157–8, *159*,
      160, 163, 164, 165,
      169, 171
  at Armstrong's funeral   158
  receives Lincoln Center
    Medallion   165
  and Ellington's
    death   165–6
  honours   165, 169, 172–4,
      183, 185
  reissues   175
  breathing
    problems   180–81
  quintuple bypass
    surgery   181
  first album for five
    years   184–5
  mystique   187
Fitzgerald, Tempie   11, 12–
    13, 14, 25, 26

Flanagan, Tommy   149–51,
    161, 162, 165, 178
Forrest, Helen   76
Four Keys   75–6, 78
Fulford, Tommy   43, *48*, 59,
    62, 72
Fuller, Harold   171
Fuqua, Charles   78
Furness, Bill   75
Furness, Peck   75
Furness, Slim   75

Gabler, Milt   58, 64, 91, 107
Gailey, Dan   165
Gaillard, Slim   51
Gale, Moe   17, 31, 33, 54, 58,
    60, 65, 81, 83, 93, 114, 115
Gale, Tim   54, 56, 91, 114,
    115
Gale Agency   65, 68, 71, 76,
    78, 79, 80, 83, *85*, 86, 98
Garcia, Russell   133
Garland, Judy   118, 131
Garner, Erroll   85, 144
Garner, Linton   85
Garroway, Dave   88
Gayles, Joe   86
Gershwin, George   88, 107,
    133, 140
Gershwin, Ira   88, 107, 140
Getz, Stan   121, 122, 137, 148,
    162
Gibbs, Georgia   51
Gillespie, Dizzy   32, 45, 59,
    71, 82, 83, 85–8, 92, 116,
    118, 119, 121, 122, *127*,
    137, 147, 176, 184
Gillespie, Lorraine   87
Glaser, Joe   83, 98, 114, 115,
    128
Goodman, Benny   34, 37,
42–5, 56, 63, 65, 116, 137, 164
Gordon, Dexter   149
Gordon, Max   115

Gorme, Edie   147
Graham, Leonard   90
Granz, Hanne   153
Granz, Norman   69, 71, 80,
    94–6, 98, 104–7, 109, 110,
    113–19, 121–4, 126, 128,
    132, 133, 138, 139, 140,
    144, 145, 146, 148–9, 150,
    152–5, 157, *159*, 161, 162,
    163, 167, 169, 171, 176,
        177, 185, 186
Grasso, Ralph   162
Grateful Dead   136
Green, Benny   44, 122
Green, Bill   162
Greer, Sonny   30
Grey, Al   164
Guild, Hazel   142

Hackett, Bobby   164
Haggart, Bob   79
Haig, Al   85, 93
Hall, Edmond   108
Hall, George   13
Hall, Jim   138, 148
Hamilton, Bernie   140
Hammerstein, Oscar   21
Hammond, John   22, 24, 25,
    80, 83, *85*, 140
Hampton, Gladys   34, 83, 101,
    115
Hampton, Lionel   34, 36, 44,
    65, 74, 81, 83, 101, 109,
    115, 116, 121, 156
Handy, W. C.   136
Hardy, Earl   66
Harlem Stompers   30
Hart, Lorenz   126, 133
Hartman, Johnny   147
Hatfield, Ernie   75
Haughton, Chauncey   *48*, 64,
    66, 164
Hawkins, Coleman   75, 96,
    105, 137, 155
Hawkins, Erskine   60

Haymes, Dick 98
Heard, J. C. 90
Heard, Jack 121
Heard, John 162
Heath, Ted 100, 101
Henderson, Fletcher 17,
    23–5, 31, 65, 74
Henry, Georgianna 26, 65, 75,
    86, 87, 99, 103, 117, 119,
    121, 146
Henry, Haywood 164
Hentoff, Nat 162
Herman, Woody 124
Higgins, Billy 27
Hill, Teddy 45
Hines, Earl 74, 78, 154
Hinsley, Jimmy 88
Hite, Les 77
Hodges, Johnny 39, 132, 148
Hogan, Carl 82
Holiday, Billie 22, 34–5, 40,
    42, 44, 45, 49, 69, 76, 101,
    102, 115, 131, 140, 146,
    173
Horne, Lena 116, 136, 184
Hughes, Howard 106
Humes, Helen 55, 94, 96
Hunter, Eddie 27
Hutton, Betty 99, 100

Ink Spots 47, 78, 79, 81, 108
Izenhall, Aaron 82

Jackson, Cliff 108
Jackson, Edgar 64
Jackson, Jesse 179
Jackson, Josh 82
Jackson, Mahalia 144
Jackson, Milt 85
Jacquet, Illinois 90, 102, 118,
    119, 121, 127
James, Governor Fob 172
James, Harry 137
Jazz at the Philharmonic
    (JATP) 94, 95, 96, 98,

103, 106, 109, 110, 111,
    113, 114, 116–19, 130,
    132, 133, 137, 138, 139,
    142, 145, 154, 155, 162,
    164
Jazz at the Philharmonic
    All Stars 105, 127
Jeffers, Jack 164
Jefferson, Hilton 59
Jeffries, Jim 15
Jimmy Rowles Trio 179
Jimmy Smith Trio 180
Johnson, Gus 136, 138, 149,
    151, 153
Johnson, J. C. 23, 36
Johnson, Jack 15
Johnson, J. J. 162
Johnson, Lyndon B. 153
Johnson, Wini 77
Johnson's Happy Pals 17–18
Jones, Hank 90, 92–3, 99,
    105, 108, 109, 111
Jones, Happy 78
Jones, Jimmy 153
Jones, Quincy 176
Jordan, Louis 48, 49, 50, 62,
    82, 89, 103
Jordan, Taft 31, 43, 45, 47, 48,
    59, 66, 164
Josephson, Arthur 107–8
Josephson, Barney 107
J. S. Trotter's Orchestra 109
Jungle Band 31

Kane, Big Daddy 176
Keith, B. F. 21
Kemp, Jack 51
Kennedy, John
    Fitzgerald 144, 156
Kennedy, Robert 156
Kenny, Bill 78
Kenton, Stan 124
Kessel, Barney 109, 110–11, 124
King, Rev Martin Luther,
    Jr 126, 145, 156, 157

King Cole Trio 109
Kirby, John 31
Kirk, Andy 65
Kitt, Eartha 116, 118
Klee, Harry 162
Knight, Gene 125
Knight, Renee de 81
Kolodin, Irving 132–3
Kornegay, Benny 72–3
Krupa, Gene 56, 113, 114, 118, 121, 122, *127*

LaGuardia, Mayor
 Fiorello 23
Laing, Margaret 152
Larkins, Ellis 107
Larsen, Thor Einar 130–31
Lawford, Peter 144
Lawrence, Steve 147
Le Jazz Hot 116
Lee, Brenda 148
Lee, Peggy 90, 173
*Let No Man Write My
 Epitaph* 140
Levey, Stan 85
Levy, Lou 138, 146, 148, 150, 153
Lewis, Carroll 162
Lewis, John 117
Lewis, Mel 74–5, 92–3, 116, 138–9, 145, 178–9
Lindbergh, Charles A. 18
Lindsay, John 157
Linton, Charlie 32, 34, 37, *38*, *39*, 48
Linton Brothers 32
Little Richard 135
Livingston, Ulysses 72
Lo Pinto, Frank 164
Logan, Dr Arthur 157–8
Logan, Chip 185
Logan, Marian 92, 106, 147, 158, 182, 185–6
Lombardo, Guy 116
Long, Slats 39

Lorillard, Elaine 124
Lorillard, Louis 124
Lou Levy Quartet 145
Louis, Joe 63
Louis Armstrong's
 All-Stars 124
Lourie, Vic 82
Lovelock, A. William 113–14
Lucy, Lawrence 164
Luft, Sid 118
Lunceford, Jimmie 40
Lunceford Band 108

McConnell, John 64, 66
McDaniel, Hattie 68
McDonough, John 95, 175, 177
McFerrin, Bobby 184
McGee (i.e. McGhee),
 John 79
McHugh, Jimmy 22
McKay, Bernie 79
McKinney's Cotton
 Pickers 63
McRae, Carmen 147
McRae, Teddy 31, 43, 44, *48*, 59, 71, 72
McTooney, Ray 86
McVan, Lillian 75
Malneck, Matt 59
Marsalis, Wynton 184
Marshall, Kaiser 62
Martin, Dean 144
Martin, Monty 62
Marty Paitch Orchestra 175
Mass, Irving 115
Mathis, Johnny 137
Matthews, George 59, 64, 66, 164
Matuleff, Norman 103–5
Mercer, Mabel 123, 135
Merry Macs, The 68
Middlebrooks,
 Wilfred 138, 148
Miller, Glen 74

Miller, Norman 'Puerto
  Rico'   106
Miller, Paul Eduard   60
Mills Brothers   13, 116
Modern Jazz Quartet   117
Monk, Thelonious   83
Monroe, Clark   85
Monroe, Marilyn   118, 145
Moody, James   85, 86, 87, 176
Morton, Billy   149
Moten, Benny   63
Murrain, Edward (Sonny)   121

Neiman, LeRoy   179–80
Nelson Riddle Orchestra   153
New York Philharmonic   124
Nicholas, Fayard   63
Nicholas, Harold   63
Noel, Dick   162
Norman, Jessye   184
Norman Granz's Jazz   94

O'Connell, Helen   76
O'Day, Anita   76
Oliver, King   17
Oliver, Sy   103
Ory, Kid   122
Oscar Peterson Trio   109, 110,
  124, 137, 145, 151, 178,
  179

Paitch, Marty   160
Pareles, Jon   180
Parish, Mitchell   59
Parker, Charlie   59, 82, 83,
  105
Parks, Rosa   118, 129
Pass, Joe   165, 167, 169, 177,
  179
Paul Smith Trio   179, 182
Paul Weston's Orchestra   133
Peer, Beverly   35, 43, 47,
  48, 58, 59, 67, 71, 72,
  164
Pete Kelly's Blues   118, 121

Peterson, Oscar   109–11, 118,
  126, 139, 142, 148, 155,
  167, 175, 177–80
Petrillo, James Cesar   76, 79,
  90, 97
Philippe, Claude   125
Phillips, Flip   105, 118, 127
Poitier, Sidney   144
Porter, Cole   122, 123, 133,
  162, 163, 170
Powell, Rev Adam
  Clayton, Jr   114–15
Powell, Bud   93
Presley, Elvis   135, 139
Previn, André   184
Prince, Maurice   186

Ramey, Gene   79
Ramirez, Roger   62, 65, 67, 71,
  72
Randolph, Irving   53–4, 65,
  66, 71, 72
Randolph, Mrs Irving   34
Randy Brooks and His
  Orchestra   81
Rawls, Lou   169
Ray Brown Trio   109
Ray Brown's Rhythm
  Group   92, 97
Reagan, Ronald   174, 183
Rector, Eddie   15, 17
Red and Curly   79
Redman, Don   24
Rich, Buddy   105, 118,
  126
Richmond, June   45
Riddle, Christopher   162
Riddle, Nelson   140, 148, 162,
  176
Ride 'Em Cowboy   68–9,
  76, 100
Riley, Governor and Mrs
  Richard W.   179
Rivera, Lino   42
Robbins, Fred   90

Robinson, Bill 'Bojangles' 15, 20, 75
Rockwell, John 10
Rodgers, Richard 126, 133, 172
Roker, Mickey 179
Rolling Stones 136
Ronstadt, Linda 184
Roseland Band 30
Ross, Allie 24
Roten, Philip 130
Rowles, Jimmy 179
Rushing, Jimmy 37
Russell, John 62
Russell, Nipsey 144
Russell, Snookum 88

Sachs, Mannie 94
St Louis Woman 136
Sampson, Edgar 31, 59
Schapp, Phil 112, 158, 182, 184
Schoenberg, Gordon 162
Schuller, Gunther 45
Schwartz, Jonathan 176
Schwartz, Nat 36
Schwartz, Wilbur 162
Scott, Cecil 108
Scott, Ronnie 169
Secunda, Victoria 154
Shaw, Artie 45, 49, 74, 110
Shearing, George 184
Sherock, Shorty 162
Short, Bobby 71
Signorelli, Frank 59
Simmons, John 90
Simon, George T. 146
Simon, William 126
Simpkins, Jesse 82
Sims, Zoot 165, 177, 179
Sinatra, Frank 98, 118, 121, 133, 134, 135, 144, 145, 151, 157, 166, 176
Smalls, Cliff 164
Smith, Bessie 64, 173

Smith, Bob 110, 141, 147, 148, 160, 161, 166
Smith, Carlton 68
Smith, Harry 92
Smith, Jimmy 171
Smith, Mamie 13
Smith, Paul 148, 150, 162, 178–9
Sokolow, Sam 74–5
Song Spinners 91, 99
Sonny Burke and His Orchestra 103, 109
Stafford, Jo 137
Stark, Bobby 39, 47
Stephens, Haig 81
Stewart, Slam 93
Stewart-Baxter, Derrick 174
Stitt, Sonny 85, 137
Story, Nat 47, 48, 59
Strayhorn, Billy 132
Sullivan, Maxine 51
Sussman, Morris 23
Swing Era, The (Schuller) 45

Tatum, Art 93, 149
Teddy Wilson and His Orchestra 34, 40, 44
Terry, Clark 165, 179, 185
Thigpen, Ed 160
Thompson, Sir Charles 90
Thornton, Terry 147
3 Sams 27
Tirro, Frank 150
Toledano, Ralph de 146
Tommy Flanagan Trio 153, 160, 163, 169
Toots Camarata and His Orchestra 121
Tormé, Mel 147
Tracy, Arthur 13, 25
Treacy, Gene 83
Tricarico, Bobby 162
Trueheart, John 28, 43, 48, 59, 67

Tucker, Earl 'Snakehips' 18
Tucker, Sophie 22
Turner, Charles 162
Tympany Five 49, 82, 103

Ulanov, Barry 30

Vallee, Rudy 51
Van Alexander (previously
  Al Feldman) 50
Vance, Dick 59, 66, 164
Vaughan, Sarah 35, 78, 98,
  149, 176, 180, 184
Vic Schoen and His
  Orchestra 81

Waller, Fats 14, 23, 93
Ward, Helen 37, 43
Waring, Fred 116
Washington, Dinah 35, 101,
  115, 131, 158
Waters, Ethel 13
Watrous, Bill 162
Watrous, Peter 185
Watson, Ivory 78
Webb, Jack 118
Webb, Sallye 34, 57, 63
Webb, William Henry
  'Chick' 28, 48, 151
  'battles' with other
    bands 17, 37, 39
  early life 28
  illness 28, 50, 53–4
  first band 30
  as bandleader 30–31
  ability as a drummer 31
  first hears Ella 32–3
  makes Ella his girl
    singer 34
  intense involvement
    with music 35
  and Ella's first recording
    session 36
  as 'King of the Savoy' 37

radio show (1936) 40
allows Ella to record
  for Goodman 42–3
plays opposite Goodman's
  band at Savoy 44
helps other musicians 45
bond with Ella 46
musicality of band 47
fires Louis Jordan 49, 50
death 56, 57, 58
memorial show in
  Baltimore 62–3
Webster, Ben 116, 132
Wein, George 33, 35, 124,
  158, 179, 181
Wettling, George 81
White, Hy 81, 90
White, Stanford 24
White, Walter 68
Whiting, George 36
Whyte's Lindy Hoppers 20
Wild Bill Davis Trio 153
Williams, Clarence 64
Williams, Cootie 79
Williams, Elmer 39, 66
Williams, Francis 66, 164
Williams, Joe 108, 184
Williams, Mary Lou 36
Williams, Sandy 31, 43, 47,
  48, 59, 64
Williams, 'Professor'
  Stanley 17
Williams, Virginia 11, 25
Wilson, John S. 166–7, 170
Wilson, Nancy 147
Wilson, Teddy 34, 40, 44, 93,
  164
Wyatt, Fred 164

X, Malcolm 156

Yancey, Bill 158
Young, Lester 90, 93, 96, 111,
  118, 119, 122